COMEDY

COMEDY

Modes of Literature Series

Edited by

Ashley Brown
John L. Kimmey

University of South Carolina

Charles E. Merrill Publishing Company
Columbus, Ohio
A Bell & Howell Company

Library of Congress Catalog Number: 69 10745

72 73 / 10 9 8 7 6 5 4 3 2

Printed in the United States of America

Preface

The *Modes of Literature* Series differs from most anthologies introducing college students to literature by stressing synthesis as well as analysis. It organizes stories, poems, and plays into modes rather than into fiction, poetry, and drama. The purpose of this arrangement is to unify the selections in an organic and meaningful way so that they relate to each other and provide a cohesive approach to a variety of works from American, English, and Continental literatures.

We define a mode both as a mood or attitude which the writer assumes toward his subject and the form or manner in which the subject reveals itself. During the 18th Century, for instance, when satire was an important mode, a poet or prose writer searched the world around him for subjects to attack or ridicule. His mood could be bitter, his attitude ironic, his tone either facetious or angry. To express his views he might use the mock-epic, such as Alexander Pope did in *The Rape of the Lock*, or the manner of a travel book which Voltaire adopted for *Candide*.

The major modes of literature are epic, tragedy, comedy, tragicomedy, satire, and romance. All of these are represented in the five volumes of this anthology with the exception of epic. Limitations of space obviously make it impossible to reprint a long poem such as the *Aeneid*. As for the novel, we do not regard it as a separate mode, for it might be epical, tragic, comic, satiric, romantic, or a combination of these. Throughout the five volumes our emphasis is on fairly long works, although we include a number of short poems and stories. Many of these long works are familiar, part of the cultural heritage of the Western World. Their association with a mode, however, places several of them in a new light. Wordsworth's "Michael" is an example of a poem that read in terms of tragedy becomes a stronger and more complex work than it is generally thought to be. Less familiar selections such as Chekhov's "Ward No. 6," Aldous Huxley's "Nuns at Luncheon,"

Elizabeth Bishop's "The Burglar of Babylon," and Robert Lowell's *Benito Cereno* add a freshness often absent from texts that usually rely on the tried and the conventional.

There are a number of advantages to our approach. Instead of viewing a literary work as having only a tenuous connection with the one preceding or following it in an anthology, we see it as belonging to a diverse group of poems, plays, and stories that exhibit the common characteristics of one of the major modes. This mode, then, becomes the precise focus of attention. In a comedy, for instance, not only does the student analyze *The Country Wife* and Hardy's "The Ruined Maid" but through them and other works he develops an understanding of what comedy is, how it has evolved, who are some of its important writers, and what kinds of experience it presents in different ages. While there is much to be said for restricting the study of literature to a concern with style and form, or centering it on significant social and moral themes, either method in itself tends to be one-sided. Our approach engages the student simultaneously in a formal interpretation of literature and a consideration of the vital themes it embodies.

Although the sequence of tragedy, comedy, tragicomedy, satire, and romance is the one we recommend, the five modes can be taken up separately and in any order. Each volume is self-sufficient and does not depend on any other. Occasionally, however, there are references in the introduction or a question to another mode, but these are kept to a minimum. Their aim is to show how the modes touch and cross despite their lines of division.

The selections in this particular volume do not in any sense attempt to represent the entire history of comedy. The introductory essay largely fulfills this function. Its purpose also is to suggest approaches to the poems, stories, and plays included and to stimulate the reader to arrive at his own conclusions about their comic nature.

We wish to thank Betty Trueblood for her assistance in preparing this manuscript. Her efficiency is exceeded only by her abundant good humor. We also wish to express our gratitude to Jane Kimmey for her suggestions and her encouragement.

A. B.

J. L. K.

Contents

COMEDY

Comedy: Introduction

It is commonly agreed that there were only two great periods when the tragic mode flourished, the 5th Century B.C. in Greece and the 17th Century in England and France. Comedy, on the other hand, has been a very recurrent phenomenon in the Western literary tradition, even though it has not always existed at the highest level. The Wife of Bath, Falstaff, Don Quixote, Tom Jones—just to name a few of the famous comic heroes—have come out of a variety of social situations in different historical periods. The range of comedy is in fact larger than some commentators have thought. Perhaps we are still awed by the great claims that Aristotle made for tragedy at the expense of comedy. Although his *Poetics* as we have it is incomplete, Aristotle's bias is obvious. He is quite categorical in stating that this mode is distinguished by its imitation of "characters of a lower type"—the ludicrous, which consists of "some defect or ugliness which is not painful or destructive." And he goes on to remark that "Comedy has had no history, because it was not at first treated seriously." We should remember that Aristotle did not have such writers as Chaucer and Cervantes to discuss in his treatise, and as a rather empirical philosopher he based his definitions on what was available to him.

It might be well, then, to establish a tentative theory of what is involved in comedy as we know it. The essence of a comic situation, high or low, is incongruity: the contradiction between an individual's actions and the laws or principles which we think he should observe. Thus in *The Way of the World* by Congreve (1670-1729) we are amused by the elderly Lady Wishfort, whose preoccupation with youth and passion is "unbecoming" to a woman of her age. Or in *Henry IV* we laugh at Falstaff's attempt to be a rogue; he is fat and cowardly and obviously cannot make a go of it. But he has his own set of values; he is loyal, and in effect he exposes the weak side of the calculating politician Prince Hal. Here is an instance of comedy turned to serious purpose. Or to take another example from English stage history: In *The Importance of Being Earnest* by Oscar Wilde (1854-1900) Lady Bracknell, in a sharp interview with her daughter's suitor, says, "You have a town house, I hope? A girl with a simple, unspoiled nature, like Gwendolyn, could hardly be expected to reside in the country." Here the commonplace notion about the "innocent" countryside and the "corrupt" city is neatly reversed in an epigram.

These comic situations may be used to make further distinctions. In comedy the persons involved do not really suffer their incongruities, and by the same token the audience does not experience pity and terror. (Aristotle states that these emotions are discharged through viewing a tragic spectacle.) At the end of a comedy one often has a sense of elation which is based on an *acceptance* of men's foibles and illusions, however ridiculous. The comic artist has so arranged things that these imperfections take their place within a design, and eventually one can be moved by the design itself. Possibly the greatest comedy lies somewhat beyond language, for example in the finales of Mozart's opera *The Marriage of Figaro* (1786) and Verdi's *Falstaff* (1892), where groups of bewildered people, singing of their different loves and disappointments in their different styles, are lifted up in a glorious complex of musical form. Then at least momentarily they transcend their essentially selfish interests and become beneficent. A small masterpiece of prose comedy, Henry James's *The Europeans* (1878), also moves toward this kind of finale: all the people in the book are brought together, properly paired off, and sent to their various rewards. Comedy does seem to depend on these social situations more than tragedy. It is possible for a tragic hero to act apart from a society: for instance, Prometheus chained to his rock in Aeschylus' *Prometheus Bound* or even Ahab in the last stages of *Moby Dick*. But one cannot imagine a comic hero in solitude for long, even though this is where he wants to be. The great tragedies are invariably given titles like *Oedipus the King* or *King Lear* or *Phaedra:* the focus is entirely on the plight of the hero who acts and suffers (even though he suffers on behalf of his society). Comedies are frequently entitled *Twelfth Night* or *The Way of the World* or *Pride and Prejudice:* the focus may very well be the social situation or the design.

With these examples in mind, one might make a further distinction between comedy and tragedy. The action of a tragedy is like a curve which seems almost inevitably to close itself. When the circle is complete, as it were, the hero is back where he started, but with a terrible difference. This is the moment of self-recognition when he knows who he is because of what he has done. The action *seems* inevitable even though the hero might have done otherwise, and the conclusion is often anticipated. (One justification of the unities of time and place so insisted upon by neo-classical critics is that the curve of the tragic action is thereby reinforced.) The action of a comedy, by contrast, is often like a series of tracks which are parallel to begin with but which begin to cross each other in unexpected and arbitrary ways—all devised by the author to exploit the most from the incongruities of the situation. The twists of a comic plot (as in *Twelfth Night* or *The Country Wife*) are almost impossible to keep in one's head, that is, to bring to a focus; whereas the jealousy of Othello, which impresses itself the first time one reads or sees that tragedy, accounts for much of the action, and one retains a single powerful image of it. The tragic artist, incidentally, always bends his energies to sustain the illusion of his hero's plight, but the comic artist sometimes deliberately breaks the illusion and draws attention to the medium itself. He says in effect, "This is language I am using and this is a play or novel I am writing for you." In the 18th Century Laurence Sterne was already doing this in *Tristram Shandy* (1759), and recent novelists like the Brazilian Machado de Assis and the Russian Vladimir Nabokov have been even more daring. These writers play a kind of superior game with the reader, and this is a final incongruity. To cite a similar example in another form, the dramatist Pirandello boldly exploits the bare, dingy stage and the actors in rehearsal in his tragicomedy *Six Characters in Search of an Author* (1921), and he thus uses the medium itself to fulfill the theme of illusion and reality.

Among the many critics and philosophers who have attempted to locate comedy in the totality of human experience, Henri Bergson in his little book *Laughter* (1900) has been outstanding. Bergson held that the individual consciousness is a continuous flow or "becoming" which participates in a universal flow of experience and systematizes it. (For example, consider the *measurements* of time, days and hours and minutes, that we impose on the actual flow of time.) The effect of this habit is to produce a mechanical rigidity in human behavior—and it is the clash of the mechanical with the living or natural, says Bergson, that is the basis of comedy. This is another way of saying that the small private habits of daily existence often turn the human being into a machine. Ben Jonson, Shakespeare's great contemporary, held a similar theory; he observed men dominated by "humors" or fixed traits such as jealousy and greed. That is, they become human machines; and out of this observation he created such comedies as *Volpone* and *The Alchemist.* An example of the human machine, as Bergson points out, is the circus clown, who tumbles and collides in a calculated rhythm. We almost lose sight of him as a man like ourselves. But this *is* an extreme case. Most of the time we see men and women whose fixed behavior makes them ridiculous only in relation to some social norm. Bergson actually goes so far as to call comedy a game, and certainly it contains a large element of the playful. Like all games it is done according to established rules.

So far we have discussed comedy as a mode which exists at a fairly high intellectual level. But, as we know, the comic impulse is often coarse and farcical, yet quite genuine. Very likely the habit of comedy, as it were, is as old as civilization, and much of the time it stays at a sub-literary level till some artist of genius, at the right moment, knows how to exploit it. Such is the case with Chaucer in "The Merchant's Tale" and elsewhere when he takes popular bawdy stories and makes them into literary art. Such is the case with William Faulkner in "Spotted Horses" when he takes the "tall tale" of the Southern frontier for his form. Some of the greatest writers, in fact, have not hesitated to use this kind of material in tragedies: Shakespeare in *King Lear* for instance. But we are concerned here mainly with the development of comic forms.

One comic writer of importance who had already finished his work before Aristotle wrote his *Poetics* was Aristophanes (ca. 448- ca. 380 B.C.). This Athenian dramatist, who lived in a period of political turmoil, was deeply involved in partisan quarrels. One of his early plays, *The Knights*, makes fun of the failure of Athenian democracy, and *Lysistrata* is the classic spoof on the pretensions of war. It is now generally agreed by scholars that the word *comedy* is derived from the Greek *komos*, meaning revel, and, at an early period at least, comedies were presented at festivals, Dionysian or otherwise. By Aristophanes' time comedy had assumed a somewhat formal character, with its episodes and choral songs and dances. All the same, the ceremony of these plays was qualified by a great deal of wit and buffoonery, some of it quite bawdy. The subjects of Aristophanes' plays were usually simple stories on some matter of current interest, such as the situation ridiculed in *The Knights*. This is usually known as Old Comedy; Aristophanes is its only exponent whose work has survived. This period of comedy gave way to so-called Greek New Comedy, which we actually know through the Roman playwrights Plautus and Terence, who adapted the work of their predecessors. (The plays of the Greek Menander, the most famous writer of New Comedy, exist only in a fragmentary way.) New Comedy is of great historical consequence because it placed such emphasis on the intricate plot which has been a feature of comedy ever since. The chorus was greatly reduced in importance, and in general the ritual character of the play disappeared. Perhaps we could say here that comedy became wholly preoccupied with human foibles and illusions; it had cut loose from its religious associations.

Although the period of Roman comedy was surprisingly short—it almost ceased to be written by the 1st Century B.C.—the surviving works of Plautus (ca. 254-184 B.C.) and Terence (ca. 190-159 B.C.) have had a considerable influence on later writers. They were written in Latin and were known in the long stretch of the Middle Ages when Aristophanes (like other Greek writers) was virtually forgotten. New Comedy, one must concede, is not the highest kind of art. With its emphasis on the neatly intricate plot it anticipates the "well-made play" of the commercial theaters today. But it was studied and brilliantly adapted by men like Molière. Shakespeare directly imitated Plautus in *The Comedy of Errors*, and Wycherley derived the main idea for *The Country Wife* from Terence's *Eunuchus*. The great comic dramatists of the Renaissance were attracted to the structure of these Roman plays; its stereotyped plot became the essence of their dramaturgy.

In at least one sense comedy did not come into its own until the Middle Ages and later. The Christian view of life, which is sacramental and redemptive, naturally finds the comic mode congenial in its acceptance of human limitations and in its beneficent conclusion. The greatest Christian poet, Dante Aligieri (1265-1321), called his poem the *Commedia;* its final vision of salvation is the ultimate happiness from the Christian point of view. (Indeed there is some question about whether tragedy could really flourish under Christian auspices, and it is significant that high tragedy emerged again—in the 17th Century—only when the Christian world-view declined.) The great English poet of the Middle Ages, Geoffrey Chaucer (ca. 1343-1400), was essentially a comic artist. During the last fourteen years of his life he worked on *The Canterbury Tales*, a collection of narratives drawn from many sources. "The Merchant's Tale" uses an episode found in many popular stories of the time—the trick played on the aged husband, who is a stock character in farce. Chaucer has set this tale in a dramatic framework by having it as one of a series of stories that present contrasting views of marriage—scholars usually call this sequence the Marriage Group. In this case the story is told by the Merchant, who has been married two months and who may be disillusioned already. In any case the narrative tone of this incongruous episode is very sophisticated, and the stock characters of farce are elevated to high comedy.

The main tradition in English literature does not necessarily develop directly from Chaucer, but his work in the comic mode has been carried forward by writers as different as the dramatist Ben Jonson and the novelists Fielding and Dickens. English stage history from Jonson to Shaw has been in fact largely a history of comedy (one wit says that it consists of comedies written by Irishmen). The classic period of English stage comedy is the Restoration (1660-1700), when the so-called "comedy of manners" flourished in the hands of such writers as Wycherley and Congreve. A recent critic, Norman N. Holland, has described the typical situation in such a play: ". . . a dashing young rake-hero lured into marriage by a witty, wealthy young heroine. These comedies hold up fops, boors, country people, older, middle-class, or serious people for unfavorable comparison to the witty lovers. There is nothing in earlier English comedy quite like this . . ." As this description suggests, the Restoration play was not intended for a popular audience, and the field of action within a play was comparatively restricted. The audience was fashionable and idle and no doubt had a low standard of sexual morality. But within these limits the playwright could achieve drama of genuine humor and social and artistic significance. Wycherley's *The Country Wife* (1675) examines the sexual pretensions of a slightly corrupt society by means of the rake Horner, who pretends to be a eunuch in order to gain the confidence of wives and divert the suspicions of their husbands. The possibilities for incongruity are endless, and Wycherley makes the most of the occasion, especially with regard to his main character, Horner, who is at once "appealing and insidious," as one critic remarks, a hero and a fool. Despite this ambiguity which pervades the play we should observe that Wycherley has presented us with a pair of lovers, Harcourt and Alithea, who are a reasonable ideal amidst the general corruption, and the audience can surely see where the dramatist's sympathies lie.

If the conventions of Restoration comedy were limited, at least the conventions existed. Since then we have probably not had a period in English history which has had the same assurance about its social and literary ideals. By contrast, the typical 19th or 20th Century writer has had to improvise his work much of the time. He has often been uncertain about his audience and its values; or he has defied the audience. No writer has been more the brilliant improviser than Byron. This poet almost immediately became a celebrity; no earlier English writer had this kind of social-literary notoriety, which undoubtedly posed problems. The heroes of his early poems—*Childe Harold* and the rest—are obsessively melancholy, and they set a new style in Europe. But Byron, a most intelligent poet, worked his way out of this phase to write *Don Juan*, the outstanding long comic poem in English. We should observe that some critics have thought the poem a satire, and certainly it contains some incidental social satire. But taken as a whole it must be seen as a comic improvisation—as Byron himself came to think of it. Recently W. H. Auden, an eminent comic poet of our generation, has stated that "[Byron's] poetic history is a quest, finally successful, to discover the right verse vehicle for a comic poet in his time." After trying the heroic couplet of Dryden and Pope (the great satirical poets) and the Spenserian stanza, he arrived at the ottava rima, a stanzaic form used with great success by Ariosto and other Italian poets of the Renaissance, and one which was altogether congenial to Byron's effect of improvisation. Part of the effect is obtained by his frequent digressions, but this is according to the practice of many comic writers.

Mr. Auden's point about the stanzaic form is worth emphasizing. All comic poetry depends on fairly rigid stanzaic forms. One could scarcely imagine *Don Juan* in blank verse. (Here we seem to have the poets in one sense agreeing with Bergson's theory about comedy based on a clash between the mechanical and the living.) The poems collected in this volume bear out the thesis. Thomas Gray's "Ode on the Death of a Favorite Cat"

(1748) and Theodore Roethke's "The Kitty-Cat Bird" are contrasting poems which use animals in absurd or exaggerated ways to symbolize human qualities. Gray, being an 18th Century poet, uses the "high style" of mock-heroic rhetoric for this purpose, but he jams it into neat stanzas which exhibit a discrepancy between rhetoric and form. Roethke, a 20th Century poet, uses the idiom of nursery rhymes and children's songs to give a form to his poem. Instead of the mock-heroic we have the diminutive. Many modern poets have likewise exploited the comic effects of dialect. The "democratizing" of poetry in the 19th Century meant that any variety of living speech could be used, and Thomas Hardy does exactly that in "The Ruined Maid," which is more successful as a poem than it would be as an episode in one of his novels. X. J. Kennedy's "In a Prominent Bar in Secaucus One Day" frankly uses the raucous and mechanical rhythms of an old popular song, "Sweet Betsy from Pike," for his form, and the speech is contemporary urban-American. Philip Larkin is more subtle about his rhymes in "If, My Darling," but his poem is carefully patterned and the stanzaic form carries forward the highly elaborated metaphor (about the girl friend jumping into his head), which takes over the poem. Hardy, Kennedy, and Larkin have written their poems on the comic potentialities of sexual experience; they continue a theme which was developed on a grander scale by Chaucer, Wycherley, and Byron.

Most of the comic writers of the last two centuries have used prose fiction as their medium. The stories in this anthology are a representative group of comedies, but one cannot easily generalize about them. Gogol, an early master of Russian fiction, already had a highly complex idea about what we now call the "absurd." The nose in his story starts out as merely one part of a man's body, but it presently is exaggerated and becomes a detachable object. Although some readers nowadays would interpret this by means of psychiatry and say that a kind of neurosis is taking place, we might refer the situation to the old writers of comedy who had an acute sense of the human being as a mechanism. Joyce's "The Boarding House," from his collection of short stories, *Dubliners* (1914), is written almost entirely in clichés, and the intelligent reader should be able to see through the vanities and illusions of the characters by what they say and think. In this story Joyce has emphasized the incongruity of the situation by switching the point of view twice (from Mrs. Mooney to Mr. Doran to Polly), an unusual procedure in a short story; the form thus renders the theme. In Ring Lardner's "Some Like Them Cold" the characters reveal themselves directly through their letters, and the author has put the old epistolary form (seldom used nowadays) to work in a modern dialect idiom. The subject undoubtedly has an inherent pathos and even sentimentality, but the form allows the author to keep his distance. Although Aldous Huxley's "Nuns at Luncheon" is almost exactly contemporary with Ring Lardner's story, it takes place in another world, where people have far more wit and eloquence, and love to exhibit them. But they can be equally as maudlin and even more pretentious. This story verges on the tragic, but the contrast between the narrator and the tale makes it otherwise. Conrad Aiken, the American poet and critic, says, "It is perhaps as triumphant an example of a dexterous and heartless *playing* with a tragic theme as one could find."

Comedy, then, contains a variety of forms and moods all the way from the sophisticated farce of "The Merchant's Tale" and "The Nose" to the comedy of manners of *The Country Wife* and *Don Juan*, from the wit of "Ode on the Death of a Favorite Cat" and "The Kitty-Cat Bird" to the bawdiness of "The Ruined Maid" and "In a Prominent Bar in Secaucus One Day." The mode is diverse, reflecting the whole spectacle of the world. If it does not touch us as deeply as tragedy, it does present more comprehensively our human condition.

Suggestions for Further Reading

Auden, W. H. "Don Juan," in *The Dyer's Hand and Other Essays.* New York: Random House, 1962.

Barber, C. L. *Shakespeare's Festive Comedy.* Princeton: The Princeton University Press, 1959.

Bergson, Henri. *Laughter*, trans. by Cloudesley Brereton and Fred Rothwell. New York: The Macmillan Company, 1911.

Cook, Albert S. *The Dark Voyage and the Golden Mean.* Cambridge, Mass.: Harvard University Press, 1949.

Cornford, Francis M. *The Origin of Attic Comedy.* London: Edward Arnold, 1914.

Duckworth, George E. *The Nature of Roman Comedy.* Princeton: The Princeton University Press, 1952.

Feibleman, James. *The Praise of Comedy.* New York: Russell & Russell, Inc., 1962.

Fergusson, Francis. "Two Comedies," in *The Human Image in Dramatic Literature.* New York: Anchor, 1962.

Frye, Northrop. "The Argument of Comedy," in *English Institute Essays: 1948*, ed. by D. A. Robertson, Jr. New York: Columbia University Press, 1949.

Holland, Norman N. *The First Modern Comedies.* Cambridge, Mass.: Harvard University Press, 1959.

Kronenberger, Louis. *The Thread of Laughter.* New York: Alfred A. Knopf, 1952.

Geoffrey Chaucer (ca. 1343-1400)

The Merchant's Tale

From *The Canterbury Tales*

TRANSLATED BY NEVILLE COGHILL

There was a knight one time of good renown
In Lombardy,[1] Pavia was the town.
He'd lived there very prosperously for more
Than sixty years and was a bachelor,
Though always taking bodily delight
On women, such as pleased his appetite,
As do these foolish worldlings, never fear.
Now when this knight had passed his sixtieth year
—Whether for holiness, or from a surge
Of dotage, who can say?—he felt an urge 10
So violent to be a wedded man
That day and night his eager fancies ran
On where and how to spy himself a bride,
Praying the Lord he might not be denied
Once to have knowledge of that blissful life
There is between a husband and his wife,
And live within the holy bond and tether
In which God first bound woman and man together.
'No other life,' he said, 'is worth a bean;
For wedlock is so easy and so clean 20
It is a very paradise on earth.'
Thus said this ageing knight, so full of worth.
  And certainly, as sure as God is King,
To take a wife is a most glorious thing,
Especially if a man is old and hoary;

[1] Province of Italy.

Then she's the fruit of all his wealth and glory.
It's then he ought to take her, young and fair.
One upon whom he might beget an heir,
And lead a life of rapture and content,
Whereas these bachelors can but lament 30
And suffer, when in some adversity
From love, which is but childish vanity.
And it's no more than right it should be so
If bachelors are beset by grief and woe:
On brittle ground they build, so all is ready
For brittle love, though they expect a steady.
Their liberty is that of bird or beast,
They've no restraint, no discipline at least,
Whereas a married man achieves a state
Of bliss that's orderly and fortunate. 40
Under the yoke of matrimony bowed,
The heart, in bliss abounding, sings aloud.
For who is so obedient as a wife?
Who is so true, so careful for his life
Whether in health or sickness, as his mate?
For weal or woe she tends upon his state,
In service, and in love, she never tires,
Though he lie bedridden till he expires.
 And yet some writers say this isn't so;
One such was Theophrastus[2] long ago. 50
Who cares if Theophrastus was a liar?
'Don't take a wife,' he said, 'from a desire
To make economies and spare expense.
A faithful servant shows more diligence
In guarding your possessions than a wife
For she claims half you have throughout her life;
And if you're sick, as God may give me joy,
Your very friends, an honest serving-boy,
Do more than she, who's watching for a way
To corner your possessions night and day. 60
And if you take a wife into your bed
You're very likely to be cuckolded.'
 Opinions such as these and hundreds worse
This fellow wrote, God lay him under curse!
But take no heed of all such vanity,

[2] Author of an anti-feminist work found in St. Jerome's *Against Jovinian.*

Defy foul Theophrastus and hear me.
  A wife is verily the gift of God.
All other kinds of gift, the fruitful sod
Of land, fair pastures, movables in store,
Rents—they're the gifts of fortune, nothing more, 70
That pass as does a shadow on a wall.
  Still, if I must speak plainly, after all
A wife does last some time, and time may lapse
A good deal slower than one likes, perhaps.
  Marriage is a momentous sacrament,
Bachelordom contemptible, and spent
In helpless desolation and remorse
—I'm speaking of the laity, of course.
I don't say this for nothing; listen why.
Woman was made to be a man's ally. 80
When God created Adam, flesh and bone,
And saw him belly-naked and alone,
He of His endless goodness thus began:
'Let us now make a help-meet for this man
Like to himself.' And He created Eve.
Here lies the proof of what we all believe,
That woman is man's helper, his resort,
His earthly paradise and his disport.
So pliant and so virtuous is she
They cannot but abide in unity. 90
One flesh they are; one flesh as I suppose
Has but a single heart in joys and woes.
  A wife! Saint Mary, what a benediction!
How can a man be subject to affliction
Who has a wife? Indeed I cannot say.
There is a bliss between them such as may
No tongue tell forth, such as no heart can judge.
If he be poor she helps her man to drudge,
Sets guard upon his goods and checks the waste;
All that her husband likes is to her taste, 100
She never once says 'no' when he says 'yes.'
'Do this,' says he; 'already done,' she says.
O blissful state of wedlock, no way vicious
But virtuous and merry, nay, delicious,
And so commended and approved withal
That any man who's worth a leek should fall
On his bare knees, to thank God, all his life,

For having ordained and given him a wife,
Or else to pray that he vouchsafe to send
A wife to last him to the very end. 110
 Then he can count upon security
And not be tricked, as far as I can see,
Provided that he works by her advice:
Jacob, the learned tell us, was precise
In following the good counsel of his mother,
And won his father's blessing from his brother,
By binding round his neck a pelt of kid.
Or Judith, one can read of what she did:
Her wisdom held God's people in its keeping
By slaying Holofernes, who was sleeping. 120
 Take Abigail, what good advice she gave!
It saved her husband Nabal from the grave.
Take Esther too, whose wisdom brought relief
To all God's people, saved them from their grief
And made Ahasuerus grant promotion
To Mordecai for his true devotion.
There's no superlative that ranks in life,
Says Seneca,[3] above a humble wife.
'The tongue of wife,' so Cato[4] was to say,
'Commands the husband: suffer and obey.' 130
And yet she will obey by courtesy.
A wife is guardian of your husbandry;
Well may a man in sickness wail and weep
Who has no wife to nurse him and to keep
His house for him; do wisely then and search
For one and love her as Christ loves His Church.
For if you love yourself you love your wife,
For no one hates his flesh, nay all his life
He fosters it, and so I bid you wive
And cherish her, or you will never thrive. 140
Husband and wife, whatever the worldly say
In ribald jest, are on the straight, sure way.
They are so knit no accident or strife
Harms them, particularly not the wife.
 So January thought, of whom I told,
Deeply considering as he grew old

---

[3] Roman dramatist and moralist who espoused the philosophy of the Stoics.
[4] Roman statesman and Stoic philosopher.

The life of lusty joy and virtuous quiet
That marriage offers in its honey-diet.
And so one day he sent for all his friends
To tell them how he meant to gain his ends. 150
  With serious face he spoke, and solemn tongue.
'My friends,' he said, 'I am no longer young;
God knows, I'm near the pit, I'm on the brink:
I have a soul, of which I ought to think.
  'My body I have foolishly expended;
Blessed be God, that still can be amended.
I have resolved to be a wedded man.
And that at once in all the haste I can
To some fair virgin; one of tender years.
Prepare yourselves to help as overseers 160
Against my wedding, for I will not wait.
I for my own part will investigate
And find a hasty match, if there be any:
But in as much as you, my friends, are many,
You may discern more readily than I
Where it would most befit me to ally.
  'But, my dear friends, you may as well be told
The woman must on no account be old,
Certainly under twenty, and demure.
Flesh should be young though fish should be mature; 170
As pike, not pickerel, makes the tastier meal,
Old beef is not so good as tender veal.
I'll have no woman thirty years of age;
That's only fodder, bean-straw for a cage.
God knows these ancient widows know their trade,
They are as tricky as the Boat of Wade[5]
With so much trouble breaking when they please
To fight, I should not have a moment's ease.
Subtle is the scholar taught in several schools;
And women taught in many are no fools, 180
Half-scholars one might say; but when they're young
A man can still control them with his tongue
And guide them, should their duty seem too lax
Just as a man may model in warm wax.
So let me sum the matter in a clause;
I will have no old woman, for this cause.

[5] Wade was a hero of the Anglo-Saxon period. The name of his boat was *Guingelot*.

For were I so unlucky as to marry
Where I could take no pleasure, I'd miscarry,
I should commit adultery and slide
Straight downwards to the devil when I died. 190
I could beget no child on her to greet me,
Yet I had rather that the dogs should eat me
Than that my fine inheritance should fall
Into strange hands, that let me tell you all.
'I'm not a fool, I know the reason why
People should wed, though I could specify
Many who prate of it, but I engage
They know about as little as my page
Touching the reasons one should take a wife.
A man unable to be chaste in life 200
Should take a wife in holy dedication
And for the sake of lawful procreation
Of children, to the honour of God above,
Not as a paramour or lady-love,
But to curb lechery, which he should eschew,
Paying his debt whenever it falls due,
Or each a willing helper to the other
In trouble, like sister to a brother
And live a life of holy chastity;
But, by your leave, sirs, that would not suit me, 210
For, God be thanked, I dare to make the claim,
I feel my limbs sufficient, strong and game
For all that is belonging to a man,
And am my own best judge in what I can.
I may seem hoary, but I'm like a tree
That blossoms white before the fruit can be;
Blossoming trees are neither dry nor dead
And I am only hoary on my head.
My heart and all my members are as green
As laurel is; all the year round, I mean. 220
And now you are informed of my intention
I beg you to agree without dissension.'
Various men gave various examples
Of classic marriages, convincing samples;
Some praised it certainly, some reprehended,
But at the last, (to get the matter ended),
As altercation happens every day
Among good friends who mean to say their say,

An argument was presently begun
Between two friends of his, Placebo one, 230
Justinus, as I recollect, the other.
  Placebo said, 'O January, dear brother,
You have no need, sweet lord, it must appear,
To take advice from anybody here,
Save that your sapience, after meditation,
Would prudently resist the inclination
To set aside the word of Solomon,
For this is what he said for everyone:
"Do all things by advice," his saying went,
"And then you'll have no reason to repent." 240
Though that may be what Solomon commends,
Dear lord, my brother, nay my best of friends,
As surely as the Lord may give me rest
I think your own opinion is the best.
Take it from me—if I can find the phrase—
You know I've been a courtier all my days,
God knows unworthily, I make admission,
Yet I have stood in quite a high position
And among lords of very great estate;
But I have never joined in a debate 250
With them, or offered contradiction. Why?
Well, obviously, my lord knows more than I,
And what he says I hold as firm and stable;
I echo it as far as I am able.
No counsellor is such a fool as he
That, serving on a lord of high degree,
Dares to presume or even thinks it fit
To be superior to him in wit.
Lords are no fools, believe me . . . May I say
That you have also shown yourself to-day 260
A man of lofty views, an eloquent,
A holy-minded man, and I consent
To all you said. It should be written down.
A speech like that—there isn't one in town,
No, nor all Italy, able to supply it!
Christ holds himself more than rewarded by it.
In anyone at all advanced in age
It shows a lively spirit to engage
In taking a young wife. Ah, Lord of grace!
You've pinned your heart up in a jolly place; 270

Follow your inclination; I protest
Whatever you decide on will be best.'
   Justinus who sat silent, having heard
Placebo speaking, then took up the word.
'Brother,' he said, 'be patient with me, pray;
You spoke your mind, now hear what I would say;
Seneca gave a lot of sound advice;
He says it's always better to think twice
Before you give away estate or pelf.
And therefore if you should advise yourself 280
In giving property away or land,
If it's important you should understand
Who is to get your goods, how much the more
You ought to think things over well before
You give away your body. If I may
I'd like to warn you; it is no child's play
Choosing a wife. It needs consideration,
In fact it asks a long investigation.
   'Is she discreet and sober? Or a drinker?
Or arrogant? Or shrewish like a tinker? 290
A scolder? Or extravagant? Too clannish?
Too poor? Too rich? Unnaturally mannish?
Although we know there isn't to be found
In all the world one that will trot quite sound,
Whether it's man or beast, the way we'd like it,
It were sufficient bargain, could we strike it,
In any women, were one sure she had
More good among her qualities than bad.
   'But all this asks some leisure to review;
God knows that many is the tear I too 300
Have wept in secret since I had a wife.
Praise whoso will the married state of life
I find it a routine, a synthesis
Of cost and care, and wholly bare of bliss.
And yet the neighbours round about, by God,
Especially the women—in a squad—
Congratulate me that I chose to wive
The constantest, the meekest soul alive.
I know where the shoe pinches; but for you,
Why, you must please yourself in what you do. 310
You're old enough—that's not what I disparage—
To think before you enter into marriage,

Especially if your wife is young and fair.
By Him that made earth, water, fire and air,
The youngest man in this distinguished rout
Will have a busy task—you need not doubt—
To keep a woman to himself. Trust me,
You will not please her more than for, say, three
Years—that is, please her to the point of fervence.
Wives ask a lot in matters of observance 320
I beg you not to take it the wrong way.'
'Well,' said old January, 'have you said your say?
Straw for your Seneca and proverbial tags;
Not worth a basketful of weeds and rags,
Your pedant-jargon! Wiser men than you,
As you have heard, take quite another view
Of my proposal. What would you reply,
Placebo?' 'An accursed man, say I,
It is that offers an impediment,'
Said he, and so, by general consent, 330
His friends then rose, declaring it was good
That he should marry when and where he would.
Busy imaginations, strange invention
And soaring fantasy obsessed the attention
Of January's soul about his wedding.
Came many a lovely form and feature shedding
A rapture through his fancies night by night.
As who should take a mirror polished bright
And set it in the common market-place,
And watch the many figures pause and pace 340
Across his mirror; in the self-same way,
Old January allowed his thoughts to play
Mirroring all the girls that lived nearby,
Still undetermined where his thought should lie.
For were there one with beauty in her face
There was another standing high in grace
With people, for her grave benignity,
Whose voices gave her the supremacy.
Others were rich, but had a tarnished name.
At last, and half in earnest, half in game, 350
He fixed on one, and setting her apart,
He banished all the others from his heart.
He chose her on his own authority,
For love is always blind and cannot see,

And when he lay in bed at night his thought
Pictured her in his heart, for he was caught
By her fresh beauty and her age so tender;
Her little waist, her arms so long and slender,
Her wise self-discipline, her gentle ways,
Her womanly bearing and her serious gaze. 360
His thought, descending on her thus, was fettered,
It seemed to him choice could not be bettered.
Once he was satisfied in this decision,
He held all other judgment in derision:
It was impossible to disagree
With him in taste, such was his fantasy.
He sent his friends a very strong request
Begging the pleasure—would they do their best?—
Of an immediate visit.
Placebo came and so did all the rest, 370
And January began with the request
That none should offer any argument
Against the purpose 'which was his intent,
Pleasing to God Almighty, and,' said he,
'The very ground of his prosperity.'
He said there was a maiden in the town
Whose beauty was indeed of great renown;
Her rank was not so great, to tell the truth,
But still she had her beauty and her youth;
She was the girl he wanted for his wife, 380
To lead a life of ease, a holy life.
And he would have her all—thank God for this!—
There would be shares for no one in his bliss.
He begged them then to labour in his need
And help to make his enterprise succeed,
For then, he said, his mind would be at rest
'With nothing to annoy me or molest,
But for one thing which pricks my conscience still,
So listen to me kindly if you will.
'I've often,' he continued, 'heard ere this 390
That none may have two perfect kinds of bliss,
Bliss in this world, I mean, and bliss in Heaven;
Though he keep clear of sin—the deadly seven
And all the branches of their dreadful tree—
Yet there's so perfect a felicity
In marriage, so much pleasure, so few tears,

That I keep fearing, though advanced in years,
I shall be leading such a happy life
So delicate, with neither grief nor strife,
That I shall have my heaven here in earth, 400
And may not that cost more than it is worth?
Since that true heaven costs a man so dear
In tribulation and in penance here,
How should I then, living in such delight,
As every married man, by day and night,
Has with his wife, attain to joys supernal
And enter into bliss with Christ Eternal?
That is my terror. Have you a suggestion,
My worthy brothers, to resolve the question?'
   Justinus, who despised his nonsense, said, 410
Jesting as ever, what was in his head;
And wishing not to spin things out in chatter
Used no authorities to support the matter.
'If there's no obstacle,' he said, 'but this,
God by some mighty miracle of His
May show you mercy as He is wont to do,
And long before they come to bury you
May cause you to bewail your married life
In which you say there never can be strife.
And God forbid that there should not be sent 420
A special grace that husbands may repent,
And sent more often than to single men.
This, sir, would be my own conclusion, then;
Never despair! You still may go to glory,
For she perhaps may prove your purgatory,
God's means of grace, as one might say, God's whip
To send your soul to Heaven with a skip
And swifter than an arrow from the bow!
   'I hope to God that you will shortly know
There's no such paramount felicity 430
In marriage, nor is ever like to be,
As to disqualify you for salvation,
Provided you observe some moderation,
Tempering down the passions of your wife
With some restriction of your amorous life,
Keeping yourself, of course, from other sin.
My tale is done, but there! My wit is thin.

Be not afraid, dear brother, that's the moral.
Let us wade out, however, of this quarrel;
The Wife of Bath,[6] if you can understand 440
Her views in the discussion now on hand,
Has put them well and briefly in this case:
And now, farewell, God have you in His Grace!'
He then took leave of January his brother
And they had no more speech with one another.
And when his friends saw that it needs must be
They made a careful marriage-treaty. She,
The girl agreed upon, whose name was May,
And with the smallest possible delay,
Was to be married to this January. 450
And I assume there is no need to tarry
Over the bonds and documents they planned
To give her the possession of his land.
Or make you listen to her rich array,
But finally there came the happy day
And off at last to church the couple went
There to receive the holy sacrament.
Out came the priest, with stole about his neck,
And bade her be like Sarah at the beck
Of Abraham in wisdom, truth and grace, 460
Said all the prayers were proper to the case,
Then signed them with the cross and bade God bless
Them both, and made all sure in holiness.
Thus they were wedded in solemnity,
And at the wedding-banquet he and she
Sat with their worthier guests upon the dais.
Joy and delight filled the entire place,
Stringed instruments, victuals of every kind,
The daintiest all Italy could find.
Music broke forth as with the sound of Zion, 470
Not Orpheus nor the Theban king Amphion
Ever achieved so sweet a melody.
At every course there came loud minstrelsy
And Joab's trumpets[7] never took the ear

---

[6] A prominent character in *The Canterbury Tales*, who has already delivered her views on marriage. She defends her right to remarry and asserts her belief that a wife should dominate her husband.

[7] Joab was an officer of King David who controlled the people with a trumpet.

So forcefully as this, nor half so clear
Those of Theodamas[8] when Thebes held out.
Bacchus himself was pouring wine about
And Venus smiled on everyone in sight,
For January had become her knight
And wished to try his courage in the carriage 480
Of his new liberty combined with marriage.
Armed with a fire-brand she danced about
Before the bride and all the happy rout;
And certainly I'll go as far as this
And say that Hymen, God of wedded bliss,
Never beheld so happy a wedded man.
Hold thou thy peace, O poet Martian,[9]
Give us no more thy marital doxology
For Mercury on wedding with Philology!
Silence the song the Muses would have sung, 490
Thine is too small a pen, too weak a tongue,
To signalize this wedding or engage
To tell of tender youth and stooping age,
Such joy it is as none may write about:
Try it yourself and you will soon find out
If I'm a liar or not in such a case.
For there sat May with so benign a face
That but to see her was a fairy-tale.
Queen Esther's eye could never so assail
Ahasuerus, never looked so meek; 500
Of so much loveliness I dare not speak,
Yet thus much of her beauty I will say
That she was like the brightest morn of May
With every grace and pleasure in her glance.
This January sat ravished, in a trance
And every time he gazed upon her face
His heart began to menace her and race;
That night his arms would strain her with the ardour
That Paris showed for Helen, aye, and harder.
And yet he felt strong qualms of pity stir 510
To think he soon must do offence to her,
That very night, and thought, 'O Tender creature!

---

[8] Prophet of Thebes who announced his prophecies with a trumpet.
[9] Martianus Capella, medieval Latin poet. He describes the wedding of Philology and Mercury.

Alas, God grant you may endure the nature
Of my desires, they are so sharp and hot.
I am aghast lest you sustain them not.
God hinder me from doing all I might!
But O I wish to God that it were night,
And the night last for ever! Oh, how slow . . .
I wish these guests would hurry up and go!'
So he began to dedicate his labours 520
To getting rid politely of his neighbours,
And to detaching them from food supplies.
At last their reason told them they should rise;
They danced and drank and, left to their devices,
They went from room to room to scatter spices
About the house. Joy rose in every man
Except in one, a squire called Damian,
Who carved for January every day.
He was so ravished by the sight of May
As to be mad with suffering; he could 530
Almost have died or fainted where he stood,
So sorely Venus burnt him with the brand
Which, as she danced, she carried in her hand.
And hastily the boy went off to bed;
No more of him at present need be said.
I leave him there to weep and to complain
Till fresh young May have pity on his pain.
O perilous fire, in the bed-straw started!
Foe in the family, home-like but false-hearted,
Pretending service and a traitor too, 540
An adder in the bosom, sly, untrue,
God shield us all from your acquaintanceship!
O January, drunk upon the lip
Of marriage, see your servant, Damian,
Who was your very squire, born your man,
Even now is meditating villainy.
O God unmask your household enemy!
Over the world no pestilence can roam
That is as foul as foe within the home.
The sun had traced his arc with golden finger 550
Across the sky, caring no more to linger
On the horizon in that latitude.
Night with her mantle which is dark and rude
Had overspread the hemisphere about,

And gone were all the merry-making rout
Of January's guests, with hearty thanks,
And homeward each convivially spanks
To undertake such business as will keep
Him happy, till it should be time for sleep.
  Soon after this the restive January 560
Demanded bed; no longer would he tarry
Except to quaff a cordial for the fire
That claret laced with spice can lend desire;
For he had many potions, drugs as fine
As those that monk, accursed Constantine,
Has numbered in his book *De Coitu*.
He drank them all; not one did he eschew,
And to his private friends who lingered on
He said, 'For God's love, hurry and be gone,
Empty the house politely if you can.' 570
And presently they did so to a man.
A toast was drunk, the curtains back were thrown;
The bride was borne to bed as still as stone.
And when the priest had blessed the wedding-bed
The room was emptied and the guests were sped.
  Fast in the arms of January lay
His mate, his paradise, his fresh young May.
He lulled her, sought to kiss away all trouble;
The bristles of his beard were thick as stubble,
Much like a dog-fish skin, and sharp as briars, 580
Being newly shaved to sweeten his desires.
He rubbed his chin against her tender cheek
And said, 'Alas, alas that I should seek
To trespass—yet I must—and to offend
You greatly too, my spouse, ere I descend.
Nevertheless consider this.' said he,
'No workman, whatsoever he may be,
Can do his work both well and in a flurry;
This shall be done in perfect ease, no hurry.
It's of no consequence how long we play, 590
We are in holy wedlock, and we may.
And blessed be the yoke that we are in
For nothing we can do will count as sin.
A man is not a sinner with his wife,
He cannot hurt himself with his own knife;
We have the law's permission thus to play.'

And so he laboured till the break of day,
Then took a sop of claret-sodden toast,
Sat up in bed as rigid as a post,
And started singing very loud and clear. 600
He kissed his wife and gave a wanton leer,
Feeling a coltish rage towards his darling
And chattering in the jargon of a starling.
The slack of skin about his neck was shaking
As thus he fell a-chanting and corn-craking.
God knows what May was thinking in her heart
Seeing him sit there in his shirt apart,
Wearing his night-cap, with his scrawny throat.
She didn't think his games were worth a groat.
At last he said, 'I think I'll take a rest; 610
Now day has come a little sleep were best.'
And down he lay and slept till half-past eight;
Then he woke up, and seeing it was late,
Old January arose; but fresh young May
Kept her apartment until the fourth day
As women will, they do it for the best.
For every labourer must have time to rest,
For otherwise he can't keep labouring;
And that is true of every living thing,
Be it a fish, a bird, a beast, or man. 620
Now I will speak of woeful Damian
Languishing in his love, as will appear.
I should address him thus, if he could hear:
'O silly Damian! Alas, alas!
Answer my question; in your present pass
How are you going to tell her of your woe?
She's absolutely bound to answer no,
And if you speak, she's certain to betray you;
I can say nothing. God be your help, and stay you!'
Sick-hearted Damian in Venus' fire 630
Is so consumed, he's dying with desire;
And so he took his courage in his hand
To end a grief he could no longer stand
And with a pen that he contrived to borrow
He wrote a letter pouring out his sorrow,
After the fashion of a song or lay,
Indited to his lady, dazzling May,
And wrapped it in a purse of silk apart

To hang inside his shirt, upon his heart.
The moon, that stood in Taurus on the day 640
When January had wedded lovely May,
Had glided into Cancer; she of whom
I speak, fresh May, had meanwhile kept her room,
As is the custom among nobles all.
A bride of course should never eat in hall
Till four days afterwards, or three at least,
But when they're over, let her go and feast.

On the fourth day, from noon to noon complete,
And when high mass was over, in his seat
Sat January in his hall with May, 650
As fresh and bright as is a summer's day.
And it so happened that this good old man
Remembered Damian, and thus began:
'Where's Damian? Saints above! How can it be
That Damian isn't here to wait on me?
Is he still sick? What's happened? Is he up?'

The squires standing there to fill his cup
Excused him on the grounds that he was ill,
He was in bed, unfit for duty still;
No other reason could have made him tarry. 660
'I'm very sorry for it', said January,
And he's a gentleman, to tell the truth,'
The old man said, 'and if he died, poor youth,
It were a pity; he's a lad of worth.
I don't know anyone of equal birth
So wise, discreet and secret, and so able;
Thrifty and serviceable too at table.
As soon as possible after meat to-day
I'll visit him myself; and so shall May.
We'll give him all the comfort that we can.' 670

Then everybody blessed the kind old man
So eager in his bounty and good breeding
To offer anything that might be needing
To comfort a sick squire; a gentle deed.

'Madam,' said January, 'take good heed
That after meat you and your women all,
When you have sought your room and left the hall,
Go up and have a look at Damian
And entertain him; he's a gentleman.
And tell him too that I shall do my best 680

To visit him myself, after my rest.
Now hurry on, be quick, and I shall bide me
Here, until you return to sleep beside me.'
And on the word he rose and gave a call
To fetch a squire (the marshal of the hall)
And gave him some instructions. Fresh young May
With all her women took the shortest way
To Damian's room and sat beside his bed;
A warmth of comfort was in all she said,
Benignity and beauty in her glance. 690
And Damian, when at last he saw his chance,
Secretly took his purse and billet-doux,
Couched in the sweetest phrases that he knew,
And put it in her hand with nothing more
Than a long sigh, as deep as to the core;
But in a whisper he contrived to say,
'Mercy, have mercy! Don't give me away!
I should be killed if this were ever known.'
The purse slid from his bosom to her own
And off she went. You get no more of me. 700
Back to old January then went she;
He was reclining on his bed by this.
He drew her to his arms with many a kiss,
Then settled back to sleep at once; and so
She then pretended that she had to go
Where everbody has to go at times.
There, after memorizing Damian's rhymes,
She tore them into pieces and she cast
Them softly down the privy-drain at last.
  Who fell into a study then but May? 710
And down beside old January she lay
Who slept until awoken by his cough.
He begged her then to strip her garments off
For he would have some pleasure of her, he said,
Her clothes were an encumbrance, to be shed.
And she obeyed, whether she would or no.
Lest I offend thc precious, I will go
No further into what he did, or tell
Whether she thought it paradise or hell.
I leave them working thus as I suppose 720
Till it was evensong, and then they rose.
  Whether by destiny or accident,

By starry influence or natural bent,
Or whether some constellation held its state
In heaven to make the hour fortunate
For giving billet-doux and lending wing
To Venus—there's a time for everything,
The learned say—and get a lady's love,
I cannot tell. But God who sits above
And knows that every action has a cause, 730
Let Him decide, for I can only pause
In silence; this at least is true of May
That such was the impression made that day
And such her pity for that sick young man
She could not rid her heart of Damian,
Or of the wish to see his troubles ended.
'Whoever else,' she thought, 'may be offended,
I do not care; but I can promise this,
To love him more than anyone there is,
Though he mayn't have a shirt. I will be kind.' 740
Pity flows swiftly in a noble mind.

Here one may see how excellently free
In bounty women, on taking thought, can be.
Some female tyrants—many I have known—
Are pitiless, their hearts are made of stone
And would have rather let him die the death
Than yield their grace or favour by a breath,
And they exult in showing cruel pride.
Calmly indifferent to homicide.

Soft May felt pity, you must understand. 750
She wrote a letter in her own fair hand
In which she granted him her very grace.
There needed nothing but the time and place
To grant the satisfactions he desired;
He was to have whatever he required.

So when she saw occasion one fine day
To visit him, off went the lovely May
And thrust this letter down with subtle skill
Under his pillow, read it if he will.
She took him by the hand and squeezed it hard, 760
(But secretly, for she was on her guard)
Bade him get well, then went without demur
To January who had called for her.

And up rose happy Damian on the morrow;

Gone was all trace of malady and sorrow.
He preens himself and prunes and combs his curls
To take the fancy of his queen of girls.
To January his master, in addition
He was a very spaniel in submission,
And was so pleasant in his general drift 770
(Craft's all that matters if you have the gift),
That people spoke him well in every way,
But above all he stood in grace with May.
Thus I leave Damian, busy with his needs,
And turn once more to how my tale proceeds.
Some writers argue that felicity
Wholly consists in pleasure; certainly
This noble January, as best he might
In all that was befitting to a knight,
Had planned to live deliciously in pleasure; 780
His house and all his finery and treasure
Were fashioned to his rank as are a king's,
And among other of his handsome things
He had a garden, walled about with stone;
So fair a garden never was there known.
For out of doubt I honestly suppose
That he who wrote the *Romance of the Rose*[10]
Could not have pictured such magnificence;
Priapus never had the eloquence,
Though he be god of gardens, to re-tell 790
The beauty of this garden and the well
Under a laurel, standing ever-green.
Many a time King Pluto and his Queen
Proserpina and all her fairy rout
Disported and made melody about
That well and held their dances, I am told.
This January, so noble, and so old,
Found walking in it such felicity
That no one was allowed to have the key
Except himself, and for its little wicket 800
He had a silver latch-key to unclick it
Or lock it up, and when his thought was set
Upon the need to pay his wife her debt

---

[10] A medieval allegorical poem by Guillaume de Lorris, which Chaucer translated from the French. It features a walled garden of love.

In summer season, thither would he go
With May his wife when there was none to know,
And anything they had not done in bed
There in the garden was performed instead,
So in this manner many a merry day
Was spent by January and lovely May.
But worldly joys, alas, may not endure 810
For January or anyone, be sure.
Changeable Fortune, O unstable Chance,
Thine is the scorpion's treacherous advance!
Thy head all flattery, about to sting,
Thy tail a death, and death by poisoning.
O brittle joy, O venom sweet and strange,
O monster that so subtly canst arrange
Thy gifts and colour them with all the dyes
Of durability to catch the wise
And foolish too! Say, why hast thou deceived 820
Old January, thy friend, as he believed?
Thou hast robbed him of his sight, his eye
Is dark, and in his grief he longs to die.
Alas this noble January, he
So generous once in his prosperity
Went blind; quite suddenly he lost his sight.
Pitiful loss! He wept it day and night,
While fires of jealousy seared his melancholy;
For fear his wife might fall into some folly.
His heart burned hot; he had been nothing loth, 830
Nay glad, if one had come to slay them both.
For neither on his death nor in his life
Was she to be the mistress or the wife
Of any other, but in weeds of state,
True as a turtle that has lost her mate,
She was to live, the garments on her back
A widow's, never anything but black.
But in the end, after a month or two,
His sorrows cooled a little, it is true,
For when he saw there was no remedy 840
He took in patience his adversity,
Save that the ineradicable sting
Of jealousy embittered everything,
For so outrageous are the thoughts it rouses

That neither when at home or in the houses
Of his acquaintance, no, nor anywhere
Would he allow his wife to take the air
Unless his hand were on her day and night.
  Ah, how she wept, fresh as she was, and bright,
Who loved her Damian, and with so benign 850
A love that sudden death was her design
Unless she could enjoy him; so at first
She wept and waited for her heart to burst.
  And Damian too, upon the other part,
Became in turn so sorrowful of heart
That none was ever like him: night or day
There never was a chance to speak to May
As to his purpose, no, nor anything near it,
Unless old January was there to hear it,
Holding her hand and never letting go. 860
  Nevertheless by writing to and fro
And private signals, Damian knew her mind,
And she was well aware what he designed.
O January, what might it thee avail
Though thou couldst see as far as ship can sail?
As well be blind and be deceived as be
Deceived as others are that still can see.
Consider Argus with his hundred eyes
Poring and prying, yet for all these spies
He was deceived, and many more I know, 870
God wot, who sagely think they are not so.
Least said is soonest mended; say no more.
  Now this fresh May of whom I spoke before
Took some warm wax and fashioned an impression
Of that same key (in January's possession)
Into the garden, where he often went.
Damian who knew exactly what she meant
Secretly forged a counterfeited key.
That's all there is to say, but presently
A wonder will befall, if you will wait, 880
Thanks to this key and to the wicket-gate.
  O noble Ovid, that was truly spoken
When you affirmed there was no cunning token
Or trickery, however long or hot,
That lovers could not find. For did they not

When Pyramus and Thisbe,[11] I recall,
Though strictly watched, held converse through a wall?
There was a trick that none could have forecast!
But to our purpose; ere a week had passed,
Before July was on them, it befell 890
That January's thoughts began to swell,
Incited by his wife, with eager wishes
To be at play with her among the bushes
In his garden, he and she alone,
And so at last one morning he made moan
To May with this intention; 'Ah,' said he,
'Rise up, my wife, my love, my lady free!
The turtle's voice is heard, my dove, my pet.
Winter is gone with all its rain and wet;
Come out with me, bright-eyes, my columbine, 900
O how far fairer are thy breasts than wine!
Our garden is enclosed and walled about;
White spouse, come forth to me; ah, never doubt
But I am wounded to the heart, dear wife,
For love of you, unspotted in your life
As well I know. Come forth to take our pleasures,
Wife of my choice and treasure of my treasures!'
He got these lewd old words out of a book.
And May at once gave Damian a look
Signalling he should go before and wait; 910
So Damian ran ahead, unlocked the gate
And darted in as swiftly as a bird,
He managed to be neither seen nor heard,
And crouched beneath the bushes on his own.
And then this January, blind as stone,
Came hand in hand with May, but unattended,
And down into the garden they descended
And having entered clapped the wicket to.
'Now wife,' he said, 'none's here but I and you,
And you are she, the creature I best love. 920
For by the Lord that sits in Heaven above,
Believe me I would die upon the knife
Rather than hurt you, truest, dearest wife.
Remember how I chose you, for God's sake;

---

[11] In classical mythology, two young lovers. Believing Thisbe killed by a lion, Pyramus killed himself, and Thisbe, finding his body, took her own life.

Not covetously nor in hope to make,
But only for the love I had to you.
And though I may be old and sightless too,
Be true to me and I will tell you why.
 'Three things for certain you shall win thereby:
First, love of Christ; next, honour to yourself; 930
Last, your inheritance, my lands and pelf,
Towers and towns; draw the agreement up,
They're yours, it shall be signed before we sup.
But first, as God may bring my soul to bliss,
I pray you seal the covenant with a kiss.
And though I may be jealous, blame me not;
You are so deeply printed in my thought
That when I see your beauty, and engage
That thought with my dislikable old age,
I cannot—though it might be death to me— 940
Forbear a moment of your company
For very love; I say it with no doubt.
Now kiss me, wife, and let us roam about.'
 Fresh-hearted May on hearing what he said
Benignly answered him with drooping head,
But first and foremost she began to weep.
'Indeed,' she said, 'I have a soul to keep
No less than you, and then there is my honour
Which for a wife is like a flower upon her.
I put it in your hands for good or ill 950
When the priest bound my body to your will,
So let me answer of my own accord
If you will give me leave, beloved lord;
I pray to God that never dawn the day
—Or let me die as foully as I may—
When I shall do my family that shame
Or bring so much dishonour on my name
As to be false. And if my love grow slack,
Take me and strip me, sew me in a sack
And drop me in the nearest lake to drown. 960
I am no common woman of the town,
I am of gentle birth, I keep aloof.
So why speak thus to me, for what reproof
Have I deserved? It's men that are untrue
And women, women ever blamed anew.
I think it a pretence that men profess;

They hide behind a charge of faithlessness.'
  And as she spoke she saw a short way off
Young Damian in his bush. She gave a cough
And signalled with a finger quickly where 970
He was to climb into a tree—a pear
Heavily charged with fruit, and up he went
Perfectly understanding what she meant,
Or any other signal, I may state,
Better than January could, her mate,
For she had written to him, never doubt it,
Telling him all and how to set about it.
And there I leave him sitting, by your pardon,
While May and January roamed the garden.
  Bright was the day and blue the firmament, 980
Down fell the golden flood that Phoebus sent
To gladden every flower with his beams;
He was in Gemini at the time, it seems,
And but a little from his declination
In Cancer, which is Jupiter's exaltation.
And so it happened through the golden tide
Into the garden from the further side
Came Pluto who is king of Fairyland
And many a lady of his elfin band
Behind his queen, the lady Proserpine, 990
Ravished by him from Aetna. I incline
To think it is in Claudian[12] you can read
How she was gathering flowers in a mead
And how he fetched her in his grisly cart.
The King of Faery sat him down apart
Upon a little bench of turfy green,
And then he turned and thus addressed his queen:
  'Dear wife,' he said, 'what no one can gainsay
And what experience shows us every day
Are the foul treacheries women do to men. 1000
Ten thousand tales, and multiply by ten,
Record your notable untruth and lightness.
O Solomon in thy wisdom, wealth and brightness,
Replete in sapience as in worldly glory,
How memorable are thy words and story

---

[12] Author of *The Rape of Proserpine*, an account of the seizure by the king of the underworld of the beautiful daughter of Ceres.

To every creature capable of reason!
Of man's true bounty and of woman's treason
Thou saidst, "Among a thousand found I one,
And yet among all women found I none."
'So said the king who knew your wickedness; 1010
And Jesus son of Sirach,[13] as I guess,
Seldom says much of you in reverence—
Wild fire and a corruptive pestilence
Fall down upon you all to burn and blight!
Do you not see that honourable knight
Who, being blind and old and unobservant,
Is to be cuckolded by his own servant?
Look, there he sits, that lecher in the tree!
Now will I grant it of my majesty
To this blind, old and estimable knight 1020
That he shall instantly receive his sight
Whenever his wife begins her villainy.
He shall know all about her harlotry
Both in rebuke of her and others too.'
'So that,' the queen replied, 'is what you'll do!
Now, by my grandsire's soul, though she is young
I'll put a ready answer on her tongue
And every woman's after, for her sake.
Though taken in their guilt they yet shall make
A bold-faced explanation to excuse them 1030
And bear down all who venture to accuse them;
For lack of answer none of them shall die.
Though a man saw things with his naked eye
We'll face it out, we women, and be bold
To weep and swear, insinuate and scold
As long as men are gullible as geese.
'What do I care for your authorities?
I'm well aware this Jew, this Solomon
Found fools among us women, many a one;
But if he never found a woman true, 1040
God knows that there are many men who do,
Who find them faithful, virtuous and good.
Witness all those in christian sisterhood
Who proved their constancy by martyrdom.
And Roman history has mentioned some,

---

[13] The reputed author of *Ecclesiasticus.*

Aye many, women of exceeding truth.
Now keep your temper, sir, though he, forsooth,
Said there were no good women, if you can.
Consider the opinion of this man.
He meant it thus that sovereign constancy 1050
Is God's alone who sits in Trinity.
Hey! God knows Solomon is only one;
Why do you make so much of Solomon?
What though he built God's temple in the story?
What though he were so rich, so high in glory?
He made a temple for false gods as well,
And what could be more reprehensible?
Plaster him over as you may, dear sir,
He was a lecher and idolater,
And in his latter days forsook the Lord; 1060
Had God not spared him, as the books record,
Because He loved his father, surely He would
Have lost his kingdom, rather than that he should.
And all the villainous terms that you apply
To women, I value at a butterfly!
I am a woman and I needs must speak
Or swell until I burst. Shall I be meek
If he has said that we were wrangleresses?
As ever I may hope to flaunt my tresses.
I will not spare for manners or politeness 1070
To rail at one who rails at woman's lightness.'
'Madam,' he said, 'be angry now no more;
I give it up. But seeing that I swore
Upon my oath to grant him sight again,
I'll stand by what I said, I tell you plain.
I am a king; it fits me not to lie.'
'And I'm the Queen of Fairyland, say I!
Her answer she shall have, I undertake.
Let us have no more words, for goodness' sake.
Indeed I don't intend to be contrary.' 1080
Now let us turn again to January
Who walked the garden with his airy May
And sang more merrily than a popinjay.
'I love you best, and ever shall, my sweet!'
So long among the paths had strayed their feet
That they at last had reached the very tree
Where Damian sat in waiting merrily,

High in his leafy bower of fresh green.
And fresh young May, so shiningly serene,
Began to sigh and said 'Oh! I've a pain! 1090
Oh Sir! Whatever happens, let me gain
One of those pears up there that I can see,
Or I shall die! I long so terribly
To eat a little pear, it looks so green.
O help me for the love of Heaven's Queen!
I warn you that a woman in my plight
May often feel so great an appetite
For fruit that she may die to go without.'
'Alas,' he said, 'that there's no boy about,
Able to climb. Alas, alas,' said he, 1100
'That I am blind,' 'No matter, sir,' said she,
'For if you would consent—there's nothing in it—
To hold the pear-tree in your arms a minute
(I know you have no confidence in me),
Then I could climb up well enough,' said she,
'If I could set my foot upon your back.'
'Of course,' he said, 'why, you shall never lack
For that, or my heart's blood to do you good.'
And down he stooped; upon his back she stood,
Catching a branch, and with a spring she thence 1110
—Ladies, I beg you not to take offence,
I can't embellish, I'm a simple man—
Went up into the tree, and Damian
Pulled up her smock at once and in he thrust.
And when King Pluto saw this shameful lust
He gave back sight to January once more
And made him see far better than before.
Never was man more taken with delight
Than January when he received his sight.
And his first thought was to behold his love. 1020
He cast eyes into the tree above
Only to see that Damian had addressed
His wife in ways that cannot be expressed
Unless I use a most discourteous word.
He gave a roaring cry, as might be heard
From stricken mothers when their babies die.
'Help! Out upon you!' he began to cry.
'Strong Madam Strumpet! What are you up to there?'
'What ails you, sir?' said she, 'what makes you swear?

Have patience, use the reason in your mind, 1130
I've helped you back to sight when you were blind!
Upon my soul I'm telling you no lies;
They told me if I wished to heal your eyes
Nothing could cure them better than for me
To struggle with a fellow in a tree.
God knows it was a kindness that I meant.'
'Struggle?' said he, 'Yes! Anyhow, in it went!'
God send you both a shameful death to die!
He had you, I saw it with my very eye,
And if I did not, hang me by the neck!' 1140
'Why then,' she said, 'my medicine's gone to wreck,
For certainly if you could really see
You'd never say such words as those to me;
You caught some glimpses, but your sight's not good.'
'I see,' he said, 'as well as ever I could,
Thanks be to God! And with both eyes, I do!
And that, I swear, is what he seemed to do.'
'You're hazy, hazy, my good sir,' said she;
'That's all I get for helping you to see.
Alas,' she said, 'that ever I was so kind!' 1150
'Dear wife,' said January, 'never mind,
Come down, dear heart, and if I've slandered you
God knows I'm punished for it. Come down, do!
But by my father's soul, it seemed to me
That Damian had enjoyed you in the tree
And that your smock was pulled up over your breast.'
'Well, think,' she said, 'as it may please you best,
But, Sir, when suddenly a man awakes,
He cannot grasp a thing at once, it takes
A little time to do so perfectly, 1160
For he is dazed at first and cannot see.
Just so a man who has been blind for long
Cannot expect his sight to be so strong
At first, or see as well as those may do
Who've had their eyesight back a day or two.
Until your sight has settled down a bit
You may be frequently deceived by it.
Be careful then, for by our heavenly King
Many a man feels sure he's seen a thing
Which was quite different really, he may fudge it; 1170
Misapprehend a thing and you'll misjudge it.'

And on the word she jumped down from the tree.
And January—who is glad but he?
Kissed her and clasped her in his arms—how often!—
And stroked her breast caressingly to soften
Her indignation. To his palace then
He led her home. Be happy, gentlemen,
That finishes my tale of January;
God and his Mother guard us, blessed Mary!

Questions for Discussion

1. The teller of the tale, the Merchant, has just explained in the prologue to his story that, although he has been married only two months, he is disillusioned with the whole institution of marriage and considers his wife a heartless shrew. What evidence of this attitude do you find in the narrative? Is it presented directly or ironically by the Merchant?

2. Is the tale a savage attack on marriage as an earthly paradise or is it a comic exposure of an all too human institution? In this regard consider the praise of marriage at the beginning of the tale.

3. Why does January not listen to Justinus' warning about the pitfalls of marriage?

4. How does the old knight think of marriage—as a sacrament or as legalized lust? In this connection see his remarks on it at the beginning of the tale and on his marriage day.

5. What is May's attitude toward January on her wedding night? How does the narrator convey this attitude?

6. Is January's blindness a device to advance the plot or does it have a thematic function? To what extent is it a source of comedy?

7. Why are Pluto and Proserpine brought into the tale? In this connection compare the mythical story of Pluto and his ravishment and abduction of Proserpine with that of January and his marriage of May.

8. How does May convince her husband she is innocent of adultery?

William Wycherley (ca. 1640-1716)

The Country Wife

CHARACTERS

MR. HORNER.
MR. HARCOURT.
MR. DORILANT.
MR. PINCHWIFE.
MR. SPARKISH.
SIR JASPER FIDGET.
QUACK.

MRS. MARGERY PINCHWIFE.
ALITHEA, sister of PINCHWIFE.
LADY FIDGET.
MRS. DAINTY FIDGET, sister of SIR JASPER.
MRS. SQUEAMISH.
OLD LADY SQUEAMISH.
LUCY, ALITHEA's maid.

A Boy, Waiters, Servants, and Attendants.

Scene—LONDON

ACT I

SCENE I: HORNER'S *Lodging.*

Enter HORNER, QUACK *following him at a distance.*

HORNER. *(Aside.)* A quack is as fit for a pimp, as a midwife for a bawd; they are still but in their way, both helpers of nature.—*(Aloud.)* Well, my dear doctor, hast thou done what I desired?

QUACK. I have undone you forever with the women, and reported you throughout the whole town as bad as an eunuch, with as much trouble as if I had made you one in earnest.

HORNER. But have you told all the midwives you know, the orange wenches[1] at the playhouses, the city husbands, and old fumbling keepers[2] of this end of the town? for they'll be the readiest to report it.

QUACK. I have told all the chambermaids, waiting-women, tire-women,[3] and old women of my acquaintance; nay, and whispered it as a secret to 'em, and to the whisperers of Whitehall; so that you need not doubt 'twill spread, and you will be as odious to the handsome young women as——

HORNER. As the small-pox. Well——

QUACK. And to the married women of this end of the town, as——

HORNER. As the great one,[4] nay, as their own husbands.

QUACK. And to the city dames, as aniseed Robin,[5] of filthy and contemptible memory; and they will frighten their children with your name, especially their females.

HORNER. And cry, Horner's coming to carry you away. I am only afraid 'twill not be believed. You told 'em it was by an English-French disaster, and an English-French surgeon, who has given me at once not only a cure, but an antidote for the future against that damned malady, and that worse distemper, love, and all other women's evils?

QUACK. Your late journey into France has made it the more credible, and your being here a fortnight before you appeared in public, looks as if you apprehended the shame, which I wonder you do not. Well, I have been hired by young gallants to belie 'em t'other way; but you are the first would be thought a man unfit for women.

1 Girls in the theater who sell oranges and other fruit to the audience.
2 Keepers of mistresses.
3 A tire-woman is a lady's maid.
4 The great pox, syphillis.
5 Famous hermaphrodite of pre-Restoration England.

HORNER. Dear Mr. Doctor, let vain rogues be contented only to be thought abler men than they are; generally 'tis all the pleasure they have; but mine lies another way.

QUACK. You take, methinks, a very preposterous way to it, and as ridiculous as if we operators in physic should put forth bills to disparage our medicaments, with hopes to gain customers.

HORNER. Doctor, there are quacks in love as well as physic, who get but the fewer and worse patients for their boasting; a good name is seldom got by giving it one's self; and women, no more than honor, are compassed by bragging. Come, come, doctor, the wisest lawyer never discovers the merits of his cause till the trial; the wealthiest man conceals his riches, and the cunning gamester his play. Shy husbands and keepers, like old rooks, are not to be cheated but by a new unpractised trick: false friendship will pass now no more than false dice upon 'em; no, not in the city.

Enter BOY.

BOY. There are two ladies and a gentleman coming up. *Exit.*

HORNER. A pox! some unbelieving sisters of my former acquaintance, who, I am afraid, expect their sense should be satisfied of the falsity of the report. No—this formal fool and women!

Enter SIR JASPER FIDGET, LADY FIDGET, *and* MRS. DAINTY FIDGET.

QUACK. His wife and sister.

SIR JASPER. My coach breaking just now before your door, sir, I look upon as an occasional reprimand to me, sir, for not kissing your hands, sir, since your coming out of France, sir; and so my disaster, sir, has been my good fortune, sir; and this is my wife and sister, sir.

HORNER. What then, sir?

SIR JASPER. My lady, and sister, sir.—Wife, this is Master Horner.

LADY FIDGET. Master Horner, husband!

SIR JASPER. My lady, my Lady Fidget, sir.

HORNER. So, sir.

SIR JASPER. Won't you be acquainted with her, sir?—*(Aside.)* So, the report is true, I find, by his coldness or aversion to the sex, but I'll play the wag with him.—*(Aloud.)* Pray salute my wife, my lady, sir.

HORNER. I will kiss no man's wife, sir, for him, sir; I have taken my eternal leave, sir, of the sex already, sir.

SIR JASPER. *(Aside.)* Ha! ha! ha! I'll plague him yet.—*(Aloud.)* Not know my wife, sir?

HORNER. I do know your wife, sir; she's a woman, sir, and consequently a monster, sir, a greater monster than a husband, sir.

SIR JASPER. A husband! how, sir?

HORNER. So, sir; but I make no more cuckolds, sir. *(Makes horns.)*[6]

SIR JASPER. Ha! ha! ha! Mercury! Mercury![7]

LADY FIDGET. Pray, Sir Jasper, let us be gone from this rude fellow.

MRS. DAINTY. Who, by his breeding, would think he had ever been in France?

LADY FIDGET. Foh! he's but too much a French fellow, such as hate women of quality and virtue for their love to their husbands. Sir Jasper, a woman is hated by 'em as much for loving her husband as for loving their money. But pray let's be gone.

HORNER. You do well, madam; for I have nothing that you came for. I have brought over not so much as a bawdy picture, no new postures, nor the second part of the *Ecole des Filles*,[8] nor——

QUACK. *(Apart to* HORNER.*)* Hold, for shame, sir! What d'ye mean? you'll ruin yourself for ever with the sex——

SIR JASPER. Ha! ha! ha! he hates women perfectly, I find.

MRS. DAINTY. What pity 'tis he should!

LADY FIDGET. Ay, he's a base fellow for't. But affectation makes not a woman more odious to them than virtue.

HORNER. Because your virtue is your greatest affectation, madam.

LADY FIDGET. How, you saucy fellow! would you wrong my honor?

HORNER. If I could.

LADY FIDGET. How d'ye mean, sir?

SIR JASPER. Ha! ha! ha! no, he can't wrong your ladyship's honor, upon my honor. He, poor man—hark you in your ear—*(Whispers.)* a mere eunuch.

LADY FIDGET. O filthy French beast! foh! foh! why do we stay? let's be gone: I can't endure the sight of him.

SIR JASPER. Stay but till the chairs come; they'll be here presently.

LADY FIDGET. No!

SIR JASPER. Nor can I stay longer. 'Tis, let me see, a quarter and half quarter of a minute past eleven. The council will be sat; I must away. Business must be preferred always before love and ceremony with the wise, Mr. Horner.

HORNER. And the impotent, Sir Jasper.

SIR JASPER. Ay, ay, the impotent, Master Horner; hah! hah! hah!

LADY FIDGET. What, leave us with a filthy man alone in his lodgings?

SIR JASPER. He's an innocent man now, you know. Pray stay, I'll hasten

---

[6] Horns are a symbol of cuckoldry, hence the significance of Horner's name since by seducing wives he makes horns sprout on the heads of their husbands.

[7] Mercury was used to treat venereal disease.

[8] A pornographic novel of the period.

the chairs to you.—Mr. Horner, your servant; I should be glad to see you at my house. Pray come and dine with me and play at cards with my wife after dinner; you are fit for women at that game yet, ha! ha!—*(Aside.)* 'Tis as much a husband's prudence to provide innocent diversion for a wife as to hinder her unlawful pleasures; and he had better employ her than let her employ herself.—*(Aloud.)* Farewell.

HORNER. Your servant, Sir Jasper. *Exit* SIR JASPER.

LADY FIDGET. I will not stay with him, foh!——

HORNER. Nay, madam, I beseech you stay, if it be but to see I can be as civil to ladies yet as they would desire.

LADY FIDGET. No, no, foh! you cannot be civil to ladies.

MRS. DAINTY. You as civil as ladies would desire?

LADY FIDGET. No, no, no, foh! foh! foh!

Exeunt LADY FIDGET *and* MRS. DAINTY FIDGET.

QUACK. Now, I think, I, or you yourself, rather, have done your business with the women.

HORNER. Thou art an ass. Don't you see already, upon the report, and my carriage, this grave man of business leaves his wife in my lodgings, invites me to his house and wife, who before would not be acquainted with me out of jealousy?

QUACK. Nay, by this means you may be the more acquainted with the husbands, but the less with the wives.

HORNER. Let me alone; if I can but abuse the husbands, I'll soon disabuse the wives. Stay—I'll reckon you up the advantages I am like to have by my stratagem. First, I shall be rid of all my old acquaintances, the most insatiable sort of duns that invade our lodgings in a morning; and next to the pleasure of making a new mistress is that of being rid of an old one, and of all old debts. Love, when it comes to be so, is paid the most unwillingly.

QUACK. Well, you may be so rid of your old acquaintances; but how will you get any new ones?

HORNER. Doctor, thou wilt never make a good chemist, thou art so incredulous and impatient. Ask but all the young fellows of the town if they do not lose more time, like huntsmen, in starting the game, than in running it down. One knows not where to find 'em; who will or will not. Women of quality are so civil you can hardly distinguish love from good breeding, and a man is often mistaken: but now I can be sure she that shows an aversion to me loves the sport, as those women that are gone, whom I warrant to be right. And then the next thing is, your women of honor, as you call 'em, are only chary of their reputations, not their persons; and 'tis scandal they would avoid, not men. Now may I have, by the reputation of an eunuch, the privileges of one, and be seen in a lady's chamber in a morning as early as her husband; kiss virgins before their parents or lovers; and may be, in short, the *passe-partout*[9] of the town. Now, doctor.

QUACK. Nay, now you shall be the doctor; and your process is so new that we do not know but it may succeed.

HORNER. Not so new either; *probatum est,*[10] doctor.

QUACK. Well, I wish you luck and many patients, whilst I go to mine. *Exit.*

Enter HARCOURT *and* DORILANT.

HARCOURT. Come, your appearance at the play yesterday has, I hope, hardened you for the future against the women's contempt and the men's raillery; and now you'll abroad as you were wont.

HORNER. Did I not bear it bravely?

DORILANT. With a most theatrical impudence, nay, more than the orange-wenches show there, or a drunken vizard-mask,[11] or a great-bellied actress; nay, or the most impudent of creatures, an ill poet; or what is yet more impudent, a second-hand critic.

HORNER. But what say the ladies? have they no pity?

HARCOURT. What ladies? The vizard-masks, you know, never pity a man when all's gone, though in their service.

DORILANT. And for the women in the boxes, you'd never pity them when 'twas in your power.

HARCOURT. They say 'tis pity but all that deal with common women should be served so.

DORILANT. Nay, I dare swear they won't admit you to play at cards with them, go to the plays with 'em, or do the little duties which other shadows of men are wont to do for 'em.

HORNER. What do you call shadows of men?

DORILANT. Half-men.

HORNER. What, boys?

DORILANT. Ay, your old boys, old *beaux garçons,*[12] who, like superannuated stallions, are suffered to run, feed, and whinny with the mares as long as they live, though they can do nothing else.

HORNER. Well, a pox on love and wenching! Women serve but to keep a man from better company. Though I can't enjoy them, I shall you the more. Good fellowship and friendship are lasting, rational, and manly pleasures.

---

9 Pass-key.
10 It has been attempted before.
11 A prostitute.
12 Playboys.

HARCOURT. For all that, give me some of those pleasures you call effeminate too; they help to relish one another.

HORNER. They disturb one another.

HARCOURT. No, mistresses are like books. If you pour upon them too much they doze you and make you unfit for company; but if used discreetly, you are the fitter for conversation by 'em.

DORILANT. A mistress should be like a little country retreat near the town; not to dwell in constantly, but only for a night and away, to taste the town the better when a man returns.

HORNER. I tell you, 'tis as hard to be a good fellow, a good friend, and a lover of women, as 'tis to be a good fellow, a good friend, and a lover of money. You cannot follow both, then choose your side. Wine gives you liberty, love takes it away.

DORILANT. Gad, he's in the right on't.

HORNER. Wine gives you joy; love, grief and tortures—besides surgeons. Wine makes us witty; love, only sots. Wine makes us sleep; love breaks it.

DORILANT. By the world he has reason, Harcourt.

HORNER. Wine makes——

DORILANT. Ay, wine makes us—makes us princes; love makes us beggars, poor rogues, egad—and wine——

HORNER. So, there's one converted.—No, no, love and wine, oil and vinegar.

HARCOURT. I grant it; love will still be uppermost.

HORNER. Come, for my part, I will have only those glorious manly pleasures of being very drunk and very slovenly.

Enter BOY.

BOY. Mr. Sparkish is below, sir. *Exit.*

HARCOURT. What, my dear friend! a rogue that is fond of me only, I think, for abusing him.

DORILANT. No, he can no more think the men laugh at him than that women jilt him; his opinion of himself is so good.

HORNER. Well, there's another pleasure by drinking I thought not of. I shall lose his acquaintance because he cannot drink: and you know 'tis a very hard thing to be rid of him; for he's one of those nauseous offerers at wit, who, like the worst fiddlers, run themselves into all companies.

HARCOURT. One that, by being in the company of men of sense, would pass for one.

HORNER. And may so to the short-sighted world, as a false jewel amongst true ones is not discerned at a distance. His company is as troublesome to us as a cuckold's when you have a mind to his wife's.

HARCOURT. No, the rogue will not let us enjoy one another, but ravishes our conversation; though he signifies no more to't than Sir Martin Mar-all's[13] gaping and awkward thrumming upon the lute does to his man's voice and music.

DORILANT. And to pass for a wit in town shows himself a fool every night to us, that are guilty of the plot.

HORNER. Such wits as he are, to a company of reasonable men, like rooks to the gamesters; who only fill a room at the table, but are so far from contributing to the play that they only serve to spoil the fancy of those that do.

DORILANT. Nay, they are used like rooks too, snubbed, checked, and abused; yet the rogues will hang on.

HORNER. A pox on 'em and all that force nature and would be still what she forbids 'em! Affectation is her greatest monster.

HARCOURT. Most men are the contraries to that they would seem. Your bully, you see, is a coward with a long sword; the little humbly fawning physician, with his ebony cane, is he that destroys men.

DORILANT. The usurer, a poor rogue, possessed of moldy bonds and mortgages; and we they call spendthrifts are only wealthy, who lay out his money upon daily new purchases of pleasure.

HORNER. Ay, your arrantest cheat is your trustee or executor; your jealous man, the greatest cuckold; your churchman, the greatest atheist; and your noisy, pert rogue of a wit, the greatest fop, dullest ass, and worst company, as you shall see; for here he comes.

Enter SPARKISH.

SPARKISH. How is't, sparks? How is't? Well, faith, Harry, I must rally thee a little, ha! ha! ha! upon the report in town of thee, ha! ha! ha! I can't hold i'faith; shall I speak?

HORNER. Yes; but you'll be so bitter then.

SPARKISH. Honest Dick and Frank here shall answer for me; I will not be extreme bitter, by the universe.

HARCOURT. We will be bound in a ten thousand pound bond, he shall not be bitter at all.

DORILANT. Nor sharp, nor sweet.

HORNER. What, not downright insipid?

SPARKISH. Nay then, since you are so brisk, and provoke me, take what follows. You must know, I was discoursing and rallying with some ladies yesterday, and they happened to talk of the fine new signs in town——

[13] A character in John Dryden's *Sir Martin Mar-all* (1667). He pretends to serenade his mistress with a lute, although his servant hiding behind him is actually singing and playing.

HORNER. Very fine ladies, I believe.

SPARKISH. Said I, I know where the best new sign is.—Where? says one of the ladies.—In Covent Garden, I replied.—Said another, In what street? —In Russel Street, answered I.—Lord, says another, I'm sure there was never a fine new sign there yesterday.—Yes, but there was, said I again; and it came out of France, and has been there a fortnight.

DORILANT. A pox! I can hear no more, prithee.

HORNER. No, hear him out; let him tune his crowd[14] a while.

HARCOURT. The worst music, the greatest preparation.

SPARKISH. Nay, faith, I'll make you laugh.—It cannot be, says a third lady.—Yes, yes, quoth I again.—Says a fourth lady——

HORNER. Look to't, we'll have no more ladies.

SPARKISH. No—then mark, mark, now. Said I to the fourth, Did you never see Mr. Horner? he lodges in Russel Street and he's a sign of a man, you know, since he came out of France; ha! ha! ha!

HORNER. But the devil take me if thine be the sign of a jest.

SPARKISH. With that they all fell a-laughing till they bepissed themselves. What, but it does not move you, methinks? Well, I see one had as good go to law without a witness, as break a jest without a laugher on one's side.—Come, come, sparks, but where do we dine? I have left at Whitehall an earl, to dine with you.

DORILANT. Why, I thought thou hadst loved a man with a title better than a suit with a French trimming to't.

HARCOURT. Go to him again.

SPARKISH. No, sir, a wit to me is the greatest title in the world.

HORNER. But go dine with your earl, sir; he may be exceptious. We are your friends, and will not take it ill to be left, I do assure you.

HARCOURT. Nay, faith, he shall go to him.

SPARKISH. Nay, pray, gentlemen.

DORILANT. We'll thrust you out, if you won't; what, disappoint anybody for us?

SPARKISH. Nay, dear gentlemen, hear me.

HORNER. No, no, sir, by no means; pray go, sir.

SPARKISH. Why, dear rogues——

DORILANT. No, no. *(They all thrust him out of the room.)*

ALL. Ha! ha! ha!

Re-enter SPARKISH.

SPARKISH. But, sparks, pray hear me. What, d'ye think I'll eat then with gay shallow fops and silent coxcombs? I think wit as necessary at dinner as

[14] Fiddle.

a glass of good wine; and that's the reason I never have any stomach when I eat alone.—Come, but where do we dine?

HORNER. Even where you will.

SPARKISH. At Chateline's?[15]

DORILANT. Yes, if you will.

SPARKISH. Or at the Cock?

DORILANT. Yes, if you please.

SPARKISH. Or at the Dog and Partridge?[16]

HORNER. Ay, if you have a mind to't; for we shall dine at neither.

SPARKISH. Pshaw! with your fooling we shall lose the new play; and I would no more miss seeing a new play the first day, than I would miss sitting in the wit's row. Therefore I'll go fetch my mistress, and away. *Exit.*

Enter PINCHWIFE.

HORNER. Who have we here? Pinchwife?

PINCHWIFE. Gentlemen, your humble servant.

HORNER. Well, Jack, by thy long absence from the town, the grumness of thy countenance, and the slovenliness of thy habit, I should give thee joy, should I not, of marriage?

PINCHWIFE. *(Aside.)* Death! does he know I'm married too? I thought to have concealed it from him at least.—*(Aloud.)* My long stay in the country will excuse my dress; and I have a suit of law that brings me up to town, that puts me out of humor. Besides, I must give Sparkish tomorrow five thousand pounds to lie with my sister.

HORNER. Nay, you country gentlemen, rather than not purchase, will buy anything; and he is a cracked title, if we may quibble. Well, but am I to give thee joy? I heard thou wert married.

PINCHWIFE. What then?

HORNER. Why, the next thing that is to be heard, is thou'rt a cuckold.

PINCHWIFE. *(Aside.)* Insupportable name!

HORNER. But I did not expect marriage from such a whoremaster as you; one that knew the town so much and women so well.

PINCHWIFE. Why, I have married no London wife.

HORNER. Pshaw! that's all one. That grave circumspection in marrying a country wife is like refusing a deceitful pampered Smithfield[17] jade, to go and be cheated by a friend in the country.

PINCHWIFE. *(Aside.)* A pox on him and his simile!—*(Aloud.)* At least we

---

[15] A French restaurant in Covent Garden.

[16] Taverns near Covent Garden.

[17] Horse market in London. A jade is not only a broken-down horse but also an immoral woman.

are a little surer of the breed there, know what her keeping has been, whether foiled or unsound.

HORNER. Come, come, I have known a clap gotten in Wales; and there are cousins, justices' clerks, and chaplains in the country—I won't say coachmen. But she's handsome and young?

PINCHWIFE. *(Aside.)* I'll answer as I should do.—*(Aloud.)* No, no; she has no beauty but her youth, no attraction but her modesty: wholesome, homely, and huswifely; that's all.

DORILANT. He talks as like a grazier as he looks.

PINCHWIFE. She's too awkard, ill-favored, and silly to bring to town.

HARCOURT. Then methinks you should bring her to be taught breeding.

PINCHWIFE. To be taught! no, sir, I thank you. Good wives and private soldiers should be ignorant—I'll keep her from your instructions, I warrant you.

HARCOURT. *(Aside.)* The rogue is as jealous as if his wife were not ignorant.

HORNER. Why, if she be ill-favored, there will be less danger here for you than by leaving her in the country. We have such variety of dainties that we are seldom hungry.

DORILANT. But they have always coarse, constant, swinging stomachs in the country.

HARCOURT. Foul feeders indeed!

DORILANT. And your hospitality is great there.

HARCOURT. Open house; every man's welcome.

PINCHWIFE. So, so, gentlemen.

HORNER. But, prithee, why shouldst thou marry her? If she be ugly, ill-bred, and silly, she must be rich then.

PINCHWIFE. As rich as if she brought me twenty thousand pounds out of this town; for she'll be as sure not to spend her moderate portion, as a London baggage would be to spend hers, let it be what it would: so 'tis all one. Then, because she's ugly, she's the likelier to be my own; and being ill-bred, she'll hate conversation; and since silly and innocent, will not know the difference betwixt a man of one-and-twenty and one of forty.

HORNER. Nine—to my knowledge. But if she be silly, she'll expect as much from a man of forty-nine, as from him of one-and-twenty. But methinks wit is more necessary than beauty; and I think no young woman ugly that has it, and no handsome woman agreeable without it.

PINCHWIFE. 'Tis my maxim, he's a fool that marries; but he's a greater that does not marry a fool. What is wit in a wife good for, but to make a man a cuckold?

HORNER. Yes, to keep it from his knowledge.

PINCHWIFE. A fool cannot contrive to make her husband a cuckold.

HORNER. No; but she'll club with a man that can: and what is worse, if she cannot make her husband a cuckold; she'll make him jealous, and pass for one: and then 'tis all one.

PINCHWIFE. Well, well, I'll take care for one. My wife shall make me no cuckold, though she had your help, Mr. Horner. I understand the town, sir.

DORILANT. *(Aside.)* His help!

HARCOURT. *(Aside.)* He's come newly to town, it seems, and has not heard how things are with him.

HORNER. But tell me, has marriage cured thee of whoring, which it seldom does?

HARCOURT. 'Tis more than age can do.

HORNER. No, the word is, I'll marry and live honest. But a marriage vow is like a penitent gamester's oath; and entering into bonds and penalties to stint himself to such a particular small sum at play for the future, which makes him but the more eager; and not being able to hold out, loses his money again, and his forfeit to boot.

DORILANT. Ay, ay, a gamester will be a gamester whilst his money lasts, and a whoremaster whilst his vigor.

HARCOURT. Nay, I have known 'em when they are broke and can lose no more, keep a fumbling with the box in their hands to fool with only, and hinder other gamesters.

DORILANT. That had wherewithal to make lusty stakes.

PINCHWIFE. Well, gentlemen, you may laugh at me; but you shall never lie with my wife. I know the town.

HORNER. But prithee, was not the way you were in better? is not keeping better than marriage?

PINCHWIFE. A pox on't! the jades would jilt me; I could never keep a whore to myself.

HORNER. So, then you only married to keep a whore to yourself. Well, but let me tell you: women, as you say, are like soldiers—made constant and loyal by good pay, rather than by oaths and covenants. Therefore I'd advise my friends to keep rather than marry; since too I find, by your example, it does not serve one's turn; for I saw you yesterday in the eighteenpenny[18] place with a pretty country-wench.

PINCHWIFE. *(Aside.)* How the devil! did he see my wife then? I sat there that she might not be seen. But she shall never go to a play again.

HORNER. What! dost thou blush, at nine-and-forty, for having been seen with a wench?

---

[18] The middle gallery of the theater occupied by clerks, women of the town, and people from the country. The most fashionable playgoers sat below in the boxes.

DORILANT. No, faith, I warrant 'twas his wife which he seated there out of sight; for he's a cunning rogue and understands the town.

HARCOURT. He blushes. Then 'twas his wife; for men are now more ashamed to be seen with them in public than with a wench.

PINCHWIFE. *(Aside.)* Hell and damnation! I'm undone, since Horner has seen her, and they know 'twas she.

HORNER. But prithee, was it thy wife? She was exceeding pretty: I was in love with her at that distance.

PINCHWIFE. You are like never to be nearer to her. Your servant, gentlemen. *(Offers to go.)*

HORNER. Nay, prithee stay.

PINCHWIFE. I cannot; I will not.

HORNER. Come, you shall dine with us.

PINCHWIFE. I have dined already.

HORNER. Come, I know thou hast not: I'll treat thee, dear rogue; thou sha't spend none of thy Hampshire money today.

PINCHWIFE. *(Aside.)* Treat me! So, he uses me already like his cuckold.

HORNER. Nay, you shall not go.

PINCHWIFE. I must; I have business at home. *Exit.*

HARCOURT. To beat his wife. He's as jealous of her as a Cheapside husband[19] of a Covent Garden wife.[20]

HORNER. Why, 'tis as hard to find an old whoremaster without jealousy and the gout, as a young one without fear, or the pox:—

As gout in age from pox in youth proceeds,
So wenching past, then jealousy succeeds;
The worst disease that love and wenching breeds.

Exeunt.

ACT II

SCENE I: *A Room in* PINCHWIFE'S *House.*

MRS. MARGERY PINCHWIFE *and* ALITHEA. PINCHWIFE *peeping behind at the door.*

MRS. PINCHWIFE. Pray, sister, where are the best fields and woods to walk in, in London?

---

[19] A husband who is a merchant.
[20] An aristocratic wife.

ALITHEA. *(Aside.)* A pretty question!—*(Aloud.)* Why, sister, Mulberry Garden and St. James's Park; and, for close walks, the New Exchange.[1]

MRS. PINCHWIFE. Pray, sister, tell me why my husband looks so grum here in town, and keeps me up so close, and will not let me go a-walking, nor let me wear my best gown yesterday.

ALITHEA. Oh, he's jealous, sister.

MRS. PINCHWIFE. Jealous! what's that?

ALITHEA. He's afraid you should love another man.

MRS. PINCHWIFE. How should he be afraid of my loving another man when he will not let me see any but himself?

ALITHEA. Did he not carry you yesterday to a play?

MRS. PINCHWIFE. Ay; but we sat amongst ugly people. He would not let me come near the gentry, who sat under us, so that I could not see 'em. He told me none but naughty women sat there, whom they toused and moused.[2] But I would have ventured, for all that.

ALITHEA. But how did you like the play?

MRS. PINCHWIFE. Indeed I was weary of the play; but I liked hugeously the actors. They are the goodliest, properest men, sister!

ALITHEA. Oh, but you must not like the actors, sister.

MRS. PINCHWIFE. Ay, how should I help it, sister? Pray, sister, when my husband comes in will you ask leave for me to go a-walking?

ALITHEA. *(Aside.)* A-walking! ha! ha! Lord, a country-gentlewoman's pleasure is the drudgery of a footpost; and she requires as much airing as her husband's horses. But here comes your husband: I'll ask, though I'm sure he'll not grant it.

MRS. PINCHWIFE. He says he won't let me go abroad for fear of catching the pox.

ALITHEA. Fy! the small-pox you should say.

Enter PINCHWIFE.

MRS. PINCHWIFE. Oh my dear, dear bud, welcome home! Why dost thou look so fropish?[3] who has nangered thee?

PINCHWIFE. You're a fool. (MRS. PINCHWIFE *goes aside, and cries.)*

ALITHEA. Faith, so she is, for crying for no fault, poor tender creature!

PINCHWIFE. What, you would have her as impudent as yourself, as arrant a jilflirt, a gadder, a magpie; and to say all, a mere notorious town-woman?

ALITHEA. Brother, you are my only censurer; and the honor of your family

---

[1] An arcade in the Strand that was the shopping center for fashionable society.

[2] Tossed and tumbled in a familiar way.

[3] Peevish.

will sooner suffer in your wife there than in me, though I take the innocent liberty of the town.

PINCHWIFE. Hark you, mistress, do not talk so before my wife.—The innocent liberty of the town!

ALITHEA. Why, pray, who boasts of any intrigue with me? what lampoon has made my name notorious? what ill women frequent my lodgings? I keep no company with any women of scandalous reputations.

PINCHWIFE. No, you keep the men of scandalous reputations company.

ALITHEA. Where? would you not have me civil? answer 'em in a box at the plays, in the drawing-room at Whitehall, in St. James's Park, Mulberry Garden, or——

PINCHWIFE. Hold, hold! Do not teach my wife where the men are to be found: I believe she's the worse for your town-documents already. I bid you keep her in ignorance, as I do.

MRS. PINCHWIFE. Indeed, be not angry with her, bud, she will tell me nothing of the town, though I ask her a thousand times a day.

PINCHWIFE. Then you are very inquisitive to know, I find?

MRS. PINCHWIFE. Not I indeed, dear; I hate London. Our place-house in the country is worth a thousand of't: would I were there again!

PINCHWIFE. So you shall, I warrant. But were you not talking of plays and players when I came in?—*(To* ALITHEA.*)* You are her encourager in such discourses.

MRS. PINCHWIFE. No, indeed, dear; she chid me just now for liking the playermen.

PINCHWIFE. *(Aside.)* Nay, if she be so innocent as to own to me her liking them, there is no hurt in't.—*(Aloud.)* Come, my poor rogue, but thou likest none better than me?

MRS. PINCHWIFE. Yes, indeed, but I do. The playermen are finer folks.

PINCHWIFE. But you love none better than me?

MRS. PINCHWIFE. You are my own dear bud and I know you. I hate a stranger.

PINCHWIFE. Ay, my dear, you must love me only; and not be like the naughty town-women who only hate their husbands and love every man else; love plays, visits, fine coaches, fine clothes, fiddles, balls, treats, and so lead a wicked town-life.

MRS. PINCHWIFE. Nay, if to enjoy all these things be a town-life, London is not so bad a place, dear.

PINCHWIFE. How! if you love me, you must hate London.

ALITHEA. *(Aside.)* The fool has forbid me discovering to her the pleasures of the town, and he is now setting her agog upon them himself.

MRS. PINCHWIFE. But, husband, do the town-women love the playermen too?

PINCHWIFE. Yes, I warrant you.

MRS. PINCHWIFE. Ay, I warrant you.

PINCHWIFE. Why, you do not, I hope?

MRS. PINCHWIFE. No, no, bud. But why have we no playermen in the country?

PINCHWIFE. Ha!—Mrs. Minx, ask me no more to go to a play.

MRS. PINCHWIFE. Nay, why, love? I did not care for going: but when you forbid me, you make me, as 'twere, desire it.

ALITHEA. *(Aside.)* So 'twill be in other things, I warrant.

MRS. PINCHWIFE. Pray let me go to a play, dear.

PINCHWIFE. Hold your peace, I wo' not.

MRS. PINCHWIFE. Why, love?

PINCHWIFE. Why, I'll tell you.

ALITHEA. *(Aside.)* Nay, if he tell her, she'll give him more cause to forbid her that place.

MRS. PINCHWIFE. Pray why, dear?

PINCHWIFE. First, you like the actors; and the gallants may like you.

MRS. PINCHWIFE. What, a homely country girl! No, bud, nobody will like me.

PINCHWIFE. I tell you yes, they may.

MRS. PINCHWIFE. No, no, you jest—I won't believe you: I will go.

PINCHWIFE. I tell you then, that one of the lewdest fellows in town, who saw you there, told me he was in love with you.

MRS. PINCHWIFE. Indeed! who, who, pray who was't?

PINCHWIFE. *(Aside.)* I've gone too far, and slipped before I was aware; how overjoyed she is!

MRS. PINCHWIFE. Was it any Hampshire gallant, any of our neighbors? I promise you, I am beholden to him.

PINCHWIFE. I promise you, you lie; for he would but ruin you, as he has done hundreds. He has no other love for women but that; such as he look upon women, like basilisks, but to destroy 'em.

MRS. PINCHWIFE. Ay, but if he loves me why should he ruin me? answer me to that. Methinks he should not, I would do him no harm.

ALITHEA. Ha! ha! ha!

PINCHWIFE. 'Tis very well; but I'll keep him from doing you any harm, or me either. But here comes company; get you in, get you in.

MRS. PINCHWIFE. But, pray, husband, is he a pretty gentleman that loves me?

PINCHWIFE. In, baggage, in. *(Thrusts her in, and shuts the door.)*

Enter SPARKISH *and* HARCOURT.

What, all the lewd libertines of the town brought to my lodging by this easy coxcomb! 'sdeath, I'll not suffer it.

SPARKISH. Here, Harcourt, do you approve my choice?—*(To* ALITHEA.*)* Dear little rogue, I told you I'd bring you acquainted with all my friends, the wits and—— *(*HARCOURT *salutes her.)*

PINCHWIFE. Ay, they shall know her, as well as you yourself will, I warrant you.

SPARKISH. This is one of those, my pretty rogue, that are to dance at your wedding tomorrow; and him you must bid welcome ever to what you and I have.

PINCHWIFE. *(Aside.)* Monstrous!

SPARKISH. Harcourt, how dost thou like her, faith? Nay, dear, do not look down; I should hate to have a wife of mine out of countenance at anything.

PINCHWIFE. *(Aside.)* Wonderful!

SPARKISH. Tell me, I say, Harcourt, how dost thou like her? Thou hast stared upon her enough to resolve me.

HARCOURT. So infinitely well, that I could wish I had a mistress too, that might differ from her in nothing but her love and engagement to you.

ALITHEA. Sir, Master Sparkish has often told me that his acquaintance were all wits and rallieurs, and now I find it.

SPARKISH. No, by the universe, madam, he does not rally now; you may believe him. I do assure you, he is the honestest, worthiest, true-hearted gentleman—a man of such perfect honor, he would say nothing to a lady he does not mean.

PINCHWIFE. *(Aside.)* Praising another man to his mistress!

HARCOURT. Sir, you are so beyond expectation obliging, that——

SPARKISH. Nay, egad, I am sure you do admire her extremely; I see't in your eyes.—He does admire you, madam.—By the world, don't you?

HARCOURT. Yes, above the world, or the most glorious part of it—her whole sex: and till now I never thought I should have envied you or any man about to marry, but you have the best excuse for marriage I ever knew.

ALITHEA. Nay, now, sir, I'm satisfied you are of the society of the wits and rallieurs; since you cannot spare your friend, even when he is but too civil to you. But the surest sign is, since you are an enemy to marriage—for that I hear you hate as much as business or bad wine.

HARCOURT. Truly, madam, I was never an enemy to marriage till now, because marriage was never an enemy to me before.

ALITHEA. But why, sir, is marriage an enemy to you now? because it robs you of your friend here? for you look upon a friend married as one gone into a monastery, that is, dead to the world.

HARCOURT. 'Tis indeed because you marry him; I see, madam, you can guess my meaning. I do confess heartily and openly, I wish it were in my power to break the match; by Heavens I would.

SPARKISH. Poor Frank!

ALITHEA. Would you be so unkind to me?

HARCOURT. No, no, 'tis not because I would be unkind to you.

SPARKISH. Poor Frank! no gad, 'tis only his kindness to me.

PINCHWIFE. *(Aside.)* Great kindness to you indeed! Insensible fop; let a man make love to his wife to his face!

SPARKISH. Come, dear Frank, for all my wife there, that shall be, thou shalt enjoy me sometimes, dear rogue. By my honor, we men of wit condole for our deceased brother in marriage as much as for one dead in earnest: I think that was prettily said of me, ha, Harcourt?—But come, Frank, be not melancholy for me.

HARCOURT. No, I assure you, I am not melancholy for you.

SPARKISH. Prithee, Frank, dost think my wife that shall be there, a fine person?

HARCOURT. I could gaze upon her till I became as blind as you are.

SPARKISH. How as I am? how?

HARCOURT. Because you are a lover, and true lovers are blind, stock blind.

SPARKISH. True, true; but by the world she has wit too, as well as beauty: go, go with her into a corner and try if she has wit; talk to her anything, she's bashful before me.

HARCOURT. Indeed, if a woman wants wit in a corner she has it nowhere.

ALITHEA. *(Aside to* SPARKISH.*)* Sir, you dispose of me a little before your time——

SPARKISH. Nay, nay, madam, let me have an earnest of your obedience, or —go, go, madam—— *(*HARCOURT *courts* ALITHEA *aside.)*

PINCHWIFE. How, sir! if you are not concerned for the honor of a wife, I am for that of a sister; he shall not debauch her. Be a pander to your own wife! bring men to her! let 'em make love before your face! thrust 'em into a corner together then leave 'em in private! is this your town wit and conduct?

SPARKISH. Ha! ha! ha! a silly wise rogue would make one laugh more than a stark fool; ha! ha! I shall burst. Nay, you shall not disturb 'em; I'll vex thee, by the world.

(Struggles with PINCHWIFE *to keep him from* HARCOURT *and* ALITHEA.*)*

ALITHEA. The writings are drawn, sir, settlements made; 'tis too late, sir, and past all revocation.

HARCOURT. Then so is my death.

ALITHEA. I would not be unjust to him.

HARCOURT. Then why to me so?

ALITHEA. I have no obligation to you.

HARCOURT. My love.

ALITHEA. I had his before.

HARCOURT. You never had it; he wants, you see, jealousy, the only infallible sign of it.

ALITHEA. Love proceeds from esteem; he cannot distrust my virtue: besides, he loves me, or he would not marry me.

HARCOURT. Marrying you is no more sign of his love than bribing your woman, that he may marry you, is a sign of his generosity. Marriage is rather a sign of interest than love; and he that marries a fortune covets a mistress, not loves her. But if you take marriage for a sign of love, take it from me immediately.

ALITHEA. No, now you have put a scruple in my head; but in short, sir, to end our dispute, I must marry him. My reputation would suffer in the world else.

HARCOURT. No; if you do marry him, with your pardon, madam, your reputation suffers in the world, and you would be thought in necessity for a cloak.

ALITHEA. Nay, now you are rude, sir.—Mr. Sparkish, pray come hither, your friend here is very troublesome, and very loving.

HARCOURT. *(Aside to* ALITHEA.*)* Hold! hold!——

PINCHWIFE. D'ye hear that?

SPARKISH. Why, d'ye think I'll seem to be jealous, like a country bumpkin?

PINCHWIFE. No, rather be a cuckold, like a credulous cit.[4]

HARCOURT. Madam, you would not have been so little generous to have told him.

ALITHEA. Yes, since you could be so little generous to wrong him.

HARCOURT. Wrong him! no man can do't. He's beneath an injury: a bubble, a coward, a senseless idiot, a wretch so contemptible to all the world but you, that——

ALITHEA. Hold, do not rail at him, for since he is like to be my husband, I am resolved to like him: nay, I think I am obliged to tell him you are not his friend.—Master Sparkish, Master Sparkish!

SPARKISH. What, what?—*(To* HARCOURT.*)* Now, dear rogue, has she not wit?

HARCOURT. *(Speaks surlily.)* Not so much as I thought, and hoped she had.

ALITHEA. Mr. Sparkish, do you bring people to rail at you?

HARCOURT. Madam——

SPARKISH. How! no; but if he does rail at me, 'tis but in jest, I warrant: what we wits do for one another, and never take any notice of it.

ALITHEA. He spoke so scurrilously of you, I had no patience to hear him; besides, he has been making love to me.

HARCOURT. *(Aside.)* True, damned tell-tale woman!

---

[4] A contemptuous term for a city dweller.

SPARKISH. Pshaw! to show his parts—we wits rail and make love often, but to show our parts: as we have no affections, so we have no malice, we——

ALITHEA. He said you were a wretch below an injury——

SPARKISH. Pshaw!

HARCOURT. *(Aside.)* Damned, senseless, impudent, virtuous jade! Well, since she won't let me have her, she'll do as good, she'll make me hate her.

ALITHEA. A common bubble——

SPARKISH. Pshaw!

ALITHEA. A coward——

SPARKISH. Pshaw, pshaw!

ALITHEA. A senseless, drivelling idiot——

SPARKISH. How! did he disparage my parts? Nay, then, my honor's concerned, I can't put up that, sir, by the world—brother, help me to kill him—*(Aside.)* I may draw now, since we have the odds of him:—'tis a good occasion, too, before my mistress—— *(Offers to draw.)*

ALITHEA. Hold, hold!

SPARKISH. What, what?

ALITHEA. *(Aside.)* I must not let 'em kill the gentleman neither, for his kindness to me: I am so far from hating him, that I wish my gallant had his person and understanding. Nay, if my honor——

SPARKISH. I'll be thy death.

ALITHEA. Hold, hold! Indeed, to tell the truth, the gentleman said after all, that what he spoke was but out of friendship to you.

SPARKISH. How! say! I am—I am a fool, that is, no wit, out of friendship to me?

ALITHEA. Yes, to try whether I was concerned enough for you; and made love to me only to be satisfied of my virtue, for your sake.

HARCOURT. *(Aside.)* Kind, however.

SPARKISH. Nay, if it were so, my dear rogue, I ask thee pardon; but why would not you tell me so, faith?

HARCOURT. Because I did not think on't, faith.

SPARKISH. Come, Horner does not come; Harcourt, let's be gone to the new play.—Come, madam.

ALITHEA. I will not go, if you intend to leave me alone in the box and run into the pit, as you use to do.

SPARKISH. Pshaw! I'll leave Harcourt with you in the box to entertain you, and that's as good; if I sat in the box, I should be thought no judge but of trimmings.—Come away, Harcourt, lead her down.

(Exeunt SPARKISH, HARCOURT, *and* ALITHEA.*)*

PINCHWIFE. Well, go thy ways, for the flower of the true town fops, such as spend their estates before they come to 'em, and are cuckolds before they're married. But let me go look to my own freehold.—How!

Enter LADY FIDGET, MRS. DAINTY FIDGET, *and* MRS. SQUEAMISH.

LADY FIDGET. Your servant, sir: where is your lady? We are come to wait upon her to the new play.

PINCHWIFE. New play!

LADY FIDGET. And my husband will wait upon you presently.

PINCHWIFE. *(Aside.)* Damn your civility.—*(Aloud.)* Madam, by no means; I will not see Sir Jasper here till I have waited upon him at home; nor shall my wife see you till she has waited upon your ladyship at your lodgings.

LADY FIDGET. Now we are here, sir?

PINCHWIFE. No, Madam.

MRS. DAINTY. Pray, let us see her.

MRS. SQUEAMISH. We will not stir till we see her.

PINCHWIFE. *(Aside.)* A pox on you all!—*(Goes to the door, and returns.)* She has locked the door and is gone abroad.

LADY FIDGET. No, you have locked the door and she's within.

MRS. DAINTY. They told us below she was here.

PINCHWIFE. *(Aside.)* Will nothing do?—*(Aloud.)* Well, it must out then. To tell you the truth, ladies, which I was afraid to let you know before, lest it might endanger your lives. My wife has just now the small-pox come out upon her; do not be frightened; but pray be gone, ladies; you shall not stay here in danger of your lives; pray get you gone, ladies.

LADY FIDGET. No, no, we have all had 'em.

MRS. SQUEAMISH. Alack, alack!

MRS. DAINTY. Come, come, we must see how it goes with her; I understand the disease.

LADY FIDGET. Come!

PINCHWIFE. *(Aside.)* Well, there is no being too hard for women at their own weapon—lying; therefore I'll quit the field. *Exit.*

MRS. SQUEAMISH. Here's an example of jealousy!

LADY FIDGET. Indeed, as the world goes, I wonder there are no more jealous, since wives are so neglected.

MRS. DAINTY. Pshaw! as the world goes, to what end should they be jealous?

LADY FIDGET. Foh! 'tis a nasty world.

MRS. SQUEAMISH. That men of parts, great acquaintance, and quality, should take up with and spend themselves and fortunes in keeping little playhouse creatures, foh!

LADY FIDGET. Nay, that women of understanding, great acquaintance, and good quality, should fall a-keeping too of little creatures, foh!

MRS. SQUEAMISH. Why, 'tis the men of quality's fault; they never visit women of honor and reputation as they used to do; and have not so much as common civility for ladies of our rank, but use us with the same indifferency and ill-breeding as if we were all married to 'em.

LADY FIDGET. She says true; 'tis an arrant shame women of quality should be so slighted; methinks birth—birth should go for something; I have known men admired, courted, and followed for their titles only.

MRS. SQUEAMISH. Ay, one would think men of honor should not love, no more than marry, out of their own rank.

MRS. DAINTY. Fy, fy, upon 'em! they are come to think cross breeding for themselves best, as well as for their dogs and horses.

LADY FIDGET. They are dogs and horses for't.

MRS. SQUEAMISH. One would think, if not for love, for vanity a little.

MRS. DAINTY. Nay, they do satisfy their vanity upon us sometimes; and are kind to us in their report—tell all the world they lie with us.

LADY FIDGET. Damned rascals, that we should be only wronged by 'em! To report a man has had a person, when he has not had a person, is the greatest wrong in the whole world that can be done to a person.

MRS. SQUEAMISH. Well, 'tis an arrant shame noble persons should be so wronged and neglected.

LADY FIDGET. But still 'tis an arranter shame for a noble person to neglect her own honor, and defame her own noble person with little inconsiderable fellows, foh!

MRS. DAINTY. I suppose the crime against our honor is the same with a man of quality as with another.

LADY FIDGET. How! no sure; the man of quality is likest one's husband, and therefore the fault should be the less.

MRS. DAINTY. But then the pleasure should be the less.

LADY FIDGET. Fy, fy, fy, for shame, sister! whither shall we ramble? Be continent in your discourse or I shall hate you.

MRS. DAINTY. Besides, an intrigue is so much the more notorious for the man's quality.

MRS. SQUEAMISH. 'Tis true that nobody takes notice of a private man, and therefore with him 'tis more secret; and the crime's the less when 'tis not known.

LADY FIDGET. You say true; i'faith, I think you are in the right on't: 'tis not an injury to a husband till it be an injury to our honors; so that a woman of honor loses no honor with a private person; and to say truth——

MRS. DAINTY. *(Apart to* MRS. SQUEAMISH.*)* So, the little fellow is grown a private person——with her——

LADY FIDGET. But still my dear, dear honor——

Enter SIR JASPER FIDGET, HORNER, *and* DORILANT.

SIR JASPER. Ay, my dear, dear of honor, thou hast still so much honor in thy mouth——

HORNER. *(Aside.)* That she has none elsewhere.

LADY FIDGET. Oh, what d'ye mean to bring in these upon us?

MRS. DAINTY. Foh! these are as bad as wits.

MRS. SQUEAMISH. Foh!

LADY FIDGET. Let us leave the room.

SIR JASPER. Stay, stay; faith, to tell you the naked truth——

LADY FIDGET. Fy, Sir Jasper! do not use that word naked.

SIR JASPER. Well, well, in short I have business at Whitehall and cannot go to the play with you; therefore would have you go——

LADY FIDGET. With those two to a play?

SIR JASPER. No, not with t'other, but with Mr. Horner; there can be no more scandal to go with him than with Mr. Tattle, or Master Limberham.[5]

LADY FIDGET. With that nasty fellow! no—no.

SIR JASPER. *(Whispers to* LADY FIDGET.*)* Nay, prithee, dear, hear me.

HORNER. Ladies——

*(*HORNER *and* DORILANT *draw near* MRS. SQUEAMISH *and* MRS. DAINTY FIDGET.*)*

MRS. DAINTY. Stand off.

MRS. SQUEAMISH. Do not approach us.

MRS. DAINTY. You herd with the wits; you are obscenity all over.

MRS. SQUEAMISH. And I would as soon look upon a picture of Adam and Eve, without fig-leaves, as any of you, if I could help it; therefore keep off, and do not make us sick.

DORILANT. What a devil are these?

HORNER. Why, these are pretenders to honor, as critics to wit, only by censuring others; and as every raw, peevish, out-of-humored, affected, dull, tea-drinking, arithmetical fop, sets up for a wit by railing at men of sense, so these for honor, by railing at the court, and ladies of as great honor as quality.

SIR JASPER. Come, Mr. Horner, I must desire you to go with these ladies to the play, sir.

HORNER. I, sir?

---

[5] Names used to denote a foolish and harmless lover.

SIR JASPER. Ay, ay, come, sir.

HORNER. I must beg your pardon, sir, and theirs; I will not be seen in women's company in public again for the world.

SIR JASPER. Ha, ha, strange aversion!

MRS. SQUEAMISH. No, he's for women's company in private.

SIR JASPER. He—poor man—he—ha! ha! ha!

MRS. DAINTY. 'Tis a greater shame amongst lewd fellows to be seen in virtuous women's company, than for the women to be seen with them.

HORNER. Indeed, madam, the time was I only hated virtuous women, but now I hate the other too; I beg your pardon, ladies.

LADY FIDGET. You are very obliging, sir, because we would not be troubled with you.

SIR JASPER. In sober sadness, he shall go.

DORILANT. Nay, if he wo' not, I am ready to call upon the ladies, and I think I am the fitter man.

SIR JASPER. You, sir! no, I thank you for that. Master Horner is a privileged man amongst the virtuous ladies; 'twill be a great while before you are so. He! he! he! he's my wife's gallant; he! he! he! No, pray withdraw, sir, for as I take it, the virtuous ladies have no business with you.

DORILANT. And I am sure he can have none with them. 'Tis strange a man can't come amongst virtuous women now, but upon the same terms as men are admitted into the Great Turk's seraglio. But heavens keep me from being an ombre player with 'em!—But where is Pinchwife? *Exit.*

SIR JASPER. Come, come, man; what, avoid the sweet society of womankind? that sweet, soft, gentle, tame, noble creature, woman made for man's companion——

HORNER. So is that soft, gentle, tame, and more noble creature a spaniel, and has all their tricks; can fawn, lie down, suffer beating, and fawn the more; barks at your friends when they come to see you, makes your bed hard, gives you fleas, and the mange sometimes. And all the difference is, the spaniel's the more faithful animal, and fawns but upon one master.

SIR JASPER. He! he! he!

MRS. SQUEAMISH. Oh the rude beast!

MRS. DAINTY. Insolent brute!

LADY FIDGET. Brute! stinking, mortified, rotten French wether,[6] to dare——

SIR JASPER. Hold, an't please your ladyship.—For shame, Master Horner! your mother was a woman—*(Aside.)* Now shall I never reconcile 'em.—*(Aside to* LADY FIDGET.*)* Hark you, madam, take my advice in your anger. You know you often want one to make up your drolling pack of ombre

[6] A eunuch.

players, and you may cheat him easily; for he's an ill gamester, and consequently loves play. Besides, you know you have but two old civil gentlemen (with stinking breaths too) to wait upon you abroad; take in the third into your service. The other are but crazy; and a lady should have a supernumerary gentleman-usher as a supernumerary coach-horse, lest sometimes you should be forced to stay at home.

LADY FIDGET. But are you sure he loves play, and has money?

SIR JASPER. He loves play as much as you, and has money as much as I.

LADY FIDGET. *(Aside.)* Then I am contented to make him pay for his scurrility. Money makes up in a measure all other wants in men.—Those whom we cannot make hold for gallants, we make fine.[7]

SIR JASPER. *(Aside.)* So, so; now to mollify, wheedle him.—*(Aside to* HORNER.*)* Master Horner, will you never keep civil company? methinks 'tis time now, since you are only fit for them. Come, come, man, you must e'en fall to visiting our wives, eating at our tables, drinking tea with our virtuous relations after dinner, dealing cards to 'em, reading plays and gazettes to 'em, picking fleas out of their shocks[8] for 'em, collecting receipts, new songs, women, pages, and footmen for 'em.

HORNER. I hope they'll afford me better employment, sir.

SIR JASPER. He! he! he! 'tis fit you know your work before you come into your place. And since you are unprovided of a lady to flatter, and a good house to eat at, pray frequent mine, and call my wife mistress, and she shall call you gallant, according to the custom.

HORNER. Who, I?

SIR JASPER. Faith, thou sha't for my sake; come, for my sake only.

HORNER. For your sake——

SIR JASPER. Come, come, here's a gamester for you; let him be a little familiar sometimes; nay, what if a little rude? Gamesters may be rude with ladies, you know.

LADY FIDGET. Yes; losing gamesters have a privilege with women.

HORNER. I always thought the contrary—that the winning gamester had most privilege with women; for when you have lost your money to a man, you'll lose anything you have, all you have, they say, and he may use you as he pleases.

SIR JASPER. He! he! he! well, win or lose, you shall have your liberty with her.

LADY FIDGET. As he behaves himself; and for your sake I'll give him admittance and freedom.

HORNER. All sorts of freedom, madam?

---

[7] Pay.

[8] Poodles.

SIR JASPER. Ay, ay, ay, all sorts of freedom thou canst take. And so go to her; begin thy new employment; wheedle her, jest with her, and be better acquainted one with another.

HORNER. *(Aside.)* I think I know her already; therefore may venture with her my secret for hers. *(*HORNER *and* LADY FIDGET *whisper.)*

SIR JASPER. Sister cuz, I have provided an innocent playfellow for you there.

MRS. DAINTY. Who, he?

MRS. SQUEAMISH. There's a playfellow, indeed!

SIR JASPER. Yes sure.—What, he is good enough to play at cards, blind-man's-buff, or the fool with, sometimes!

MRS. SQUEAMISH. Foh! we'll have no such playfellows.

MRS. DAINTY. No, sir; you shan't choose playfellows for us, we thank you.

SIR JASPER. Nay, pray hear me. *(Whispering to them.)*

LADY FIDGET. But, poor gentleman, could you be so generous, so truly a man of honor, as for the sakes of us women of honor, to cause yourself to be reported no man? No man! and to suffer yourself the greatest shame that could fall upon a man, that none might fall upon us women by your conversation? but, indeed, sir, as perfectly, perfectly the same man as before your going into France, sir? as perfectly, perfectly, sir?

HORNER. As perfectly, perfectly, madam. Nay, I scorn you should take my word; I desire to be tried only, madam.

LADY FIDGET. Well, that's spoken again like a man of honor: all men of honor desire to come to the test. But, indeed, generally you men report such things of yourselves, one does not know how or whom to believe; and it is come to that pass, we dare not take your words no more than your tailor's, without some staid servant of yours be bound with you. But I have so strong a faith in your honor, dear, dear, noble sir, that I'd forfeit mine for yours, at any time, dear sir.

HORNER. No, madam, you should not need to forfeit it for me; I have given you security already to save you harmless, my late reputation being so well known in the world, madam.

LADY FIDGET. But if upon any future falling-out, or upon a suspicion of my taking the trust out of your hands, to employ some other, you yourself should betray your trust, dear sir? I mean, if you'll give me leave to speak obscenely, you might tell, dear sir.

HORNER. If I did, nobody would believe me. The reputation of impotency is as hardly recovered again in the world as that of cowardice, dear madam.

LADY FIDGET. Nay, then, as one may say, you may do your worst, dear, dear sir.

SIR JASPER. Come, is your ladyship reconciled to him yet? have you agreed on matters? for I must be gone to Whitehall.

LADY FIDGET. Why, indeed, Sir Jasper, Master Horner is a thousand, thousand times a better man than I thought him. Cousin Squeamish, sister Dainty, I can name him now. Truly, not long ago, you know, I thought his very name obscenity; and I would as soon have lain with him as have named him.

SIR JASPER. Very likely, poor madam.

MRS. DAINTY. I believe it.

MRS. SQUEAMISH. No doubt on't.

SIR JASPER. Well, well—that your ladyship is as virtuous as any she, I know, and him all the town knows—he! he! he! therefore now you like him, get you gone to your business together, go, go to your business, I say, pleasure, whilst I go to my pleasure, business.

LADY FIDGET. Come, then, dear gallant.

HORNER. Come away, my dearest mistress.

SIR JASPER. So, so; why 'tis as I'd have it. *Exit.*

HORNER. And as I'd have it.

LADY FIDGET. Who for his business from his wife will run,
Takes the best care to have her business done. *Exeunt.*

ACT III

SCENE I: *A Room in* PINCHWIFE'S *House.*

Enter ALITHEA *and* MRS. PINCHWIFE.

ALITHEA. Sister, what ails you? you are grown melancholy.

MRS. PINCHWIFE. Would it not make any one melancholy to see you go every day fluttering about abroad, whilst I must stay at home like a poor lonely sullen bird in a cage?

ALITHEA. Ay, sister; but you came young, and just from the nest to your cage: so that I thought you liked it, and could be as cheerful in't as others that took their flight themselves early, and are hopping abroad in the open air.

MRS. PINCHWIFE. Nay, I confess I was quiet enough till my husband told me what pure[1] lives the London ladies live abroad, with their dancing, meetings, and junketings, and dressed every day in their best gowns; and I warrant you, play at nine-pins every day of the week, so they do.

---

[1] Fine.

Enter PINCHWIFE.

PINCHWIFE. Come, what's here to do? you are putting the town-pleasures in her head, and setting her a-longing.

ALITHEA. Yes, after nine-pins. You suffer none to give her those longings you mean but yourself.

PINCHWIFE. I tell her of the vanities of the town like a confessor.

ALITHEA. A confessor! just such a confessor as he that, by forbidding a silly ostler to grease the horse's teeth, taught him to do't.

PINCHWIFE. Come, Mrs. Flippant, good precepts are lost when bad examples are still before us: the liberty you take abroad makes her hanker after it, and out of humor at home. Poor wretch! she desired not to come to London; I would bring her.

ALITHEA. Very well.

PINCHWIFE. She has been this week in town, and never desired till this afternoon to go abroad.

ALITHEA. Was she not at a play yesterday?

PINCHWIFE. Yes; but she ne'er asked me; I was myself the cause of her going.

ALITHEA. Then if she ask you again, you are the cause of her asking, and not my example.

PINCHWIFE. Well, tomorrow night I shall be rid of you; and the next day, before 'tis light, she and I'll be rid of the town and my dreadful apprehensions.—Come, be not melancholy; for thou sha't go into the country after tomorrow, dearest.

ALITHEA. Great comfort!

MRS. PINCHWIFE. Pish! what d'ye tell me of the country for?

PINCHWIFE. How's this! what! pish at the country?

MRS. PINCHWIFE. Let me alone; I am not well.

PINCHWIFE. Oh, if that be all—what ails my dearest?

MRS. PINCHWIFE. Truly, I don't know: but I have not been well since you told me there was a gallant at the play in love with me.

PINCHWIFE. Ha!——

ALITHEA. That's by my example too!

PINCHWIFE. Nay, if you are not well, but are so concerned because a lewd fellow chanced to lie and say he liked you, you'll make me sick too.

MRS. PINCHWIFE. Of what sickness?

PINCHWIFE. Oh, of that which is worse than the plague, jealousy.

MRS. PINCHWIFE. Pish, you jeer! I'm sure there's no such disease in our receipt-book at home.

PINCHWIFE. No, thou never met'st with it, poor innocent.—*(Aside.)* Well, if thou cuckold me, 'twill be my own fault—for cuckolds and bastards are generally makers of their own fortune.

MRS. PINCHWIFE. Well, but pray, bud, let's go to a play tonight.

PINCHWIFE. 'Tis just done, she comes from it. But why are you so eager to see a play?

MRS. PINCHWIFE. Faith, dear, not that I care one pin for their talk there; but I like to look upon the player-men, and would see, if I could, the gallant you say loves me: that's all, dear bud.

PINCHWIFE. Is that all, dear bud?

ALITHEA. This proceeds from my example!

MRS. PINCHWIFE. But if the play be done, let's go abroad, however, dear bud.

PINCHWIFE. Come, have a little patience and thou shalt go into the country on Friday.

MRS. PINCHWIFE. Therefore I would see first some sights to tell my neighbors of. Nay, I will go abroad, that's once.

ALITHEA. I'm the cause of this desire too!

PINCHWIFE. But now I think on't, who, who was the cause of Horner's coming to my lodgings today? That was you.

ALITHEA. No, you, because you would not let him see your handsome wife out of your lodging.

MRS. PINCHWIFE. Why, O Lord! did the gentleman come hither to see me indeed?

PINCHWIFE. No, no.—You are not the cause of that damned question too, Mistress Alithea?—*(Aside.)* Well, she's in the right of it. He is in love with my wife—and comes after her—'tis so—but I'll nip his love in the bud; lest he should follow us into the country and break his chariot-wheel near our house, on purpose for an excuse to come to't. But I think I know the town.

MRS. PINCHWIFE. Come, pray, bud, let's go abroad before 'tis late; for I will go, that's flat and plain.

PINCHWIFE. *(Aside.)* So! the obstinacy already of the townwife; and I must, whilst she's here, humor her like one.—*(Aloud.)* Sister, how shall we do, that may not be seen or known?

ALITHEA. Let her put on her mask.

PINCHWIFE. Pshaw! a mask makes people but the more inquisitive and is as ridiculous a disguise as a stage-beard: her shape, stature, habit will be known. And if we should meet with Horner, he would be sure to take acquaintance with us, must wish her joy, kiss her, talk to her, leer upon her, and the devil and all. No, I'll not use her to a mask, 'tis dangerous; for masks have made more cuckolds than the best faces that ever were known.

ALITHEA. How will you do then?

MRS. PINCHWIFE. Nay, shall we go? The Exchange will be shut, and I have a mind to see that.

PINCHWIFE. So—I have it—I'll dress her up in the suit we are to carry down to her brother, little Sir James; nay, I understand the town-tricks. Come, let's go dress her. A mask! no—a woman masked, like a covered dish, gives a man curiosity and appetite; when, it may be, uncovered, 'twould turn his stomach: no, no.

ALITHEA. Indeed your comparison is something a greasy one: but I had a gentle gallant used to say, A beauty masked, like the sun in eclipse, gathers together more gazers than if it shined out. *Exeunt.*

SCENE II: *The New Exchange.*

Enter HORNER, HARCOURT, *and* DORILANT.

DORILANT. Engaged to women, and not sup with us!

HORNER. Ay, a pox on 'em all!

HARCOURT. You were much a more reasonable man in the morning, and had as noble resolutions against 'em as a widower of a week's liberty.

DORILANT. Did I ever think to see you keep company with women in vain?

HORNER. In vain: no—'tis since I can't love 'em, to be revenged on 'em.

HARCOURT. Now your sting is gone, you looked in the box amongst all those women like a drone in the hive; all upon you, shoved and ill-used by 'em all, and thrust from one side to t'other.

DORILANT. Yet he must be buzzing amongst 'em still, like other beetle-headed liquorish drones. Avoid 'em, and hate 'em, as they hate you.

HORNER. Because I do hate 'em, and would hate 'em yet more, I'll frequent 'em. You may see by marriage, nothing makes a man hate a woman more than her constant conversation. In short, I converse with 'em, as you do with rich fools, to laugh at 'em and use 'em ill.

DORILANT. But I would no more sup with women, unless I could lie with 'em, than sup with a rich coxcomb, unless I could cheat him.

HORNER. Yes, I have known thee sup, with a fool for his drinking; if he could set out your hand[2] that way only, you were satisfied, and if he were a wine-swallowing mouth, 'twas enough.

HARCOURT. Yes, a man drinks often with a fool, as he tosses with a marker, only to keep his hand in use. But do the ladies drink?

HORNER. Yes, sir; and I shall have the pleasure at least of laying 'em flat with a bottle, and bring as much scandal that way upon 'em as formerly t'other.

---

[2] If he would place a glass of wine in your hand.

HARCOURT. Perhaps you may prove as weak a brother among 'em that way as t'other.

DORILANT. Foh! drinking with women is as unnatural as scolding with 'em. But 'tis a pleasure of decayed fornicators, and the basest way of quenching love.

HARCOURT. Nay, 'tis drowning love, instead of quenching it. But leave us for civil women too!

DORILANT. Ay, when he can't be the better for 'em. We hardly pardon a man that leaves his friend for a wench, and that's a pretty lawful call.

HORNER. Faith, I would not leave you for 'em, if they would not drink.

DORILANT. Who would disappoint his company at Lewis's[3] for a gossiping?

HARCOURT. Foh! Wine and women, good apart, together are as nauseous as sack and sugar. But hark you, sir, before you go, a little of your advice; an old maimed general, when unfit for action, is fittest for counsel. I have other designs upon women than eating and drinking with them; I am in love with Sparkish's mistress, whom he is to marry tomorrow; now how shall I get her?

Enter SPARKISH, *looking about.*

HORNER. Why, here comes one will help you to her.

HARCOURT. He! he, I tell you, is my rival, and will hinder my love.

HORNER. No; a foolish rival and a jealous husband assist their rival's designs; for they are sure to make their women hate them, which is the first step to their love for another man.

HARCOURT. But I cannot come near his mistress but in his company.

HORNER. Still the better for you; for fools are most easily cheated when they themselves are accessories: and he is to be bubbled[4] of his mistress as of his money, the common mistress, by keeping him company.

SPARKISH. Who is that that is to be bubbled? Faith, let me snack; I han't met with a bubble since Christmas. 'Gad, I think bubbles are like their brother woodcocks,[5] go out with the cold weather.

HARCOURT. *(Apart to* HORNER.*)* A pox! he did not hear all, I hope.

SPARKISH. Come, you bubbling rogues you, where do we sup?—Oh, Harcourt, my mistress tells me you have been making fierce love to her all the play long: ha! ha!—But I——

HARCOURT. I make love to her!

---

[3] Not identified but probably a tavern.

[4] Cheated.

[5] Gullible fools who are easily cheated.

SPARKISH. Nay, I forgive thee, for I think I know thee, and I know her; but I am sure I know myself.

HARCOURT. Did she tell you so? I see all women are like these of the Exchange; who, to enhance the prize of their commodities, report to their fond customers offers which were never made 'em.

HORNER. Ay, women are apt to tell before the intrigue, as men after it, and so show themselves the vainer sex. But hast thou a mistress, Sparkish? 'Tis as hard for me to believe it, as that thou ever hadst a bubble, as you bragged just now.

SPARKISH. Oh, your servant, sir: are you at your raillery, sir? But we are some of us beforehand with you today at the play. The wits were something bold with you, sir; did you not hear us laugh?

HORNER. Yes; but I thought you had gone to plays to laugh at the poet's wit, not at your own.

SPARKISH. Your servant, sir: no, I thank you. 'Gad, I go to a play as to a country treat; I carry my own wine to one, and my own wit to t'other, or else I'm sure I should not be merry at either. And the reason why we are so often louder than the players is because we think we speak more wit, and so become the poet's rivals in his audience: for to tell you the truth, we hate the silly rouges; nay, so much, that we find fault even with their bawdy upon the stage, whilst we talk nothing else in the pit as loud.

HORNER. But why shouldst thou hate the silly poets? Thou hast too much wit to be one: and they, like whores, are only hated by each other: and thou dost scorn writing, I'm sure.

SPARKISH. Yes; I'd have you to know I scorn writing: but women, women, that make men do all foolish things, make 'em write songs too. Everybody does it. 'Tis even as common with lovers as playing with fans; and you can no more help rhyming to your Phyllis, than drinking to your Phyllis.

HARCOURT. Nay, poetry in love is no more to be avoided than jealousy.

DORILANT. But the poets damned your songs, did they?

SPARKISH. Damn the poets! they have turned 'em into burlesque, as they call it. That burlesque is a hocus-pocus trick they have got, which, by the virtue of *Hictius doctius topsy turvy*, they make a wise and witty man in the world, a fool upon the stage you know not how: and 'tis therefore I hate 'em too, for I know not but it may be my own case; for they'll put a man into a play for looking asquint. Their predecessors were contented to make serving-men only their stage-fools: but these rogues must have gentlemen, with a pox to 'em, nay, knights; and, indeed, you shall hardly see a fool upon the stage but he's a knight. And to tell you the truth, they have kept me these six years from being a knight in earnest, for fear of being knighted in a play, and dubbed a fool.

DORILANT. Blame 'em not, they must follow their copy, the age.

HARCOURT. But why shouldst thou be afraid of being in a play, who expose yourself every day in the play-houses, and at public places?

HORNER. 'Tis but being on the stage, instead of standing on a bench in the pit.

DORILANT. Don't you give money to painters to draw you like? and are you afraid of your pictures at length in a playhouse, where your mistresses may see you?

SPARKISH. A pox! painters don't draw the small-pox or pimples in one's face. Come, damn all your silly authors whatever, all books and booksellers, by the world; and all readers, courteous or uncourteous!

HARCOURT. But who comes here, Sparkish?

Enter PINCHWIFE *and* MRS. PINCHWIFE *in man's clothes,* ALITHEA *and* LUCY.

SPARKISH. Oh, hide me! There's my mistress too.

(SPARKISH *hides himself behind* HARCOURT.)

HARCOURT. She sees you.

SPARKISH. But I will not see her. 'Tis time to go to Whitehall and I must not fail the drawing-room.

HARCOURT. Pray, first carry me, and reconcile me to her.

SPARKISH. Another time. Faith, the king will have supped.

HARCOURT. Not with the worse stomach for thy absence. Thou art one of those fools that think their attendance at the king's meals as necessary as his physicians, when you are more troublesome to him than his doctors or his dogs.

SPARKISH. Pshaw! I know my interest, sir. Prithee hide me.

HORNER. Your servant, Pinchwife.—What, he knows us not!

PINCHWIFE. *(To his Wife aside.)* Come along.

MRS. PINCHWIFE. Pray, have you any ballads? give me six-penny worth.

BOOKSELLER. We have no ballads.

MRS. PINCHWIFE. Then give me *Covent Garden Drollery*, and a play or two—Oh, here's *Tarugo's Wiles*, and *The Slighted Maiden;*[6] I'll have them.

PINCHWIFE. *(Apart to her.)* No; plays are not for your reading. Come along; will you discover yourself?

HORNER. Who is that pretty youth with him, Sparkish?

SPARKISH. I believe his wife's brother, because he's something like her: but I never saw her but once.

HORNER. Extremely handsome; I have seen a face like it too. Let us follow 'em.

---

[6] *Covent Garden Drollery* (1672) is a collection of songs and poems. *Tarugo's Wiles* (1668) by Sir Thomas St. Serf and *The Slighted Maiden* (1663) by Sir Robert Stapylton are comedies of the period.

Exeunt PINCHWIFE, MRS. PINCHWIFE, ALITHEA, *and* LUCY; HORNER *and* DORILANT *following them.*

HARCOURT. Come, Sparkish, your mistress saw you, and will be angry you go not to her. Besides, I would fain be reconciled to her, which none but you can do, dear friend.

SPARKISH. Well, that's a better reason, dear friend. I would not go near her now for hers or my own sake; but I can deny you nothing: for though I have known thee a great while, never go, if I do not love thee as well as a new acquaintance.

HARCOURT. I am obliged to you indeed, dear friend. I would be well with her, only to be well with thee still; for these ties to wives usually dissolve all ties to friends. I would be contented she should enjoy you a-nights, but I would have you to myself a-days as I have had, dear friend.

SPARKISH. And thou shalt enjoy me a-days, dear, dear friend, never stir: and I'll be divorced from her, sooner than from thee. Come along.

HARCOURT. *(Aside.)* So, we are put to't, when we make our rival our procurer; but neither she nor her brother would let me come near her now. When all's done, a rival is the best cloak to steal to a mistress under, without suspicion; and when we have once got to her as we desire, we throw him off like other cloaks. *Exit* SPARKISH, HARCOURT *following him.*

Enter PINCHWIFE, MRS. PINCHWIFE.

PINCHWIFE. *(To* ALITHEA, *behind.)* Sister, if you will not go, we must leave you.—*(Aside.)* The fool her gallant and she will muster up all the young saunterers of this place, and they will leave their dear seamstresses to follow us. What a swarm of cuckolds and cuckold-makers are here!—Come, let's be gone, Mistress Margery.

MRS. PINCHWIFE. Don't you believe that; I han't half my bellyful of sights yet.

PINCHWIFE. Then walk this way.

MRS. PINCHWIFE. Lord, what a power of brave signs are here! stay—the Bull's-Head, the Ram's-Head, and the Stag's-Head, dear——

PINCHWIFE. Nay, if every husband's proper sign here were visible, they would be all alike.

MRS. PINCHWIFE. What d'ye mean by that, bud?

PINCHWIFE. 'Tis no matter—no matter, bud.

MRS. PINCHWIFE. Pray tell me: nay, I will know.

PINCHWIFE. They would be all Bulls, Stags, and Rams-heads.

Exeunt PINCHWIFE *and* MRS. PINCHWIFE.

Enter SPARKISH, HARCOURT, ALITHEA, *and* LUCY, *at the other side.*

SPARKISH. Come, dear madam, for my sake you shall be reconciled to him.

ALITHEA. For your sake I hate him.

HARCOURT. That's something too cruel, madam, to hate me for his sake.

SPARKISH. Ay indeed, madam, too, too cruel to me, to hate my friend for my sake.

ALITHEA. I hate him because he is your enemy; and you ought to hate him too, for making love to me, if you love me.

SPARKISH. That's a good one! I hate a man for loving you! If he did love you, 'tis but what he can't help; and 'tis your fault, not his, if he admires you. I hate a man for being of my opinion! I'll n'er do't, by the world.

ALITHEA. Is it for your honor, or mine, to suffer a man to make love to me, who am to marry you tomorrow?

SPARKISH. Is it for your honor, or mine, to have me jealous? That he makes love to you is a sign you are handsome, and that I am not jealous is a sign you are virtuous. That I think is for your honor.

ALITHEA. But 'tis your honor too I am concerned for.

HARCOURT. But why, dearest madam, will you be more concerned for his honor than he is himself? Let his honor alone, for my sake and his. He! he has no honor——

SPARKISH. How's that?

HARCOURT. But what my dear friend can guard himself.

SPARKISH. Oh, ho—that's right again.

HARCOURT. Your care of his honor argues his neglect of it, which is no honor to my dear friend here. Therefore once more, let his honor go which way it will, dear madam.

SPARKISH. Ay, ay; were it for my honor to marry a woman whose virtue I suspected, and could not trust her in a friend's hands?

ALITHEA. Are you not afraid to lose me?

HARCOURT. He afraid to lose you, madam! No, no—you may see how the most estimable and most glorious creature in the world is valued by him. Will you not see it?

SPARKISH. Right, honest Frank, I have that noble value for her that I cannot be jealous of her.

ALITHEA. You mistake him. He means, you care not for me, nor who has me.

SPARKISH. Lord, madam, I see you are jealous! Will you wrest a poor man's meaning from his words?

ALITHEA. You astonish me, sir, with your want of jealousy.

SPARKISH. And you make me giddy, madam, with your jealousy and fears, and virtue and honor. 'Gad, I see virtue makes a woman as troublesome as a little reading or learning.

ALITHEA. Monstrous!

LUCY. *(Aside.)* Well, to see what easy husbands these women of quality can meet with! a poor chambermaid can never have such ladylike luck. Besides, he's thrown away upon her. She'll make no use of her fortune, her blessing none to a gentleman, for a pure cuckold; for it requires good breeding to be a cuckold.

ALITHEA. I tell you then plainly, he pursues me to marry me.

SPARKISH. Pshaw!

HARCOURT. Come, madam, you see you strive in vain to make him jealous of me. My dear friend is the kindest creature in the world to me.

SPARKISH. Poor fellow!

HARCOURT. But his kindness only is not enough for me, without your favor, your good opinion, dear madam: 'tis that must perfect my happiness. Good gentleman, he believes all I say: would you would do so! Jealous of me! I would not wrong him nor you for the world.

SPARKISH. Look you there. Hear him, hear him, and do not walk away so. (ALITHEA *walks carelessly to and fro.*)

HARCOURT. I love you, madam, so——

SPARKISH. How's that? Nay, now you begin to go too far indeed.

HARCOURT. So much, I confess, I say, I love you, that I would not have you miserable, and cast yourself away upon so unworthy and inconsiderable a thing as what you see here.

(Clapping his hand on his breast, points at SPARKISH.*)*

SPARKISH. No, faith, I believe thou wouldst not: now his meaning is plain: but I knew before thou wouldst not wrong me, nor her.

HARCOURT. No, no, Heavens forbid the glory of her sex should fall so low, as into the embraces of such a contemptible wretch, the least of mankind—my friend here—I injure him! (*Embracing* SPARKISH.)

ALITHEA. Very well.

SPARKISH. No, no, dear friend, I knew it.—Madam, you see he will rather wrong himself than me, in giving himself such names.

ALITHEA. Do not you understand him yet?

SPARKISH. Yes: how modestly he speaks of himself, poor fellow!

ALITHEA. Methinks he speaks impudently of yourself, since—before yourself too; insomuch that I can no longer suffer his scurrilous abusiveness to you, no more than his love to me. *(Offers to go.)*

SPARKISH. Nay, nay, madam, pray stay—his love to you! Lord, madam, has he not spoke yet plain enough?

ALITHEA. Yes, indeed, I should think so.

SPARKISH. Well then, by the world, a man can't speak civilly to a woman now, but presently she says he makes love to her. Nay. madam, you shall stay, with your pardon, since you have not yet understood him, till he has made an *eclaircissement*[7] of his love to you; that is—what kind of love it is. Answer to thy catechism, friend; do you love my mistress here?

HARCOURT. Yes, I wish she would not doubt it.

SPARKISH. But how do you love her?

HARCOURT. With all my soul.

ALITHEA. I thank him. Methinks he speaks plain enough now.

SPARKISH. *(To* ALITHEA.*)* You are out still.—But with what kind of love, Harcourt?

HARCOURT. With the best and truest love in the world.

SPARKISH. Look you there then, that is with no matrimonial love, I'm sure.

ALITHEA. How's that? do you say matrimonial love is not best?

SPARKISH. 'Gad, I went too far ere I was aware. But speak for thyself, Harcourt; you said you would not wrong me nor her.

HARCOURT. No, no, madam, e'en take him for Heaven's sake—

SPARKISH. Look you there, madam.

HARCOURT. Who should in all justice be yours: he that loves you most.

(Claps his hand on his breast.)

ALITHEA. Look you there, Mr. Sparkish, who's that?

SPARKISH. Who should it be?—Go on, Harcourt.

HARCOURT. Who loves you more than women, titles; or fortune, fools.

(*Points at* SPARKISH.)

SPARKISH. Look you there, he means me still, for he points at me.

ALITHEA. Ridiculous!

HARCOURT. Who can only match your faith and constancy in love.

SPARKISH. Ay.

HARCOURT. Who knows, if it be possible, how to value so much beauty and virtue.

SPARKISH. Ay.

HARCOURT. Whose love can no more be equalled in the world, than that heavenly form of yours.

SPARKISH. No.

HARCOURT. Who could no more suffer a rival, than your absence; and yet could no more suspect your virtue, than his own constancy in his love to you.

SPARKISH. No.

HARCOURT. Who, in fine, loves you better than his eyes, that first made him love you.

---

[7] Explanation.

SPARKISH. Ay—Nay, madam, faith, you shan't go till——

ALITHEA. Have a care, lest you make me stay too long.

SPARKISH. But till he has saluted you; that I may be assured you are friends, after his honest advice and declaration. Come, pray, madam, be friends with him.

Enter PINCHWIFE *and* MRS. PINCHWIFE.

ALITHEA. You must pardon me, sir, that I am not yet so obedient to you.

PINCHWIFE. What, invite your wife to kiss men? Monstrous! are you not ashamed? I will never forgive you.

SPARKISH. Are you not ashamed, that I should have more confidence in the chastity of your family than you have? You must not teach me; I am a man of honor, sir, though I am frank and free; I am frank, sir——

PINCHWIFE. Very frank, sir, to share your wife with your friends.

SPARKISH. He is an humble, menial friend, such as reconciles the differences of the marriage bed; you know man and wife do not always agree; I design him for that use, therefore would have him well with my wife.

PINCHWIFE. A menial friend!—you will get a great many menial friends by showing your wife as you do.

SPARKISH. What then? It may be I have a pleasure in't, as I have to show fine clothes at a play-house the first day, and count money before poor rogues.

PINCHWIFE. He that shows his wife or money will be in danger of having them borrowed sometimes.

SPARKISH. I love to be envied and would not marry a wife that I alone could love; loving alone is as dull as eating alone. Is it not a frank age? and I am a frank person; and to tell you the truth, it may be, I love to have rivals in a wife—they make her seem to a man still but a kept mistress; and so good night, for I must to Whitehall.—Madam, I hope you are now reconciled to my friend; and so I wish you a good night, madam, and sleep if you can: for to-morrow you know I must visit you early with a canonical gentleman. Good night, dear Harcourt. *Exit.*

HARCOURT. Madam, I hope you will not refuse my visit to-morrow, if it should be earlier with a canonical gentleman than Mr. Sparkish's.

PINCHWIFE. This gentlewoman is yet under my care, therefore you must yet forbear your freedom with her, sir.

(Coming between ALITHEA *and* HARCOURT.*)*

HARCOURT. Must, sir?

PINCHWIFE. Yes, sir, she is my sister.

HARCOURT. 'Tis well she is, sir—for I must be her servant, sir.—Madam—

PINCHWIFE. Come away, sister, we had been gone, if it had not been for you, and so avoided these lewd rake-hells who seem to haunt us.

Enter HORNER *and* DORILANT.

HORNER. How now, Pinchwife!

PINCHWIFE. Your servant.

HORNER. What! I see a little time in the country makes a man turn wild and unsociable, and only fit to converse with his horses, dogs, and his herds.

PINCHWIFE. I have business, sir, and must mind it; your business is pleasure, therefore you and I must go different ways.

HORNER. Well, you may go on, but this pretty young gentleman——
(Takes hold of MRS. PINCHWIFE.*)*

HARCOURT. The lady——

DORILANT. And the maid——

HORNER. Shall stay with us; for I suppose their business is the same with ours, pleasure.

PINCHWIFE. *(Aside.)* 'Sdeath, he knows her, she carries it so sillily! yet if he does not, I should be more silly to discover it first.

ALITHEA. Pray, let us go, sir.

PINCHWIFE. Come, come——

HORNER. *(To* MRS. PINCHWIFE.*)* Had you not rather stay with us?—Prithee, Pinchwife, who is this pretty young gentleman?

PINCHWIFE. One to whom I'm a guardian.—*(Aside.)* I wish I could keep her out of your hands.

HORNER. Who is he? I never saw anything so pretty in all my life.

PINCHWIFE. Pshaw! do not look upon him so much, he's a poor bashful youth, you'll put him out of countenance.—Come away, brother. *(Offers to take her away.)*

HORNER. Oh, your brother!

PINCHWIFE. Yes, my wife's brother.—Come, come, she'll stay supper for us.

HORNER. I thought so, for he is very like her I saw you at the play with, whom I told you I was in love with.

MRS. PINCHWIFE. *(Aside.)* Oh, jeminy! is that he that was in love with me? I am glad on't, I vow, for he's a curious fine gentleman, and I love him already, too.—*(To* PINCHWIFE.*)* Is this he, bud?

PINCHWIFE. *(To his* Wife.*)* Come away, come away.

HORNER. Why, what haste are you in? why won't you let me talk with him?

PINCHWIFE. Because you'll debauch him; he's yet young and innocent, and I would not have him debauched for anything in the world.—*(Aside.)* How she gazes on him! the devil!

HORNER. Harcourt, Dorilant, look you here, this is the likeness of that dowdy he told us of his wife; did you ever see a lovelier creature? The rogue has reason to be jealous of his wife, since she is like him, for she would make all that see her in love with her.

HARCOURT. And, as I remember now, she is as like him here as can be.

DORILANT. She is indeed very pretty, if she be like him.

HORNER. Very pretty? a very pretty commendation!—she is a glorious creature, beautiful beyond all things I ever beheld.

PINCHWIFE. So, so.

HARCOURT. More beautiful than a poet's first mistress of imagination.

HORNER. Or another man's last mistress of flesh and blood.

MRS. PINCHWIFE. Nay, now you jeer, sir; pray don't jeer me.

PINCHWIFE. Come, come.—*(Aside.)* By Heavens, she'll discover herself!

HORNER. I speak of your sister, sir.

PINCHWIFE. Ay, but saying she was handsome, if like him, made him blush.—*(Aside.)* I am upon a rack!

HORNER. Methinks he is so handsome he should not be a man.

PINCHWIFE. *(Aside.)* Oh there 'tis out! he has discovered her! I am not able to suffer any longer.—*(To his* Wife.*)* Come, come away, I say.

HORNER. Nay, by your leave, sir, he shall not go yet.—*(Aside to them.)* Harcourt, Dorilant, let us torment this jealous rogue a little.

HARCOURT. DORILANT. How?

HORNER. I'll show you.

PINCHWIFE. Come, pray let him go, I cannot stay fooling any longer; I tell you his sister stays supper for us.

HORNER. Does she? Come then, we'll all go to sup with he and thee.

PINCHWIFE. No, now I think on't, having stayed so long for us, I warrant she's gone to bed.—*(Aside.)* I wish she and I were well out of their hands. —(*To his* Wife.) Come, I must rise early tomorrow, come.

HORNER. Well then, if she be gone to bed, I wish her and you a good night. But pray, young gentleman, present my humble service to her.

MRS. PINCHWIFE. Thank you heartily, sir.

PINCHWIFE. *(Aside.)* 'Sdeath, she will discover herself yet in spite of me. —*(Aloud.)* He is something more civil to you, for your kindness to his sister, than I am, it seems.

HORNER. Tell her, dear sweet little gentleman, for all your brother there, that you have revived the love I had for her at first sight in the playhouse.

MRS. PINCHWIFE. But did you love her indeed, and indeed?

PINCHWIFE. *(Aside.)* So, so.—*(Aloud.)* Away, I say.

HORNER. Nay, stay.—Yes, indeed, and indeed, pray do you tell her so, and give her this kiss from me. *(Kisses her.)*

PINCHWIFE. *(Aside.)* Oh Heavens! what do I suffer? Now 'tis too plain he knows her, and yet——

HORNER. And this, and this—— *(Kisses her again.)*

MRS. PINCHWIFE. What do you kiss me for? I am no woman.

PINCHWIFE. *(Aside.)* So, there, 'tis out.—*(Aloud.)* Come, I cannot, nor will stay any longer.

HORNER. Nay, they shall send your lady a kiss too. Here Harcourt, Dorilant, will you not? *(They kiss her.)*

PINCHWIFE. *(Aside.)* How! do I suffer this? Was I not accusing another just now for this rascally patience, in permitting his wife to be kissed before his face? Ten thousand ulcers gnaw away their lips.—*(Aloud.)* Come, come.

HORNER. Good night, dear little gentleman; madam, good night; farewell, Pinchwife—(*Apart to* HARCOURT *and* DORILANT). Did not I tell you I would raise his jealous gall? *Exeunt* HORNER, HARCOURT, *and* DORILANT.

PINCHWIFE. So, they are gone at last; stay, let me see first if the coach be at this door. *Exit.*

Enter HORNER, HARCOURT, *and* DORILANT.

HORNER. What, not gone yet? Will you be sure to do as I desired you, sweet sir?

MRS. PINCHWIFE. Sweet sir, but what will you give me then?

HORNER. Anything. Come away into the next walk.

(*Exit, haling away* MRS. PINCHWIFE.)

ALITHEA. Hold! hold! what d'ye do?

LUCY. Stay, stay, hold——

HARCOURT. Hold, madam, hold, let him present him—he'll come presently; nay, I will never let you go till you answer my question.

LUCY. For God's sake, sir, I must follow 'em.

(ALITHEA *and* LUCY, *struggling with* HARCOURT *and* DORILANT.)

DORILANT. No, I have something to present you with too; you shan't follow them.

Enter PINCHWIFE.

PINCHWIFE. Where?—how—what's become of?—gone!—whither?

LUCY. He's only gone with the gentleman, who will give him something, an't please your worship.

PINCHWIFE. Something!—give him something, with a pox!—where are they?

ALITHEA. In the next walk only, brother.

PINCHWIFE. Only, only! where, where?

(Exit and returns presently, then goes out again.)

HARCOURT. What's the matter with him? why so much concerned? But, dearest madam——

ALITHEA. Pray let me go, sir; I have said and suffered enough already.

HARCOURT. Then you will not look upon, nor pity, my sufferings?

ALITHEA. To look upon 'em, when I cannot help 'em, were cruelty, not pity; therefore, I will never see you more.

HARCOURT. Let me then, madam, have my privilege of a banished lover, complaining or railing, and giving you but a farewell reason why, if you cannot condescend to marry me, you should not take that wretch, my rival.

ALITHEA. He only, not you, since my honor is engaged so far to him, can give me a reason why I should not marry him; but if he be true, and what I think him to me, I must be so to him. Your servant, sir.

HARCOURT. Have women only constancy when 'tis a vice, and are, like Fortune, only true to fools?

DORILANT. *(To* LUCY, *who struggles to get from him.)* Thou sha't not stir, thou robust creature; you see I can deal with you, therefore you should stay the rather, and be kind.

Enter PINCHWIFE.

PINCHWIFE. Gone, gone, not to be found! quite gone! ten thousand plagues go with 'em! Which way went they?

ALITHEA. But into t'other walk, brother.

LUCY. Their business will be done presently sure, an't please your worship; it can't be long in doing, I'm sure on't.

ALITHEA. Are they not there?

PINCHWIFE. No, you know where they are, you infamous wretch, eternal shame of your family, which you do not dishonor enough yourself you think, but you must help her to do it too, thou legion of bawds!

ALITHEA. Good brother—

PINCHWIFE. Damned, damned sister!

ALITHEA. Look you here, she's coming.

Enter MRS. PINCHWIFE *running, with her hat full of oranges and dried fruit under her arm,* HORNER *following.*

MRS. PINCHWIFE. Oh dear bud, look you here what I have got, see!

PINCHWIFE. *(Aside, rubbing his forehead.)* And what I have got here too, which you can't see.

MRS. PINCHWIFE. The fine gentleman has given me better things yet.

PINCHWIFE. Has he so?—*(Aside.)* Out of breath and colored!—I must hold yet.

HORNER. I have only given your little brother an orange, sir.

PINCHWIFE. *(To* HORNER.*)* Thank you, sir.—*(Aside.)* You have only squeezed my orange, I suppose, and given it me again; yet I must have a city patience.[8]—*(To his* Wife.*)* Come, come away.

MRS. PINCHWIFE. Stay, till I have put up my fine things, bud.

Enter SIR JASPER FIDGET.

SIR JASPER. Oh, Master Horner, come, come, the ladies stay for you; your mistress, my wife, wonders you make not more haste to her.

HORNER. I have stayed this half hour for you here, and 'tis your fault I am not now with your wife.

SIR JASPER. But, pray, don't let her know so much; the truth on't is, I was advancing a certain project to his majesty about—I'll tell you.

HORNER. No, let's go, and hear it at your house. Good night, sweet little gentleman; one kiss more, you'll remember me now, I hope. *(Kisses her.)*

DORILANT. What, Sir Jasper, will you separate friends? He promised to sup with us, and if you take him to your house, you'll be in danger of our company too.

SIR JASPER. Alas! gentlemen, my house is not fit for you; there are none but civil women there, which are not for your turn. He, you know, can bear with the society of civil women now, ha! ha! ha! besides, he's one of my family—he's—he! he! he!

DORILANT. What is he?

SIR JASPER. Faith, my eunuch, since you'll have it; he! he!

Exeunt SIR JASPER FIDGET *and* HORNER.

DORILANT. I rather wish thou wert his or my cuckold. Harcourt, what a good cuckold is lost there for want of a man to make him one? Thee and I cannot have Horner's privilege, who can make use of it.

HARCOURT. Ay, to poor Horner 'tis like coming to an estate at three-score, when a man can't be the better for't.

PINCHWIFE. Come.

MRS. PINCHWIFE. Presently, bud.

DORILANT. Come, let us go too.—(*To* ALITHEA.) Madam, your servant. —(*To* LUCY.) Good night, strapper.

HARCOURT. Madam, though you will not let me have a good day or night, I wish you one; but dare not name the other half of my wish.

ALITHEA. Good night, sir, for ever.

MRS. PINCHWIFE. I don't know where to put this here, dear bud, you shall

---

[8] The patience of a husband who is a cuckold yet does not want anyone to know it.

eat it; nay, you shall have part of the fine gentleman's good things, or treat, as you call it, when we come home.

PINCHWIFE. Indeed, I deserve it, since I furnished the best part of it.
(Strikes away the orange.)

The gallant treats presents, and gives the ball;
But 'tis the absent cuckold pays for all. *Exeunt.*

ACT IV

SCENE I: PINCHWIFE'S *House in the morning.*

Enter ALITHEA *dressed in new clothes, and* LUCY.

LUCY. Well—madam, now have I dressed you, and set you out with so many ornaments and spent upon you ounces of essence and pulvillio;[1] and all this for no other purpose but as people adorn and perfume a corpse for a stinking second-hand grave: such, or as bad, I think Master Sparkish's bed.

ALITHEA. Hold your peace.

LUCY. Nay, madam, I will ask you the reason why you would banish poor Master Harcourt for ever from your sight; how could you be so hard-hearted?

ALITHEA. 'Twas because I was not hard-hearted.

LUCY. No, no; 'twas stark love and kindness, I warrant.

ALITHEA. It was so; I would see him no more because I love him.

LUCY. Hey day, a very pretty reason!

ALITHEA. You do not understand me.

LUCY. I wish you may yourself.

ALITHEA. I was engaged to marry, you see, another man, whom my justice will not suffer me to deceive or injure.

LUCY. Can there be a greater cheat or wrong done to a man than to give him your person without your heart? I should make a conscience of it.

ALITHEA. I'll retrieve it for him after I am married a while.

LUCY. The woman that marries to love better, will be as much mistaken as the wencher that marries to live better. No, madam, marrying to increase love is like gaming to become rich; alas! you only lose what little stock you had before.

---

[1] Perfumed powder.

ALITHEA. I find by your rhetoric you have been bribed to betray me.

LUCY. Only by his merit, that has bribed your heart, you see, against your word and rigid honor. But what a devil is this honor! 'tis sure a disease in the head, like the megrim or falling-sickness,[2] that always hurries people away to do themselves mischief. Men lose their lives by it; women, what's dearer to 'em, their love, the life of life.

ALITHEA. Come, pray talk you no more of honor, nor Master Harcourt; I wish the other would come to secure my fidelity to him and his right in me.

LUCY. You will marry him then?

ALITHEA. Certainly. I have given him already my word, and will my hand too, to make it good, when he comes.

LUCY. Well, I wish I may never stick pin more, if he be not an arrant natural,[3] to t'other fine gentleman.

ALITHEA. I own he wants the wit of Harcourt, which I will dispense withal for another want he has, which is want of jealousy, which men of wit seldom want.

LUCY. Lord, madam, what should you do with a fool to your husband? You intend to be honest, don't you? then that husbandly virtue, credulity, is thrown away upon you.

ALITHEA. He only that could suspect my virtue should have cause to do it; 'tis Sparkish's confidence in my truth that obliges me to be so faithful to him.

LUCY. You are not sure his opinion may last.

ALITHEA. I am satisfied; 'tis impossible for him to be jealous after the proofs I have had of him. Jealousy in a husband—Heaven defend me from it! it begets a thousand plagues to a poor woman, the loss of her honor, her quiet, and her——

LUCY. And her pleasure.

ALITHEA. What d'ye mean, impertinent?

LUCY. Liberty is a great pleasure, madam.

ALITHEA. I say, loss of her honor, her quiet, nay, her life sometimes; and what's as bad almost, the loss of this town; that is, she is sent into the country, which is the last ill-usage of a husband to a wife, I think.

LUCY. *(Aside.)* Oh, does the wind lie there?—*(Aloud.)* Then of necessity, madam, you think a man must carry his wife into the country, if he be wise. The country is as terrible, I find, to our young English ladies, as a monastery to those abroad; and on my virginity, I think they would rather marry a London jailer, than a high sheriff of a county, since neither can stir from his employment. Formerly women of wit married fools for a great estate, a

---

[2] Epilepsy.
[3] A fool.

fine seat, or the like; but now 'tis for a pretty seat only in Lincoln's Inn Fields, St. James's Fields, or the Pall Mall.

Enter SPARKISH, *and* HARCOURT, *dressed like a* PARSON.

SPARKISH. Madam, your humble servant, a happy day to you, and to us all.

HARCOURT. Amen.

ALITHEA. Who have we here?

SPARKISH. My chaplain, faith—Oh madam, poor Harcourt remembers his humble service to you; and, in obedience to your last commands, refrains coming into your sight.

ALITHEA. Is not that he?

SPARKISH. No, fy, no; but to show that he ne'er intended to hinder our match, has sent his brother here to join our hands. When I get me a wife, I must get her a chaplain, according to the custom; that is his brother, and my chaplain.

ALITHEA. His brother!

LUCY. *(Aside.)* And your chaplain, to preach in your pulpit then——

ALITHEA. His brother!

SPARKISH. Nay, I knew you would not believe it.—I told you, sir, she would take you for your brother Frank.

ALITHEA. Believe it!

LUCY. *(Aside.)* His brother! ha! ha! he! He has a trick left still, it seems.

SPARKISH. Come, my dearest, pray let us go to church before the canonical hour is past.[4]

ALITHEA. For shame, you are abused still.

SPARKISH. By the world, 'tis strange now you are so incredulous.

ALITHEA. 'Tis strange you are so credulous.

SPARKISH. Dearest of my life, hear me. I tell you this is Ned Harcourt of Cambridge, by the world; you see he has a sneaking college look. 'Tis true he's something like his brother Frank; and they differ from each other no more than in their ages, for they were twins.

LUCY. Ha! ha! ha!

ALITHEA. Your servant, sir; I cannot be so deceived, though you are. But come, let's hear, how do you know what you affirm so confidently?

SPARKISH. Why I'll tell you all. Frank Harcourt coming to me this morning to wish me joy, and present his service to you, I asked him if he could help me to a parson. Whereupon he told me, he had a brother in town who was in orders; and he went straight away, and sent him, you see there, to me.

---

[4] Church law decreed marriages could only take place between 8 a.m. and noon.

ALITHEA. Yes, Frank goes and put on a black coat, then tells you he is Ned; that's all you have for't.

SPARKISH. Pshaw! pshaw! I tell you, by the same token, the midwife put her garter about Frank's neck to know 'em asunder, they were so like.

ALITHEA. Frank tells you this too?

SPARKISH. Ay, and Ned there too; nay, they are both in a story.

ALITHEA. So, so; very foolish.

SPARKISH. Lord, if you won't believe one, you had best try him by your chambermaid there; for chambermaids must needs know chaplains from other men, they are so used to 'em.

LUCY. Let's see: nay, I'll be sworn he has the canonical smirk, and the filthy clammy palm of a chaplain.

ALITHEA. Well, most reverend doctor, pray let us make an end of this fooling.

HARCOURT. With all my soul, divine heavenly creature, when you please.

ALITHEA. He speaks like a chaplain indeed.

SPARKISH. Why, was there not soul, divine, heavenly, in what he said?

ALITHEA. Once more, most impertinent black coat, cease your persecution, and let us have a conclusion of this ridiculous love.

HARCOURT. *(Aside.)* I had forgot, I must suit my style to my coat, or I wear it in vain.

ALITHEA. I have no more patience left; let us make once an end of this troublesome love, I say.

HARCOURT. So be it, seraphic lady, when your honor shall think it meet and convenient so to do.

SPARKISH. 'Gad, I'm sure none but a chaplain could speak so, I think.

ALITHEA. Let me tell you, sir, this dull trick will not serve your turn; though you delay our marriage, you shall not hinder it.

HARCOURT. Far be it from me, munificent patroness, to delay your marriage; I desire nothing more than to marry you presently, which I might do, if you yourself would; for my noble, good-natured, and thrice generous patron here would not hinder it.

SPARKISH. No, poor man, not I, faith.

HARCOURT. And now, madam, let me tell you plainly nobody else shall marry you; by Heavens! I'll die first, for I'm sure I should die after it.

LUCY. How his love has made him forget his function, as I have seen it in real parsons!

ALITHEA. That was spoken like a chaplain too? now you understand him, I hope.

SPARKISH. Poor man, he takes it heinously to be refused; I can't blame him, 'tis putting an indignity upon him, not to be suffered; but you'll pardon me, madam, it shan't be; he shall marry us; come away, pray, madam.

LUCY. Ha! ha! he! more ado! 'tis late.

ALITHEA. Invincible stupidity! I tell you, he would marry me as your rival, not as your chaplain.

SPARKISH. *(Pulling her away.)* Come, come, madam.

LUCY. I pray, madam, do not refuse this reverend divine the honor and satisfaction of marrying you; for dare I say, he has set his heart upon't, good doctor.

ALITHEA. What can you hope or design by this?

HARCOURT. *(Aside.)* I could answer her, a reprieve for a day only, oftener revokes a hasty doom. At worst, if she will not take mercy on me and let me marry her, I have at least the lover's second pleasure—hindering my rival's enjoyment, though but for a time.

SPARKISH. Come, madam, 'tis e'en twelve o'clock, and my mother charged me never to be married out of the canonical hours. Come, come; Lord, here's such a deal of modesty, I warrant, the first day.

LUCY. Yes, an't please your worship, married women show all their modesty the first day, because married men show all their love the first day. *Exeunt.*

SCENE II: *A Bedchamber in* PINCHWIFE'S *House.*

PINCHWIFE *and* MRS. PINCHWIFE *discovered.*

PINCHWIFE. Come, tell me, I say.

MRS. PINCHWIFE. Lord! han't I told it a hundred times over?

PINCHWIFE. *(Aside.)* I would try, if in the repetition of the ungrateful tale, I could find her altering it in the least circumstance; for if her story be false, she is so too.—*(Aloud.)* Come, how was't, baggage?

MRS. PINCHWIFE. Lord, what pleasure you take to hear it sure!

PINCHWIFE. No, you take more in telling it I find; but speak, how was't?

MRS. PINCHWIFE. He carried me up into the house next to the Exchange.

PINCHWIFE. So, and you two were only in the room!

MRS. PINCHWIFE. Yes, for he sent away a youth that was there, for some dried fruit, and China oranges.

PINCHWIFE. Did he so? Damn him for it—and for——

MRS. PINCHWIFE. But presently came up the gentlewoman of the house.

PINCHWIFE. Oh, 'twas well she did; but what did he do whilst the fruit came?

MRS. PINCHWIFE. He kissed me a hundred times, and told me he fancied he kissed my fine sister, meaning me, you know, whom he said he loved with all his soul, and bid me to be sure to tell her so, and to desire her to be at her window by eleven of the clock this morning, and he would walk under it at that time.

PINCHWIFE. *(Aside.)* And he was as good as his word, very punctual; a pox reward him for't.

MRS. PINCHWIFE. Well, and he said if you were not within, he would come up to her, meaning me, you know, bud, still.

PINCHWIFE. *(Aside.)* So—he knew her certainly; but for this confession, I am obliged to her simplicity.—*(Aloud.)* But what, you stood very still when he kissed you?

MRS. PINCHWIFE. Yes, I warrant you; would you have had me discovered myself?

PINCHWIFE. But you told me he did some beastliness to you, as you call it; what was't?

MRS. PINCHWIFE. Why, he put——

PINCHWIFE. What?

MRS. PINCHWIFE. Why, he put the tip of his tongue between my lips, and so mousled[5] me—and I said, I'd bite it.

PINCHWIFE. An eternal canker seize it, for a dog!

MRS. PINCHWIFE. Nay, you need not be so angry with him neither, for to say the truth, he has the sweetest breath I ever knew.

PINCHWIFE. The devil! you were satisfied with it then, and would do it again.

MRS. PINCHWIFE. Not unless he should force me.

PINCHWIFE. Force you, changeling![6] I tell you, no woman can be forced.

MRS. PINCHWIFE. Yes, but she may sure, by such a one as he, for he's a proper, goodly, strong man; 'tis hard, let me tell you, to resist him.

PINCHWIFE. *(Aside.)* So, 'tis plain she loves him, yet she has not love enough to make her conceal it from me; but the sight of him will increase her aversion for me and love for him; and that love instruct her how to deceive me and satisfy him, all idiot as she is. Love! 'twas he gave women first their craft, their art of deluding. Out of Nature's hands they came plain, open, silly, and fit for slaves, as she and Heaven intended 'em; but damned Love—well—I must strangle that little monster whilst I can deal with him. —*(Aloud.)* Go fetch pen, ink, and paper out of the next room.

MRS. PINCHWIFE. Yes, bud. *Exit.*

PINCHWIFE. Why should women have more invention in love than men? It can only be because they have more desires, more soliciting passions, more lust, and more of the devil.

---

[5] Muzzled.

[6] Idiot.

Enter MRS. PINCHWIFE.

Come, minx, sit down and write.

MRS. PINCHWIFE. Ay, dear bud, but I can't do't very well.

PINCHWIFE. I wish you could not at all.

MRS. PINCHWIFE. But what should I write for?

PINCHWIFE. I'll have you write a letter to your lover.

MRS. PINCHWIFE. Oh lord, to the fine gentleman a letter!

PINCHWIFE. Yes, to the fine gentleman.

MRS. PINCHWIFE. Lord, you do but jeer: sure you jest.

PINCHWIFE. I am not so merry: come, write as I bid you.

MRS. PINCHWIFE. What, do you think I am a fool?

PINCHWIFE. *(Aside.)* She's afraid I would not dictate any love to him, therefore she's unwilling.—*(Aloud.)* But you had best begin.

MRS. PINCHWIFE. Indeed, and indeed, but I won't, so I won't.

PINCHWIFE. Why?

MRS. PINCHWIFE. Because he's in town; you may send for him if you will.

PINCHWIFE. Very well, you would have him brought to you; is it come to this? I say, take the pen and write, or you'll provoke me.

MRS. PINCHWIFE. Lord, what d'ye make a fool of me for? Don't I know that letters are never writ but from the country to London, and from London into the country? Now he's in town, and I am in town too; therefore I can't write to him, you know.

PINCHWIFE. *(Aside.)* So, I am glad it is no worse; she is innocent enough yet.—*(Aloud.)* Yes, you may, when your husband bids you, write letters to people that are in town.

MRS. PINCHWIFE. Oh, may I so? then I'm satisfied.

PINCHWIFE. Come, begin: *(Dictates.)*—"Sir"——

MRS. PINCHWIFE. Shan't I say, "Dear Sir?"—You know one says always something more than bare "Sir."

PINCHWIFE. Write as I bid you, or I will write whore with this penknife in your face.

MRS. PINCHWIFE. Nay, good bud *(Writes.)*—"Sir"——

PINCHWIFE. "Though I suffered last night your nauseous, loathed kisses and embraces"—Write!

MRS. PINCHWIFE. Nay, why should I say so? You know I told you he had a sweet breath.

PINCHWIFE. Write!

MRS. PINCHWIFE. Let me but put out "loathed."

PINCHWIFE. Write, I say!

MRS. PINCHWIFE. Well then. *(Writes.)*

PINCHWIFE. Let's see, what have you writ?—*(Takes the paper and reads.)* "Though I suffered last night your kisses and embraces"—Thou impudent creature! where is "nauseous" and "loathed?"

MRS. PINCHWIFE. I can't abide to write such filthy words.

PINCHWIFE. Once more write as I'd have you, and question it not, or I will spoil thy writing with this. I will stab out those eyes that cause my mischief. *(Holds up the penknife.)*

MRS. PINCHWIFE. Oh lord! I will.

PINCHWIFE. So—so—let's see now.—*(Reads.)* "Though I suffered last night your nauseous, loathed kisses and embraces"—go on—"yet I would not have you presume that you shall ever repeat them"—so——

(She writes.)

MRS. PINCHWIFE. I have writ it.

PINCHWIFE. On, then—"I then concealed myself from your knowledge, to avoid your insolencies."—— *(She writes.)*

MRS. PINCHWIFE. So——

PINCHWIFE. "The same reason, now I am out of your hands"——

(She writes.)

MRS. PINCHWIFE. So——

PINCHWIFE. "Makes me own to you my unfortunate, though innocent frolic, of being in man's clothes"—— *(She writes.)*

MRS. PINCHWIFE. So——

PINCHWIFE. "That you may for evermore cease to pursue her, who hates and detests you"—— *(She writes on.)*

MRS. PINCHWIFE. So—heigh! *(Sighs.)*

PINCHWIFE. What, do you sigh?—"detests you—as much as she loves her husband and her honor."

MRS. PINCHWIFE. I vow, husband, he'll ne'er believe I should write such a letter.

PINCHWIFE. What, he'd expect a kinder from you? Come, now your name only.

MRS. PINCHWIFE. What, shan't I say "Your most faithful humble servant till death?"

PINCHWIFE. No, tormenting fiend!—*(Aside.)* Her style, I find, would be very soft.—*(Aloud.)* Come, wrap it up now, whilst I go fetch wax and a candle; and write on the backside, "For Mr. Horner." *Exit.*

MRS. PINCHWIFE. "For Mr. Horner."—So, I am glad he has told me his name. Dear Mr. Horner! but why should I send thee such a letter that will vex thee, and make thee angry with me?—Well, I will not send it.—Ay, but then my husband will kill me—for I see plainly he won't let me love Mr. Horner—but what care I for my husband?—I won't, so I won't, send poor Mr. Horner such a letter—But then my husband—but oh, what if I writ at bottom my husband made me write it?—Ay, but then my husband would see't—Can one have no shift? ah, a London woman would have had a hundred presently. Stay—what if I should write a letter, and wrap it up like this, and write upon't too? Ay, but then my husband would see't—I don't know what to do.—But yet evads[7] I'll try, so I will—for I will not send this letter to poor Mr. Horner, come what will on't.

"Dear sweet Mr. Horner"—*(Writes and repeats what she writes.)*—so—"my husband would have me send you a base, rude, unmannerly letter; but I won't"—so—"and would have me forbid you loving me; but I won't"—so " and would have me say to you, I hate you, poor Mr. Horner; but I won't tell a lie for him"—there—"for I'm sure if you and I were in the country at cards together"—so—"I could not help treading on your toe under the table"—so—"or rubbing knees with you, and staring in your face, till you saw me"—very well—"and then looking down, and blushing for an hour together"—so—"but I must make haste before my husband comes: and now he has taught me to write letters, you shall have longer ones from me, who am, dear, dear, poor, dear Mr. Horner, your most humble friend, and servant to command till death,—Margery Pinchwife."

Stay, I must give him a hint at bottom—so—now wrap it up just like t'other—so—now write "For Mr. Horner"—But oh now, what shall I do with it? for here comes my husband.

Enter PINCHWIFE.

PINCHWIFE. *(Aside.)* I have been detained by a sparkish coxcomb who pretended a visit to me; but I fear 'twas to my wife—*(Aloud.)* What, have you done?

MRS. PINCHWIFE. Ay, ay, bud, just now.

PINCHWIFE. Let's see't: what d'ye tremble for? what, you would not have it go?

MRS. PINCHWIFE. Here—*(Aside.)* No, I must not give him that: so I had been served if I had given him this. *(He opens and reads the first letter.)*

PINCHWIFE. Come, where's the wax and seal?

MRS. PINCHWIFE. *(Aside.)* Lord, what shall I do now? Nay, then I have it—*(Aloud.)* Pray let me see't. Lord, you will think me so arrant a fool, I cannot seal a letter; I will do't, so I will.

(Snatches the letter from him, changes it for the other, seals it, and delivers it to him.)

PINCHWIFE. Nay, I believe you will learn that, and other things too, which I would not have you.

---

[7] An oath meaning "in faith."

MRS. PINCHWIFE. So, han't I done it curiously?[8]—*(Aside.)* I think I have; there's my letter going to Mr. Horner, since he'll needs have me send letters to folks.

PINCHWIFE. 'Tis very well; but I warrant, you would not have it go now?

MRS. PINCHWIFE. Yes, indeed, but I would, bud, now.

PINCHWIFE. Well, you are a good girl then. Come, let me lock you up in your chamber, till I come back; and be sure you come not within three strides of the window when I am gone, for I have a spy in the street.—*(Exit* MRS. PINCHWIFE, PINCHWIFE *locks the door.)* At least, 'tis fit she thinks so. If we do not cheat women, they'll cheat us, and fraud may be justly used with secret enemies, of which a wife is the most dangerous; and he that has a handsome one to keep, and a frontier town, must provide against treachery, rather than open force. Now I have secured all within, I'll deal with the foe without, with false intelligence. *Holds up the letter.* *Exit.*

SCENE III: HORNER'S *Lodging.*

Enter HORNER *and* QUACK.

QUACK. Well, sir, how fadges[9] the new design? have you not the luck of all your brother projectors, to deceive only yourself at last?

HORNER. No, good domine doctor, I deceive you, it seems, and others too; for the grave matrons, and old, rigid husbands think me unfit for love, as they are; but their wives, sisters, and daughters know, some of 'em, better things already.

QUACK. Already!

HORNER. Already, I say. Last night I was drunk with half-a-dozen of your civil persons, as you call 'em, and people of honor, and so was made free of their society and dressing-rooms forever hereafter; and am already come to the privileges of sleeping upon their pallets, warming smocks, tying shoes and garters, and the like, doctor, already, already, doctor.

QUACK. You have made good use of your time, sir.

HORNER. I tell thee, I am now no more interruption to 'em, when they sing, or talk bawdy, than a little squab French page who speaks no English.

QUACK. But do civil persons and women of honor drink, and sing bawdy songs?

HORNER. Oh, amongst friends, amongst friends. For your bigots in honor are just like those in religion; they fear the eye of the world more than the eye of Heaven; and think there is no virtue, but railing at vice, and no sin,

---

[8] Cleverly.

[9] Succeeds.

but giving scandal. They rail at a poor, little, kept player, and keep themselves some young, modest pulpit comedian[10] to be privy to their sins in their closets, not to tell 'em of them in their chapels.

QUACK. Nay, the truth on't is, priests, amongst the women now, have quite got the better of us lay-confessors, physicians.

HORNER. And they are rather their patients; but—

Enter LADY FIDGET, *looking about her.*

Now we talk of women of honor, here comes one. Step behind the screen there, and but observe, if I have not particular privileges with the women of reputation already, doctor, already. (QUACK *retires.*)

LADY FIDGET. Well, Horner, am not I a woman of honor? you see, I'm as good as my word.

HORNER. And you shall see, madam, I'll not be behind-hand with you in honor; and I'll be as good as my word too, if you please but to withdraw into the next room.

LADY FIDGET. But first, my dear sir, you must promise to have a care of my dear honor.

HORNER. If you talk a word more of your honor, you'll make me incapable to wrong it. To talk of honor in the mysteries of love, is like talking of Heaven or the Diety, in an operation of witchcraft, just when you are employing the devil: it makes the charm impotent.

LADY FIDGET. Nay, fy! let us not be smutty. But you talk of mysteries and bewitching to me; I don't understand you.

HORNER. I tell you, madam, the word money in a mistress's mouth, at such a nick of time, is not a more disheartening sound to a younger brother, than that of honor to an eager lover like myself.

LADY FIDGET. But you can't blame a lady of my reputation to be chary.

HORNER. Chary! I have been chary of it already, by the report I have caused of myself.

LADY FIDGET. Ay, but if you should ever let other women know that dear secret, it would come out. Nay, you must have a great care of your conduct; for my acquaintance are so censorious (oh, 'tis a wicked, censorius world, Mr. Horner!), I say, are so censorious, and detracting, that perhaps they'll talk to the prejudice of my honor, though you should not let them know the dear secret.

HORNER. Nay, madam, rather than they shall prejudice your honor, I'll prejudice theirs; and, to serve you, I'll lie with 'em all, make the secret their own, and then they'll keep it. I am a Machiavel in love, madam.

LADY FIDGET. Oh, no, sir, not that way.

---

[10] A chaplain.

HORNER. Nay, the devil take me, if censorious women are to be silenced any other way.

LADY FIDGET. A secret is better kept, I hope, by a single person than a multitude; therefore pray do not trust anybody else with it, dear, dear Mr. Horner. *(Embracing him.)*

Enter SIR JASPER FIDGET.

SIR JASPER. How now!

LADY FIDGET. *(Aside.)* Oh my husband!—prevented—and what's almost as bad, found with my arms about another man—that will appear too much—what shall I say?—*(Aloud.)* Sir Jasper, come hither: I am trying if Mr. Horner were ticklish, and he's as ticklish as can be. I love to torment the confounded toad; let you and I tickle him.

SIR JASPER. No, your ladyship will tickle him better without me I suppose. But is this your buying china? I thought you had been at the china-house.

HORNER. *(Aside.)* China-house! that's my cue, I must take it.—*(Aloud.)* A pox! can't you keep your impertinent wives at home? Some men are troubled with the husbands, but I with the wives; but I'd have you to know, since I cannot be your journeyman by night, I will not be your drudge by day, to squire your wife about, and be your man of straw, or scarecrow only to pies and jays, that would be nibbling at your forbidden fruit; I shall be shortly the hackney[11] gentleman-usher of the town.

SIR JASPER. *(Aside.)* He! he! he! poor fellow, he's in the right on't, faith. To squire women about for other folks is as ungrateful an employment, as to tell money for other folks.—*(Aloud.)* He! he! he! be'n't angry, Horner.

LADY FIDGET. No, 'tis I have more reason to be angry, who am left by you to go abroad indecently alone; or, what is more indecent, to pin myself upon such ill-bred people of your acquaintance as this is.

SIR JASPER. Nay, prithee, what has he done?

LADY FIDGET. Nay, he has done nothing.

SIR JASPER. But what d'ye take ill, if he has done nothing?

LADY FIDGET. Ha! ha! ha! faith, I can't but laugh however; why, d'ye think the unmannerly toad would come down to me to the coach? I was fain to come up to fetch him, or go without him, which I was resolved not to do; for he knows china very well, and has himself very good, but will not let me see it, lest I should beg some; but I will find it out, and have what I came for yet.

HORNER. *(Apart to* LADY FIDGET, *as he follows her to the door.)* Lock the door, madam.—*(Exit* LADY FIDGET, *and locks the door.)*—*(Aloud.)* So, she

[11] A hired hack.

has got into my chamber and locked me out. Oh the impertinency of woman-kind! Well, Sir Jasper, plain-dealing is a jewel; if ever you suffer your wife to trouble me again here, she shall carry you home a pair of horns; by my lord mayor she shall; though I cannot furnish you myself, you are sure, yet I'll find a way.

SIR JASPER. Ha! ha! he!—*(Aside.)* At my first coming in, and finding her arms about him, tickling him it seems, I was half jealous, but now I see my folly.—*(Aloud.)* He! he! he! poor Horner.

HORNER. Nay, though you laugh now, 'twill be my turn ere long. Oh women, more impertinent, more cunning, and more mischievous than their monkeys, and to me almost as ugly!—Now is she throwing my things about and rifling all I have; but I'll get in to her the back way, and so rifle her for it.

SIR JASPER. Ha! ha! ha! poor angry Horner.

HORNER. Stay here a little, I'll ferret her out to you presently, I warrant.

Exit at the other door.

*(*SIR JASPER *talks through the door to his* Wife, *she answers from within.)*

SIR JASPER. Wife! my Lady Fidget! wife! he is coming into you the back way.

LADY FIDGET. Let him come, and welcome, which way he will.

SIR JASPER. He'll catch you, and use you roughly, and be too strong for you.

LADY FIDGET. Don't you trouble yourself, let him if he can.

QUACK. *(Aside.)* This indeed I could not have believed from him, nor any but my own eyes.

Enter MRS. SQUEAMISH.

MRS. SQUEAMISH. Where's this woman-hater, this toad, this ugly, greasy, dirty sloven?

SIR JASPER. *(Aside.)* So, the women all will have him ugly: methinks he is a comely person, but his wants make his form contemptible to 'em; and 'tis e'en as my wife said yesterday, talking of him, that a proper handsome eunuch was as ridiculous a thing as a gigantic coward.

MRS. SQUEAMISH. Sir Jasper, your servant: where is the odious beast?

SIR JASPER. He's within in his chamber, with my wife; she's playing the wag with him.

MRS. SQUEAMISH. Is she so? and he's a clownish beast; he'll give her no quarter, he'll play the wag with her again, let me tell you: come, let's go help her.—What, the door's locked?

SIR JASPER. Ay, my wife locked it.

MRS. SQUEAMISH. Did she so? let's break it open then.

SIR JASPER. No, no, he'll do her no hurt.

MRS. SQUEAMISH. *(Aside.)* But is there no other way to get in to 'em? wither goes this? I will disturb 'em. *Exit at another door.*

Enter OLD LADY SQUEAMISH.

LADY SQUEAMISH. Where is this harlotry, this impudent baggage, this rambling tomrigg[12]? Oh Sir Jasper, I'm glad to see you here; did you not see my vile grandchild come in hither just now?

SIR JASPER. Yes.

LADY SQUEAMISH. Ay, but where is she then? where is she? Lord, Sir Jasper, I have e'en rattled myself to pieces in pursuit of her: but can you tell what she makes here? they say below, no woman lodges here.

SIR JASPER. No.

LADY SQUEAMISH. No! what does she here then? say, if it be not a woman's lodging, what makes she here? But are you sure no woman lodges here?

SIR JASPER. No, nor no man neither, this is Mr. Horner's lodging.

LADY SQUEAMISH. Is it so, are you sure?

SIR JASPER. Yes, yes.

LADY SQUEAMISH. So; then there's no hurt in't, I hope. But where is he?

SIR JASPER. He's in the next room with my wife.

LADY SQUEAMISH. Nay, if you trust him with your wife, I may with my Biddy. They say, he's a merry harmless man now, e'en as harmless a man as ever came out of Italy with a good voice,[13] and as pretty, harmless company for a lady, as a snake without his teeth.

SIR JASPER. Ay, ay, poor man.

Enter MRS. SQUEAMISH.

MRS. SQUEAMISH. I can't find 'em.—Oh, are you here, grandmother? I followed, you must know, my Lady Fidget hither; 'tis the prettiest lodging, and I have been staring on the prettiest pictures——

Enter LADY FIDGET *with a piece of china in her hand, and* HORNER *following.*

LADY FIDGET. And I have been toiling and moiling for the prettiest piece of china, my dear.

HORNER. Nay, she has been too hard for me, do what I could.

MRS. SQUEAMISH. Oh, lord, I'll have some china too. Good Mr. Horner,

---

[12] Tomboy.
[13] A eunuch.

don't think to give other people china, and me none; come in with me too.

HORNER. Upon my honor, I have none left now.

MRS. SQUEAMISH. Nay, nay, I have known you deny your china before now, but you shan't put me off so. Come.

HORNER. This lady had the last there.

LADY FIDGET. Yes indeed, madam, to my certain knowledge, he has no more left.

MRS. SQUEAMISH. Oh, but it may be he may have some you could not find.

LADY FIDGET. What, d'ye think if he had had any left I would not have had it too? for we women of quality never think we have china enough.

HORNER. Do not take it ill, I cannot make china for you all, but I will have a roll-waggon[14] for you too, another time.

MRS. SQUEAMISH. Thank you, dear toad.

LADY FIDGET. *(Aside to* HORNER.*)* What do you mean by that promise?

HORNER. *(Aside to* LADY FIDGET.*)* Alas, she has an innocent, literal understanding.

LADY SQUEAMISH. Poor Mr. Horner! he has enough to do to please you all, I see.

HORNER. Ay, madam, you see how they use me.

LADY SQUEAMISH. Poor gentleman, I pity you.

HORNER. I thank you, madam: I could never find pity, but from such reverend ladies as you are; the young ones will never spare a man.

MRS. SQUEAMISH. Come, come, beast, and go dine with us; for we shall want a man at ombre after dinner.

HORNER. That's all their use of me, madam, you see.

MRS. SQUEAMISH. Come, sloven, I'll lead you, to be sure of you.

(Pulls him by the cravat.)

LADY SQUEAMISH. Alas, poor man, how she tugs him! Kiss, kiss her; that's the way to make such nice women quiet.

HORNER. No, madam, that remedy is worse than the torment; they know I dare suffer anything rather than do it.

LADY SQUEAMISH. Prithee kiss her, and I'll give you her picture in little, that you admired so last night; prithee do.

HORNER. Well, nothing but that could bribe me: I love a woman only in effigy, and good painting as much as I hate them.—I'll do't, for I could adore the devil well painted. *(Kisses* MRS. SQUEAMISH.*)*

MRS. SQUEAMISH. Foh, you filthy toad! nay, now I've done jesting.

LADY SQUEAMISH. Ha! ha! ha! I told you so.

MRS. SQUEAMISH. Foh! a kiss of his——

SIR JASPER. Has no more hurt in't than one of my spaniel's.

---

14 A vase.

MRS. SQUEAMISH. Nor no more good neither.

QUACK. *(Aside.)* I will now believe anything he tells me.

Enter PINCHWIFE.

LADY FIDGET. Oh lord, here's a man! Sir Jasper, my mask, my mask! I would not be seen here for the world.

SIR JASPER. What, not when I am with you?

LADY FIDGET. No, no, my honor—let's be gone.

MRS. SQUEAMISH. Oh grandmother, let's be gone; make haste, make haste, I know not how he may censure us.

LADY FIDGET. Be found in the lodging of anything like a man!—Away.

Exeunt SIR JASPER FIDGET, LADY FIDGET, OLD LADY SQUEAMISH, *and* MRS. SQUEAMISH.

QUACK. *(Aside.)* What's here? another cuckold? he looks like one, and none else sure have any business with him.

HORNER. Well, what brings my dear friend hither?

PINCHWIFE. Your impertinency.

HORNER. My impertinency!—why, you gentlemen that have got handsome wives, think you have a privilege of saying anything to your friends, and are as brutish as if you were our creditors.

PINCHWIFE. No, sir, I'll ne'er trust you any way.

HORNER. But why not, dear Jack? why diffide[15] in me thou know'st so well?

PINCHWIFE. Because I do know you so well.

HORNER. Han't I been always thy friend, honest Jack, always ready to serve thee, in love or battle, before thou wert married, and am so still?

PINCHWIFE. I believe so, you would be my second now, indeed.

HORNER. Well then, dear Jack, why so unkind, so grum, so strange to me? Come, prithee kiss me, dear rogue: gad, I was always, I say, and am still as much thy servant as——

PINCHWIFE. As I am yours, sir. What, you would send a kiss to my wife, is that it?

HORNER. So, there 'tis—a man can't show his friendship to a married man, but presently he talks of his wife to you. Prithee, let thy wife alone, and let thee and I be all one, as we were wont. What, thou art as shy of my kindness as a Lombard Street alderman of a courtier's civility at Locket's![16]

---

[15] Mistrust me.

[16] A Lombard Street merchant would be suspicious of a courtier's request for a loan.

Locket—a tavern frequented by the wits of the town.

PINCHWIFE. But you are overkind to me, as kind as if I were your cuckold already; yet I must confess you ought to be kind and civil to me, since I am so civil to you, as to bring you this; look you there, sir.

(Delivers him a letter.)

HORNER. What is't?

PINCHWIFE. Only a love letter, sir.

HORNER. From whom?—how! this is from your wife—hum—and hum—

(Reads.)

PINCHWIFE. Even from my wife, sir: am I not wondrous kind and civil to you now too?—*(Aside.)* But you'll not think her so.

HORNER. *(Aside.)* Ha! is this a trick of his or hers?

PINCHWIFE. The gentleman's surprised I find.—What, you expected a kinder letter?

HORNER. No faith, not I, how could I?

PINCHWIFE. Yes, yes, I'm sure you did. A man so well made as you are, must needs be disappointed, if the women declare not their passion at first sight or opportunity.

HORNER. *(Aside.)* But what should this mean? Stay, the postscript. *(Reads aside.)* "Be sure you love me, whatsoever my husband says to the contrary, and let him not see this, lest he should come home and pinch me, or kill my squirrel."—It seems he knows not what the letter contains.

PINCHWIFE. Come, ne'er wonder at it so much.

HORNER. Faith, I can't help it.

PINCHWIFE. Now, I think I have deserved your infinite friendship and kindness, and have showed myself sufficiently an obliging kind friend and husband; am I not so, to bring a letter from my wife to her gallant?

HORNER. Ay, the devil take me, art thou, the most obliging, kind friend and husband in the world, ha! ha!

PINCHWIFE. Well, you may be merry, sir; but in short I must tell you, sir, my honor will suffer no jesting.

HORNER. What dost thou mean?

PINCHWIFE. Does the letter want a comment? Then, know, sir, though I have been so civil a husband, as to bring you a letter from my wife, to let you kiss and court her to my face, I will not be a cuckold, sir, I will not.

HORNER. Thou art mad with jealousy. I never saw thy wife in my life but at the play yesterday, and I know not if it were she or no. I court her, kiss her!

PINCHWIFE. I will not be a cuckold, I say: there will be danger in making me a cuckold.

HORNER. Why, wert thou not well cured of thy last clap?

PINCHWIFE. I wear a sword.

HORNER. It should be taken from thee, less thou should'st do thyself a mischief with it; thou art mad, man.

PINCHWIFE. As mad as I am, and as merry as you are, I must have more reason from you ere we part. I say again, though you kissed and courted last night my wife in man's clothes, as she confesses in her letter——

HORNER. *(Aside.)* Ha!

PINCHWIFE. Both she and I say, you must not design it again, for you have mistaken your woman, as you have done your man.

HORNER. *(Aside.)* Oh—I understand something now—*(Aloud.)* Was that thy wife! Why would'st thou not tell me 'twas she? Faith, my freedom with her was your fault, not mine.

PINCHWIFE. *(Aside.)* Faith, so 'twas.

HORNER. Fy! I'd never do't to a woman before her husband's face, sure.

PINCHWIFE. But I had rather you should do't to my wife before my face, than behind my back; and that you shall never do.

HORNER. No—you will hinder me.

PINCHWIFE. If I would not hinder you, you see by her letter she would.

HORNER. Well, I must e'en acquiesce then, and be contented with what she writes.

PINCHWIFE. I'll assure you 'twas voluntarily writ; I had no hand in't you may believe me.

HORNER. I do believe thee, faith.

PINCHWIFE. And I believe her too, for she's an innocent creature, has no dissembling in her: and so fare you well, sir.

HORNER. Pray, however, present my humble service to her, and tell her I will obey her letter to a tittle, and fulfill her desires, be what they will, or with what difficulty soever I do't; and you shall be no more jealous of me, I warrant her, and you.

PINCHWIFE. Well then, fare you well; and play with any man's honor but mine, kiss any man's wife but mine, and welcome. *Exit.*

HORNER. Ha! ha! ha! doctor.

QUACK. It seems, he has not heard the report of you, or does not believe it.

HORNER. Ha! ha!—now, doctor, what think you?

QUACK. Pray let's see the letter—hum—"for—dear—love you——"

(Reads the letter.)

HORNER. I wonder how she could contrive it! What say'st thou to't? 'tis an original.[17]

QUACK. So are your cuckolds too originals: for they are like no other common cuckolds, and I will henceforth believe it not impossible for you to cuckold the Grand Signior[18] amidst his guards of eunuchs, that I say.

HORNER. And I say for the letter, 'tis the first love-letter that ever was without flames, darts, fates, destinies, lying and dissembling in't.

---

[17] A natural fool.
[18] A Turkish Ruler.

Enter SPARKISH *pulling in* PINCHWIFE.

SPARKISH. Come back, you are a pretty brother-in-law, neither go to church nor to dinner with your sister bride!

PINCHWIFE. My sister denies her marriage, and you see is gone away from you dissatisfied.

SPARKISH. Pshaw! upon a foolish scruple, that our parson was not in lawful orders, and did not say all the common-prayer; but 'tis her modesty only I believe. But let all women be never so modest the first day, they'll be sure to come to themselves by night, and I shall have enough of her then. In the meantime, Harry Horner, you must dine with me: I keep my wedding at my aunt's in the Piazza.[19]

HORNER. Thy wedding! what stale maid has lived to despair of a husband, or what young one of a gallant?

SPARKISH. Oh, your servant, sir—this gentleman's sister then,—no stale maid.

HORNER. I'm sorry for't.

PINCHWIFE. *(Aside.)* How comes he so concerned for her?

SPARKISH. You sorry for't? why, do you know any ill by her?

HORNER. No, I know none but by thee; 'tis for her sake, not yours, and another man's sake that might have hoped, I thought.

SPARKISH. Another man! another man! what is his name?

HORNER. *(Aside.)* Nay, since 'tis past, he shall be nameless.—Poor Harcourt! I am sorry thou hast missed her.

PINCHWIFE. *(Aside.)* He seems to be much troubled at the match.

SPARKISH. Prithee, tell me—Nay, you shan't go, brother.

PINCHWIFE. I must of necessity, but I'll come to you to dinner. *Exit.*

SPARKISH. But, Harry, what, have I a rival in my wife already? But with all my heart, for he may be of use to me hereafter; for though my hunger is now my sauce, and I can fall on heartily without, the time will come when a rival will be as good sauce for a married man to a wife, as an orange to veal.

HORNER. Oh thou damned rogue! thou hast set my teeth on edge with thy orange.

SPARKISH. Then let's to dinner—there I was with you again. Come.

HORNER. But who dines with thee?

SPARKISH. My friends and relations, my brother Pinchwife, you see, of your acquaintance.

HORNER. And his wife?

SPARKISH. No, 'gad, he'll ne'er let her come amongst us good fellows; your

---

[19] An open arcade in Covent Garden used as a meeting place for fashionable society.

stingy country coxcomb keeps his wife from his friends as he does his little firkin of ale for his own drinking, and a gentleman can't get a smack on't; but his servants, when his back is turned, broach it at their pleasures, and dust it away, ha! ha! ha!—'Gad, I am witty, I think, considering I was married today, by the world; but come——

HORNER. No, I will not dine with you, unless you can fetch her too.

SPARKISH. Pshaw! what pleasure canst thou have with women now, Harry?

HORNER. My eyes are not gone; I love a good prospect yet, and will not dine with you unless she does too; go fetch her therefore, but do not tell her husband 'tis for my sake.

SPARKISH. Well, I'll go try what I can do; in the meantime, come away to my aunt's lodging, 'tis in the way to Pinchwife's.

HORNER. The poor woman has called for aid, and stretched forth her hand, doctor; I cannot but help her over the pale out of the briars. *Exeunt.*

SCENE IV: *A Room in* PINCHWIFE'S *House.*

MRS. PINCHWIFE *alone, leaning on her elbow.—A table, pen, ink, and paper.*

MRS. PINCHWIFE. Well, 'tis e'en so, I have got the London disease they call love; I am sick of my husband, and for my gallant. I have heard this distemper called a fever, but methinks 'tis like an ague; for when I think of my husband, I tremble, and am in a cold sweat, and have inclinations to vomit; but when I think of my gallant, dear Mr. Horner, my hot fit comes, and I am all in a fever indeed; and, as in other fevers, my own chamber is tedious to me, and I would fain be removed to his, and then methinks I should be well. Ah, poor Mr. Horner! Well, I cannot, will not stay here; therefore I'll make an end of my letter to him, which shall be a finer letter than my last, because I have studied it like anything. Oh sick, sick!

(Takes the pen and writes.)

Enter PINCHWIFE, *who seeing her writing, steals softly behind her and looking over her shoulder, snatches the paper from her.*

PINCHWIFE. What, writing more letters?

MRS. PINCHWIFE. Oh lord, bud, why d'ye fright me so?

(She offers to run out; he stops her, and reads.)

PINCHWIFE. How's this? nay, you shall not stir, madam:—"Dear, dear, dear Mr. Horner"—very well—I have taught you to write letters to good purpose—but let us see't. "First, I am to beg your pardon for my boldness in writing to you, which I'd have you to know I would not have done, had not you said first you loved me so extremely, which if you do, you will suffer me to lie in the arms of another man whom I loathe, nauseate, and detest." —Now you can write these filthy words. But what follows?—"Therefore, I hope you will speedily find some way to free me from this unfortunate match, which was never, I assure you, of my choice, but I'm afraid 'tis already too far gone; however, if you love me, as I do you, you will try what you can do; but you must help me away before tomorrow, or else, alas! I shall be forever out of your reach, for I can defer no longer our— our——" what is to follow "our"?—speak, what—our journey into the country I suppose—Oh woman, damned woman! and Love, damned Love, their old tempter! for this is one of his miracles; in a moment he can make those blind that could see, and those see that were blind, those dumb that could speak, and those prattle who were dumb before; nay, what is more than all, make these dough-baked, senseless, indocile animals, women, too hard for us their politic lords and rulers, in a moment. But make an end to your letter, and then I'll make an end of you thus, and all my plagues together. *(Draws his sword.)*

MRS. PINCHWIFE. Oh lord, Oh lord, you are such a passionate man, bud!

Enter SPARKISH.

SPARKISH. How now, what's here to do?

PINCHWIFE. This fool here now!

SPARKISH. What! drawn upon your wife? You should never do that, but at night in the dark, when you can't hurt her. This is my sister-in-law, is it not? ay, faith, e'en our country Margery *(pulls aside her handkerchief)*; one may know her. Come, she and you must go dine with me; dinner's ready, come. But where's my wife? is she not come home yet? where is she?

PINCHWIFE. Making you a cuckold; 'tis that they all do, as soon as they can.

SPARKISH. What, the wedding-day? no, a wife that designs to make a cully[20] of her husband will be sure to let him win the first stake of love, by the world. But come, they stay dinner for us: come, I'll lead down our Margery.

PINCHWIFE. No—sir, go, we'll follow you.

SPARKISH. I will not wag without you.

PINCHWIFE. *(Aside.)* This coxcomb is a sensible torment to me amidst the greatest in the world.

SPARKISH. Come, come, Madam Margery.

PINCHWIFE. No; I'll lead her my way: what, would you treat your friends with mine, for want of your own wife?—*(Leads her to the other door, and*

---

[20] A fool.

locks her in and returns.) I am contented my rage should take breath——

SPARKISH. *(Aside.)* I told Horner this.

PINCHWIFE. Come now.

SPARKISH. Lord, how shy you are of your wife! but let me tell you, brother, we men of wit have amongst us a saying, that cuckolding, like the small-pox, comes with a fear; and you may keep your wife as much as you will out of danger of infection, but if her constitution incline her to't, she'll have it sooner or later, by the world, say they.

PINCHWIFE. *(Aside.)* What a thing is a cuckold, that every fool can make him ridiculous!—*(Aloud.)* Well, sir—but let me advise you, now you are come to be concerned, because you suspect the danger, not to neglect the means to prevent it, especially when the greatest share of the malady will light upon your own head, for

Hows'e'er the kind wife's belly comes to swell,
The husband breeds[21] for her, and first is ill. *Exeunt.*

ACT V

SCENE I: PINCHWIFE'S *House.*

Enter PINCHWIFE *and* MRS. PINCHWIFE. *A table and candle.*

PINCHWIFE. Come, take the pen and make an end of the letter, just as you intended; if you are false in a tittle, I shall soon perceive it, and punish you as you deserve.—*(Lays his hand on his sword.)* Write what was to follow—let's see—"You must make haste, and help me away before to-morrow, or else I shall be for ever out of your reach, for I can defer no longer our"—What follows "our"?

MRS. PINCHWIFE. Must all out, then, bud?—Look you there, then.

(MRS. PINCHWIFE *takes the pen and writes.)*

PINCHWIFE. Let's see—"For I can defer no longer our—wedding—Your slighted Alithea."—What's the meaning of this? my sister's name to't? speak, unriddle.

MRS. PINCHWIFE. Yes, indeed, bud.

PINCHWIFE. But why her name to't? speak—speak, I say.

MRS. PINCHWIFE. Ay, but you'll tell her then again. If you would not tell her again——

PINCHWIFE. I will not:—I am stunned, my head turns round.—Speak.

MRS. PINCHWIFE. Won't you tell her, indeed, and indeed?

---

[21] Grows horns.

PINCHWIFE. No; speak, I say.

MRS. PINCHWIFE. She'll be angry with me; but I had rather she should be angry with me than you, bud; and, to tell you the truth, 'twas she made me write the letter, and taught me what I should write.

PINCHWIFE. *(Aside.)* Ha! I thought the style was somewhat better than her own.—*(Aloud.)* Could she come to teach you, since I had locked you up alone?

MRS. PINCHWIFE. Oh, through the key-hole, bud.

PINCHWIFE. But why should she make you write a letter for her to him, since she can write herself?

MRS. PINCHWIFE. Why, she said because—for I was unwilling to do it——

PINCHWIFE. Because what—because?

MRS. PINCHWIFE. Because, lest Mr. Horner should be cruel, and refuse her; or be vain afterwards, and show the letter, she might disown it, the hand not being hers.

PINCHWIFE. *(Aside.)* How's this? Ha!—then I think I shall come to myself again. This changeling could not invent this lie: but if she could, why should she? she might think I should soon discover it.—Stay—now I think on't too, Horner said he was sorry she had married Sparkish; and her disowning her marriage to me makes me think she has evaded it for Horner's sake: yet why should she take this course? But men in love are fools; women may well be so—*(Aloud.)* But hark you, madam, your sister went out in the morning, and I have not seen her within since.

MRS. PINCHWIFE. Alack-a-day, she has been crying all day above, it seems, in a corner.

PINCHWIFE. Where is she? let me speak with her.

MRS. PINCHWIFE. *(Aside.)* Oh lord, then she'll discover all!—*(Aloud.)* Pray hold, bud; what, d'ye mean to discover me? she'll know I have told you then. Pray, bud, let me talk with her first.

PINCHWIFE. I must speak with her, to know whether Horner ever made her any promise, and whether she be married to Sparkish or no.

MRS. PINCHWIFE. Pray, dear bud, don't till I have spoken with her and told her that I have told you all; for she'll kill me else.

PINCHWIFE. Go then, and bid her come out to me.

MRS. PINCHWIFE. Yes, yes, bud.

PINCHWIFE. Let me see——

MRS. PINCHWIFE. *(Aside.)* I'll go, but she is not within to come to him: I have just got time to know of Lucy her maid, who first set me on work, what lie I shall tell next; for I am e'en at my wit's end. *Exit.*

PINCHWIFE. Well, I resolve it, Horner shall have her: I'd rather give him my sister than lend him my wife; and such an alliance will prevent his pretensions to my wife, sure. I'll make him of kin to her, and then he won't care for her.

Enter MRS. PINCHWIFE

MRS. PINCHWIFE. Oh lord, bud! I told you what anger you would make me with my sister.

PINCHWIFE. Won't she come hither?

MRS. PINCHWIFE. No, no. Lack-a-day, she's ashamed to look you in the face: and she says, if you go in to her, she'll run away downstairs, and shamefully go herself to Mr. Horner, who has promised her marriage, she says; and she will have no other, so she won't.

PINCHWIFE. Did he so?—promise her marriage!—then she shall have no other. Go tell her so; and if she will come and discourse with me a little concerning the means, I will about it immediately. Go—(*Exit* MRS. PINCHWIFE.) His estate is equal to Sparkish's, and his extraction much better than his, as his parts are; but my chief reason is, I'd rather be akin to him by the name of brother-in-law than that of cuckold.

Enter MRS. PINCHWIFE

Well, what says she now?

MRS. PINCHWIFE. Why, she says she would only have you lead her to Horner's lodging; with whom she first will discourse the matter before she talks with you, which yet she cannot do; for alack, poor creature, she says she can't so much as look you in the face, therefore, she'll come to you in a mask. And you must excuse her, if she make you no answer to any question of yours, till you have brought her to Mr. Horner; and if you will not chide her, nor question her, she'll come out to you immediately.

PINCHWIFE. Let her come: I will not speak a word to her, nor require a word from her.

MRS. PINCHWIFE. Oh, I forgot: besides, she says she cannot look you in the face, though through a mask; therefore would desire you to put out the candle.

PINCHWIFE. I agree to all. Let her make haste.—There, 'tis out.—(*Puts out the candle. Exit* MRS. PINCHWIFE.) My case is something better: I'd rather fight with Horner for not lying with my sister, than for lying with my wife; and of the two, I had rather find my sister too forward than my wife. I expected no other from her free education, as she calls it, and her passion for the town. Well, wife and sister are names which make us expect love and duty, pleasure and comfort; but we find 'em plagues and torments, and are equally, though differently, troublesome to their keeper; for we have as much ado to get people to lie with our sisters as to keep 'em from lying with our wives.

Enter MRS. PINCHWIFE *masked, and in hoods and scarfs, and a nightgown and petticoat of* ALITHEA'S.

What, are you come, sister? let us go then.—But first, let me lock up my wife. Mrs. Margery, where are you?

MRS. PINCHWIFE. Here, bud.

PINCHWIFE. Come hither, that I may lock you up: get you in.—*(Locks the door.)* Come, sister, where are you now?

(MRS. PINCHWIFE *give him her hand; but when he lets her go, she steals softly on to the other side of him, and is led away by him for his sister,* ALITHEA.)

SCENE II: HORNER'S *Lodging.*

HORNER *and* QUACK.

QUACK. What, all alone? not so much as one of your cuckolds here, nor one of their wives! They use to take their turns with you, as if they were to watch you.

HORNER. Yes, it often happens that a cuckold is but his wife's spy, and is more upon family duty when he is with her gallant abroad, hindering his pleasure, than when he is at home with her playing the gallant. But the hardest duty a married woman imposes upon a lover is keeping her husband company always.

QUACK. And his fondness wearies you almost as soon as hers.

HORNER. A pox! keeping a cuckold company, after you have had his wife, is as tiresome as the company of a country squire to a witty fellow of the town, when he has got all his money.

QUACK. And as at first a man makes a friend of the husband to get the wife, so at last you are fain to fall out with the wife to be rid of the husband.

HORNER. Ay, most cuckold-makers are true courtiers; when once a poor man has cracked his credit for 'em, they can't abide to come near him.

QUACK. But at first, to draw him in, are so sweet, so kind, so dear! just as you are to Pinchwife. But what becomes of that intrigue with his wife?

HORNER. A pox! he's as surly as an alderman that has been bit; and since he's so coy, his wife's kindness is in vain, for she's a silly innocent.

QUACK. Did she not send you a letter by him?

HORNER. Yes; but that's a riddle I have not yet solved. Allow the poor creature to be willing, she is silly too, and he keeps her up so close——

QUACK. Yes, so close, that he makes her but the more willing, and adds but revenge to her love; which two, when met, seldom fail of satisfying each other one way or another.

HORNER. What! here's the man we are talking of, I think.

Enter PINCHWIFE, *leading in* MRS. PINCHWIFE, *masked, muffled, and in her sister's gown.*

Pshaw!

QUACK. Bringing his wife to you is the next thing to bringing a love-letter from her.

HORNER. What means this?

PINCHWIFE. The last time, you know, sir, I brought you a love-letter; now, you see, a mistress; I think you'll say I am a civil man to you.

HORNER. Ay, the devil take me, will I say thou art the civilest man I ever met with; and I have known some. I fancy I understand thee now better than I did the letter. But, hark thee, in thy ear——

PINCHWIFE. What?

HORNER. Nothing but the usual question, man: is she sound, on thy word?

PINCHWIFE. What, you take her for a wench, and me for a pimp?

HORNER. Pshaw! wench and pimp, paw[1] words; I know thou art an honest fellow, and hast a great acquaintance among the ladies, and perhaps hast made love for me, rather than let me make love to thy wife.

PINCHWIFE. Come, sir, in short, I am for no fooling.

HORNER. Nor I neither: there prithee, let's see her face presently. Make her show, man: art thou sure I don't know her?

PINCHWIFE. I am sure you do know her.

HORNER. A pox! why dost thou bring her to me then?

PINCHWIFE. Because she's a relation of mine——

HORNER. Is she, faith, man? then thou art still more civil and obliging, dear rogue.

PINCHWIFE. Who desired me to bring her to you.

HORNER. Then she is obliging, dear rogue.

PINCHWIFE. You'll make her welcome for my sake, I hope.

HORNER. I hope she is handsome enough to make herself welcome. Prithee let her unmask.

PINCHWIFE. Do you speak to her; she would never be ruled by me.

HORNER. Madam——(MRS. PINCHWIFE *Whispers to* HORNER.) She says she must speak with me in private. Withdraw, prithee.

PINCHWIFE. *(Aside.)* She's unwilling, it seems, I should know all her in-

---

[1] Naughty.

decent conduct in this business.—*(Aloud.)* Well then, I'll leave you together, and hope when I am gone, you'll agree; if not, you and I shan't agree, sir.

HORNER. What means the fool? if she and I agree 'tis no matter what you and I do.

(Whispers to MRS. PINCHWIFE, *who makes signs with her hand for him to be gone.)*

PINCHWIFE. In the meantime I'll fetch a parson, and find out Sparkish, and disabuse him. You would have me fetch a parson, would you not? Well then—now I think I am rid of her and shall have no more trouble with her—our sisters and daughters, like userers' money, are safest when put out; but our wives, like their writings, never safe, but in our closets under lock and key. *Exit.*

Enter BOY.

BOY. Sir Jasper Fidget, sir, is coming up. *Exit.*

HORNER. Here's the trouble of a cuckold now we are talking of. A pox on him! has he not enough to do to hinder his wife's sport, but he must other women's too?—Step in here, madam. *(Exit* MRS. PINCHWIFE.*)*

Enter SIR JASPER FIDGET.

SIR JASPER. My best and dearest friend.

HORNER. *(Aside to* QUACK.*)* The old style, doctor.—*(Aloud.)* Well, be short, for I am busy. What would your impertinent wife have now?

SIR JASPER. Well guessed, i'faith; for I do come from her.

HORNER. To invite me to supper! Tell her, I can't come: go.

SIR JASPER. Nay, now you are out, faith; for my lady, and the whole knot of the virtuous gang, as they call themselves, are resolved upon a frolic of coming to you tonight in masquerade, and are all dressed already.

HORNER. I shan't be at home.

SIR JASPER. *(Aside.)* Lord, how churlish he is to women!—*(Aloud.)* Nay, prithee don't disappoint 'em; they'll think 'tis my fault: prithee don't. I'll send in the banquet and the fiddles. But make no noise on't; for the poor virtuous rogues would not have it known, for the world, that they go a-masquerading; and they would come to no man's ball but yours.

HORNER. Well, well—get you gone; and tell 'em, if they come, 'will be at the peril of their honor and yours.

SIR JASPER. He! he! he!—we'll trust you for that: farewell. *Exit.*

HORNER. Doctor, anon you too shall be my guest,
But now I'm going to a private feast. *Exeunt.*

SCENE III: *The Piazza of Covent Garden.*

Enter SPARKISH *with a letter in his hand,* PINCHWIFE *following.*

SPARKISH. But who would have thought a woman could have been false to me? By the world, I could not have thought it.

PINCHWIFE. You were for giving and taking liberty: she has taken it only, sir, now you find in that letter. You were a frank person, and so is she, you see there.

SPARKISH. Nay, if this be her hand—for I never saw it.

PINCHWIFE. 'Tis no matter whether that be her hand or no; I am sure this hand, at her desire, led her to Mr. Horner, with whom I left her just now, to go fetch a parson to 'em at their desire too, to deprive you of her for ever; for it seems yours was but a mock marriage.

SPARKISH. Indeed, she would needs have it that 'twas Harcourt himself, in a parson's habit, that married us; but I'm sure he told me 'twas his brother Ned.

PINCHWIFE. Oh, there 'tis out; and you were deceived, not she: for you are such a frank person. But I must be gone.—You'll find her at Mr. Horner's. Go, and believe your eyes. *Exit.*

SPARKISH. Nay, I'll to her, and call her as many crocodiles, sirens, harpies, and other heathenish names, as a poet would do a mistress who had refused to hear his suit; nay more, his verses on her.—But stay, is not that she following a torch at t'other end of the Piazza? and from Horner's certainly—'tis so.

Enter ALITHEA *following a torch, and* LUCY *behind.*

You are well met, madam, though you don't think so. What, you have made a short visit to Mr. Horner? but I suppose you'll return to him presently, by that time the parson can be with him.

ALITHEA. Mr. Horner and the parson, sir!

SPARKISH. Come, madam, no more dissembling, no more jilting; for I am no more a frank person.

ALITHEA. How's this?

LUCY. *(Aside.)* So. 'twill work, I see.

SPARKISH. Could you find out no easy country fool to abuse? none but me, a gentleman of wit and pleasure about the town? But it was your pride to be too hard for a man of parts, unworthy false woman! false as a friend that lends a man money to lose; false as dice, who undo those that trust all they have to 'em.

LUCY. *(Aside.)* He has been a great bubble, by his similes, as they say.

ALITHEA. You have been too merry, sir, at your wedding-dinner, sure.

SPARKISH. What, d'ye mock me too?

ALITHEA. Or you have been deluded.

SPARKISH. By you.

ALITHEA. Let me understand you.

SPARKISH. Have you the confidence (I should call it something else, since you know your guilt) to stand my just reproaches? you did not write an impudent letter to Mr. Horner? who I find now has clubbed with you in deluding me with his aversion for women, that I might not, forsooth, suspect him for my rival.

LUCY. *(Aside.)* D'ye think the gentleman can be jealous now, madam?

ALITHEA. I write a letter to Mr. Horner!

SPARKISH. Nay, madam, do not deny it. Your brother showed it me just now; and told me likewise, he left you at Horner's lodging to fetch a parson to marry you to him: and I wish you joy, madam, joy, joy; and to him too, much joy; and to myself more joy, for not marrying you.

ALITHEA. *(Aside.)* So, I find my brother would break off the match; and I can consent to't, since I see this gentleman can be made jealous.—*(Aloud.)* Oh Lucy, by his rude usage and jealousy, he makes me almost afraid I am married to him. Art thou sure 'twas Harcourt himself, and no parson, that married us?

SPARKISH. No, madam, I thank you. I suppose, that was a contrivance too of Mr. Horner's and yours, to make Harcourt play the parson; but I would as little as you have him one now, no, not for the world. For, shall I tell you another truth? I never had any passion for you till now, for now I hate you. 'Tis true, I might have married your portion, as other men of parts of the town do sometimes: and so, your servant. And to show my unconcernedness, I'll come to your wedding and resign you with as much joy as I would a stale wench to a new cully; nay, with as much joy as I would after the first night, if I had been married to you. There's for you; and so your servant, servant.

Exit.

ALITHEA. How was I deceived in a man!

LUCY. You'll believe then a fool may be made jealous now? for that easiness in him that suffers him to be led by a wife, will likewise permit him to be persuaded against her by others.

ALITHEA. But marry Mr. Horner! my brother does not intend it, sure: if I thought he did, I would take thy advice, and Mr. Harcourt for my husband. And now I wish, that if there be any overwise woman of the town, who, like me, would marry a fool for fortune, liberty, or title, first, that her husband may love play, and be a cully to all the town but her, and suffer none but Fortune to be mistress of his purse; then, if for liberty, that he may send her into the country, under the conduct of some huswifely mother-in-law; and if for title, may the world give 'em none but that of cuckold.

LUCY. And for her greater curse, madam, may he not deserve it.

ALITHEA. Away, impertinent! Is not this my old Lady Lanterlu's?[2]

LUCY. Yes, madam.—*(Aside.)* And here I hope we shall find Mr. Harcourt. *Exeunt.*

SCENE IV: HORNER'S *Lodging: a table, banquet, and bottles.*

Enter HORNER, LADY FIDGET, MRS. DAINTY FIDGET, *and* MRS. SQUEAMISH.

HORNER. *(Aside.)* A pox! they are come too soon—before I have sent back my new mistress. All that I have now to do is to lock her in, that they may not see her.

LADY FIDGET. That we may be sure of our welcome, we have brought our entertainment with us, and are resolved to treat thee, dear toad.

MRS. DAINTY. And that we may be merry to purpose, have left Sir Jasper and my old Lady Squeamish quarrelling at home at backgammon.

MRS. SQUEAMISH. Therefore let us make use of our time, lest they should chance to interrupt us.

LADY FIDGET. Let us sit then.

HORNER. First, that you may be private, let me lock this door and that, and I'll wait upon you presently.

LADY FIDGET. No, sir, shut 'em only, and your lips for ever; for we must trust you as much as our women.

HORNER. You know all vanity's killed in me; I have no occasion for talking.

LADY FIDGET. Now, ladies, supposing we had drank each of us two bottles, let us speak the truth of our hearts.

MRS. DAINTY AND MRS. SQUEAMISH. Agreed.

LADY FIDGET. By this brimmer,[3] for truth is nowhere else to be found—*(aside to* HORNER.*)* not in thy heart, false man!

HORNER. *(Aside to* LADY FIDGET.*)* You have found me a true man, I'm sure.

LADY FIDGET. *(Aside to* HORNER.*)* Not every way.—But let us sit and be merry. *(Sings.)*

---

[2] A card game.
[3] A glass or cup filled with wine.

Why should our damned tyrants oblige us to live
On the pittance of pleasure which they only give?
 We must not rejoice
 With wine and with noise:
In vain we must wake in a dull bed alone,
Whilst to our warm rival the bottle they're gone.
 Then lay aside charms,
 And take up these arms.[4]
'Tis wine only gives 'em their courage and wit;
Because we live sober, to men we submit.
 If for beauties you'd pass,
 Take a lick of the glass,
'Twill mend your complexions, and when they are gone,
 The best red we have is the red of the grape:
Then, sisters, lay't on,
 And damn a good shape.

MRS. DAINTY. Dear brimmer! Well, in token of our openness and plain-dealing, let us throw our masks over our heads.

HORNER. *(Aside.)* So, 'twill come to the glasses anon.

MRS. SQUEAMISH. Lovely brimmer! let me enjoy him first.

LADY FIDGET. No, I never part with a gallant till I've tried him. Dear brimmer! that makest our husbands short-sighted.

MRS. DAINTY. And our bashful gallants bold.

MRS. SQUEAMISH. And, for want of a gallant, the butler lovely in our eyes. —Drink, eunuch.

LADY FIDGET. Drink, thou representative of a husband. Damn a husband!

MRS. DAINTY. And, as it were a husband, an old keeper.

MRS. SQUEAMISH. And an old grandmother.

HORNER. And an English bawd, and a French surgeon.

LADY FIDGET. Ay, we have all reason to curse 'em.

HORNER. For my sake, ladies?

LADY FIDGET. No, for our own; for the first spoils all young gallants' industry.

MRS. DAINTY. And the other's art makes 'em bold only with common women.

MRS. SQUEAMISH. And rather run the hazard of the vile distemper amongst them, than of a denial amongst us.

MRS. DAINTY. The filthy toads choose mistresses now as they do stuffs, for having been fancied and worn by others.

---

[4] The glasses.

MRS. SQUEAMISH. For being common and cheap.

LADY FIDGET. Whilst women of quality, like the richest stuffs, lie untumbled, and unasked for.

HORNER. Ay, neat, and cheap, and new, often they think best.

MRS. DAINTY. No, sir, the beasts will be known by a mistress longer than by a suit.

MRS. SQUEAMISH. And 'tis not for cheapness neither.

LADY FIDGET. No; for the vain fops will take up druggets[5] and embroider 'em. But I wonder at the depraved appetites of witty men; they used to be out of the common road, and hate imitation. Pray tell me, beast, when you were a man, why you rather chose to club with a multitude in a common house for an entertainment, than to be the only guest at a good table.

HORNER. Why, faith, ceremony and expectation are unsufferable to those that are sharp bent. People always eat with the best stomach at an ordinary,[6] where every man is snatching for the best bit.

LADY FIDGET. Though he get a cut over the fingers.—But I have heard, that people eat most heartily of another man's meat, that is, what they do not pay for.

HORNER. When they are sure of their welcome and freedom; for ceremony in love and eating is as ridiculous as in fighting: falling on briskly is all should be done on those occasions.

LADY FIDGET. Well, then, let me tell you, sir, there is nowhere more freedom than in our houses; and we take freedom, from a young person as a sign of good breeding, and a person may be as free as he pleases with us, as frolic, as gamesome, as wild as he will.

HORNER. Han't I heard you all declaim against wild men?

LADY FIDGET. Yes, but for all that, we think wildness in a man as desirable a quality as in a duck or rabbit; a tame man! foh!

HORNER. I know not, but your reputations frightened me as much as your faces invite me.

LADY FIDGET. Our reputation! Lord, why should you not think that we women make use of our reputation, as you men of yours, only to deceive the world with less suspicion? Our virtue is like the statesman's religion, the quaker's word, the gamester's oath, and the great man's honor; but to cheat those that trust us.

MRS. SQUEAMISH. And that demureness, coyness, and modesty, that you see in our faces in the boxes at plays, is as much a sign for a kind woman, as a vizard-mask in the pit.

MRS. DAINTY. For, I assure you, women are least masked when they have the velvet vizard on.

---

5 Coarse woolen fabrics.
6 A meal at a fixed price provided by a tavern.

LADY FIDGET. You would have found us modest women in our denials only.

MRS. SQUEAMISH. Our bashfulness is only the reflection of the men's.

MRS. DAINTY. We blush when they are shamefaced.

HORNER. I beg your pardon, ladies, I was deceived in you devilishly. But why that mighty pretence to honor?

LADY FIDGET. We have told you; but sometimes 'twas for the same reason you men pretend business often, to avoid ill company, to enjoy the better and more privately those you love.

HORNER. But why would you ne'er give a friend a wink then?

LADY FIDGET. Faith, your reputation frightened us, as much as ours did you, you were so notoriously lewd.

HORNER. And you so seemingly honest.

LADY FIDGET. Was that all that deterred you?

HORNER. And so expensive—you allow freedom, you say.

LADY FIDGET. Ay, ay.

HORNER. That I was afraid of losing my little money, as well as my little time, both which my other pleasures required.

LADY FIDGET. Money! foh! you talk like a little fellow now: do such as we expect money?

HORNER. I beg your pardon, madam, I must confess, I have heard that great ladies, like great merchants, set but the higher prices upon what they have, because they are not in necessity of taking the first offer.

MRS. DAINTY. Such as we make sale of our hearts?

MRS. SQUEAMISH. We bribed for our love? foh!

HORNER. With your pardon, ladies, I know, like great men in offices, you seem to exact flattery and attendance only from your followers; but you have receivers[7] about you, and such fees to pay, a man is afraid to pass your grants.[8] Besides, we must let you win at cards, or we lose your hearts; and if you make an assignation, 'tis at a goldsmith's, jeweler's, or china-house; where for your honor you deposit to him, he must pawn his to the punctual cit,[9] and so paying for what you take up, pays for what he takes up.

MRS. DAINTY. Would you not have us assured of our gallants' love?

MRS. SQUEAMISH. For love is better known by liberality than by jealousy.

LADY FIDGET. For one may be dissembled, the other not.—*(Aside.)* But my jealousy can be no longer dissembled, and they are telling ripe.—*(Aloud.)*—Come, here's to our gallants in waiting, whom we must name, and I'll begin. This is my false rogue. *(Claps him on the back.)*

---

[7] Servants who collect bribes.

[8] Receive your favors.

[9] A shopkeeper who demands that the bills owed to him be paid on time.

MRS. SQUEAMISH. How!

HORNER. *(Aside.)* So, all will out now.

MRS. SQUEAMISH. *(Aside to* HORNER.*)* Did you not tell me, 'twas for my sake only you reported yourself no man?

MRS. DAINTY. *(Aside to* HORNER.*)* Oh, wretch! did you not swear to me, 'twas for my love and honor you passed for that thing you do?

HORNER. So, so.

LADY FIDGET. Come, speak, ladies: this is my false villain.

MRS. SQUEAMISH. And mine too.

MRS. DAINTY. And mine.

HORNER. Well then, you are all three my false rogues too, and there's an end on't.

LADY FIDGET. Well then, there's no remedy; sister sharers, let us not fall out, but have a care of our honor. Though we get no presents, no jewels of him, we are savers of our honor, the jewel of most value and use, which shines yet to the world unsuspected, though it be counterfeit.

HORNER. Nay, and is e'en as good as if it were true, provided the world think so; for honor, like beauty now, only depends on the opinion of others.

LADY FIDGET. Well, Harry Common, I hope you can be true to three. Swear; but 'tis to no purpose to require your oath, for you are as often forsworn as you swear to new women.

HORNER. Come, faith, madam, let us e'en pardon one another; for all the difference I find betwixt we men and you women, we forswear ourselves at the beginning of an amour, you as long as it lasts.

Enter SIR JASPER FIDGET, *and* OLD LADY SQUEAMISH.

SIR JASPER. Oh, my Lady Fidget, was this your cunning, to come to Mr. Horner without me? but you have been nowhere else, I hope.

LADY FIDGET. No, Sir Jasper.

LADY SQUEAMISH. And you came straight hither, Biddy?

MRS. SQUEAMISH. Yes, indeed, lady grandmother.

SIR JASPER. 'Tis well, 'tis well; I knew when once they were thoroughly acquainted with poor Horner, they'd ne'er be from him: you may let her masquerade it with my wife and Horner, and I warrant her reputation safe.

Enter BOY.

BOY. Oh, sir, here's the gentleman come, whom you bid me not suffer to come up, without giving you notice, with a lady too, and other gentlemen.

HORNER. Do you all go in there, whilst I send 'em away; and, boy, do you desire 'em to stay below till I come, which shall be immediately.

(Exeunt SIR JASPER FIDGET, LADY FIDGET, LADY SQUEAMISH, MRS. SQUEAMISH, *and* MRS. DAINTY FIDGET.*)*

BOY. Yes, sir. *Exit.*

(Exit HORNER *at the other door, and returns with* MRS. PINCHWIFE.*)*

HORNER. You would not take my advice, to be gone home before your husband came back. He'll now discover all; yet pray, my dearest, be persuaded to go home and leave the rest to my management; I'll let you down the back way.

MRS. PINCHWIFE. I don't know the way home, so I don't.

HORNER. My man shall wait upon you.

MRS. PINCHWIFE. No, don't you believe that I'll go at all; what, are you weary of me already?

HORNER. No, my life, 'tis that I may love you long, 'tis to secure my love, and your reputation with your husband; he'll never receive you again else.

MRS. PINCHWIFE. What care I? d'ye think to frighten me with that? I don't intend to go to him again; you shall be my husband now.

HORNER. I cannot be your husband, dearest, since you are married to him.

MRS. PINCHWIFE. Oh, would you make me believe that? Don't I see every day at London here, women leave their first husbands and go and live with other men as their wives? pish, pshaw! you'd make me angry, but that I love you so mainly.

HORNER. So, they are coming up—In again, in, I hear 'em.—*(Exit* MRS. PINCHWIFE.*)* Well, a silly mistress is like a weak place, soon got, soon lost—a man has scarce time for plunder; she betrays her husband first to her gallant, and then her gallant to her husband.

Enter PINCHWIFE, ALITHEA, HARCOURT, SPARKISH, LUCY, *and a* PARSON.

PINCHWIFE. Come, madam, 'tis not the sudden change of your dress, the confidence of your asseverations, and your false witness there shall persuade me I did not bring you hither just now; here's my witness, who cannot deny it, since you must be confronted.—Mr. Horner, did not I bring this lady to you just now?

HORNER. *(Aside.)* Now must I wrong one woman for another's sake,—but that's no new thing with me, for in these cases I am still on the criminal's side against the innocent.

ALITHEA. Pray speak, sir.

HORNER. *(Aside.)* It must be so. I must be impudent, and try my luck; impudence uses to be too hard for truth.

PINCHWIFE. What, you are studying an evasion or excuse for her! Speak, sir.

HORNER. No, faith; I am something backward only to speak in women's affairs or disputes.

PINCHWIFE. She bids you speak.

ALITHEA. Ah, pray, sir, do, pray satisfy him.

HORNER. Then truly, you did bring that lady to me just now.

PINCHWIFE. Oh ho!

ALITHEA. How, sir?

HARCOURT. How, Horner?

ALITHEA. What mean you, sir? I always look you for a man of honor.

HORNER. *(Aside.)* Ay, so much a man of honor, that I must save my mistress, I thank you, come what will on't.

SPARKISH. So, if I had had her, she'd have made me believe the moon had been made of a Christmas pie.

LUCY. *(Aside.)* Now could I speak, if I durst, and solve the riddle, who am the author of it.

ALITHEA. Oh unfortunate woman! A combination against my honor! which most concerns me now, because you share in my disgrace, sir, and it is your censure, which I must now suffer, that troubles me, not theirs.

HARCOURT. Madam, then have no trouble, you shall now see 'tis possible for me to love too, without being jealous; I will not only believe your innocence myself, but make all the world believe it.—*(Aside to* HORNER.*)* Horner, I must now be concerned for this lady's honor.

HORNER. And I must be concerned for a lady's honor too.

HARCOURT. This lady has her honor, and I will protect it.

HORNER. My lady has not her honor, but has given it me to keep, and I will preserve it.

HARCOURT. I understand you not.

HORNER. I would not have you.

MRS. PINCHWIFE. What's the matter with 'em all? *(Peeping in behind.)*

PINCHWIFE. Come, come, Mr. Horner, no more disputing; here's the parson, I brought him not in vain.

HARCOURT. No, sir, I'll employ him, if this lady please.

PINCHWIFE. How! what d'ye mean?

SPARKISH. Ay, what does he mean?

HORNER. Why, I have resigned your sister to him, he has my consent.

PINCHWIFE. But he has not mine, sir; a woman's injured honor, no more than a man's, can be repaired or satisfied by any but him that first wronged it; and you shall marry her presently, or—— *(Lays his hand on his sword.)*

Enter MRS. PINCHWIFE.

MRS. PINCHWIFE. Oh lord, they'll kill poor Mr. Horner! besides, he shan't marry her whilst I stand by, and look on; I'll not lose my second husband so.

PINCHWIFE. What do I see?

ALITHEA. My sister in my clothes!

SPARKISH. Ha!

MRS. PINCHWIFE. *(To* PINCHWIFE.*)* Nay, pray now don't quarrel about finding work for the parson, he shall marry me to Mr. Horner; for now, I believe, you have enough of me.

HORNER. *(Aside.)* Damned, damned loving changeling!

MRS. PINCHWIFE. Pray, sister, pardon me for telling so many lies of you.

HORNER. I suppose the riddle is plain now.

LUCY. No, that must be my work.—Good sir, hear me.

(Kneels to PINCHWIFE, *who stands doggedly with his hat over his eyes.)*

PINCHWIFE. I will never hear woman again, but make 'em all silent thus—— *(Offers to draw upon his* Wife.*)*

HORNER. No, that must not be.

PINCHWIFE. You then shall go first, 'tis all one to me.

(Offers to draw on HORNER, *but is stopped by* HARCOURT.*)*

HARCOURT. Hold!

Enter SIR JASPER FIDGET, LADY FIDGET, LADY SQUEAMISH, MRS. DAINTY FIDGET, *and* MRS. SQUEAMISH.

SIR JASPER. What's the matter? what's the matter? pray, what's the matter, sir? I beseech you communicate, sir.

PINCHWIFE. Why, my wife has communicated, sir, as your wife may have done too, sir, if she knows him, sir.

SIR JASPER. Pshaw, with him! ha! ha! he!

PINCHWIFE. D'ye mock me, sir? a cuckold is a kind of a wild beast; have a care, sir.

SIR JASPER. No, sure, you mock me, sir. He cuckold you! it can't be, ha! ha! he! why, I'll tell you, sir—— *(Offers to whisper.)*

PINCHWIFE. I tell you again, he has whored my wife, and yours too, if he knows her, and all the women he comes near; 'tis not his dissembling, his hypocrisy, can wheedle me.

SIR JASPER. How! does he dissemble! is he a hypocrite? Nay, then—how —wife—sister, is he a hypocrite?

LADY SQUEAMISH. A hypocrite! a dissembler! Speak, young harlotry, speak, how?

SIR JASPER. Nay, then—Oh my head too!—Oh thou libidinous lady!

LADY SQUEAMISH. Oh thou harloting harlotry! hast thou done't then?

SIR JASPER. Speak, good Horner, art thou a dissembler, a rogue? hast thou——

HORNER. So!

LUCY. *(Apart to* HORNER.*)* I'll fetch you off, and her too, if she will but hold her tongue.

HORNER. *(Apart to* LUCY.*)* Canst thou? I'll give thee——

LUCY. *(To* PINCHWIFE.*)* Pray have but patience to hear me, sir, who am the unfortunate cause of all this confusion. Your wife is innocent, I only culpable; for I put her upon telling you all these lies concerning my mistress, in order to the breaking off the match between Mr. Sparkish and her, to make way for Mr. Harcourt.

SPARKISH. Did you so, ternal rotten tooth? Then, it seems, my mistress was not false to me, I was only deceived by you. Brother, that should have been, now man of conduct, who is a frank person now, to bring your wife to her lover, ha?

LUCY. I assure you, sir, she came not to Mr. Horner out of love, for she loves him no more——

MRS. PINCHWIFE. Hold, I told lies for you, but you shall tell none for me, for I do love Mr. Horner with all my soul, and nobody shall say me nay; pray, don't you go to make poor Mr. Horner believe to the contrary; 'tis spitefully done of you, I'm sure.

HORNER. (*Aside to* MRS. PINCHWIFE.) Peace, dear idiot.

MRS. PINCHWIFE. Nay, I will not peace.

PINCHWIFE. Not till I make you.

Enter DORILANT and QUACK.

DORILANT. Horner, your servant; I am the doctor's guest, he must excuse our intrusion.

QUACK. But what's the matter, gentlemen? for Heaven's sake, what's the matter?

HORNER. *(Whispers.)* Oh, 'tis well you are come. 'Tis a censorious world we live in; you may have brought me a reprieve, or else I had died for a crime I never committed, and these innocent ladies had suffered with me; therefore, pray satisfy these worthy, honorable, jealous gentlemen—that—

QUACK. Oh, I understand you, is that all?—Sir Jasper, by Heavens, and upon the word of a physician, sir——*(Whispers to* SIR JASPER.*)*

SIR JASPER. Nay, I do believe you truly.—Pardon me, my virtuous lady, and dear of honor.

LADY SQUEAMISH. What, then all's right again?

SIR JASPER. Ay, ay, and now let us satisfy him too.

(They whisper with PINCHWIFE.*)*

PINCHWIFE. An eunuch! Pray, no fooling with me.

QUACK. I'll bring half the surgeons in town to swear it.

PINCHWIFE. They!—they'll swear a man that bled to death through his wounds died of an apoplexy.

QUACK. Pray, hear me, sir—why, all the town has heard the report of him.

PINCHWIFE. But does all the town believe it?

QUACK. Pray, inquire a little, and first of all these.

PINCHWIFE. I'm sure when I left the town, he was the lewdest fellow in't.

QUACK. I tell you, sir, he has been in France since; pray, ask but these ladies and gentlemen, your friend Mr. Dorilant. Gentlemen and ladies, han't you all heard the late sad report of poor Mr. Horner?

ALL THE LADIES. Ay, ay, ay.

DORILANT. Why, thou jealous fool, dost thou doubt it? he's an arrant French capon.

MRS. PINCHWIFE. 'Tis false, sir, you shall not disparage poor Mr. Horner, for to my certain knowledge——

LUCY. Oh, hold!

MRS. SQUEAMISH. *(Aside to* LUCY.*)* Stop her mouth!

LADY FIDGET. (*To* PINCHWIFE.) Upon my honor, sir, 'tis as true——

MRS. DAINTY. D'ye think we would have been seen in his company?

MRS. SQUEAMISH. Trust our unspotted reputations with him?

LADY FIDGET. *(Aside to* HORNER.*)* This you get, and we too, by trusting your secret to a fool.

HORNER. Peace, madam.—(*Aside to* QUACK.) Well, doctor, is not this a good design, that carries a man on unsuspected, and brings him off safe?

PINCHWIFE. *(Aside.)* Well, if this were true—but my wife——(DORILANT *whispers with* MRS. PINCHWIFE.)

ALITHEA. Come, brother, your wife is yet innocent, you see; but have a care of too strong an imagination, lest, like an over-concerned timorous gamester, by fancying an unlucky cast, it should come. Women and fortune are truest still to those that trust 'em.

LUCY. And any wild thing grows but the more fierce and hungry for being kept up, and more dangerous to the keeper.

ALITHEA. There's doctrine for all husbands, Mr. Harcourt.

HARCOURT. I edify, madam, so much, that I am impatient till I am one.

DORILANT. And I edify so much by example, I will never be one.

SPARKISH. And because I will not disparage my parts, I'll ne'er be one.

HORNER. And I, alas! can't be one.

PINCHWIFE. But I must be one—against my will to a country wife, with a country murrain[10] to me!

MRS. PINCHWIFE. *(Aside.)* And I must be a country wife still too, I find; for I can't, like a city one, be rid of my musty husband, and do what I list.

HORNER. Now, sir, I must pronounce your wife innocent, though I blush whilst I do it; and I am the only man by her now exposed to shame which I will straight drown in wine, as you shall your suspicion; and the ladies' troubles we'll divert with a ballad.—Doctor, where are your maskers?

LUCY. Indeed, she's innocent, sir, I am her witness; and her end of coming out was but to see her sister's wedding; and what she has said to your face of her love to Mr. Horner, was but the usual innocent revenge on a husband's jealousy—was it not, madam, speak?

MRS. PINCHWIFE. (*Aside to* LUCY *and* HORNER.) Since you'll have me tell more lies—*(Aloud.)* Yes, indeed, bud.

PINCHWIFE. For my own sake fain I would all believe;

Cuckolds, like lovers, should themselves deceive.

But—— *(Sighs.)*

His honor is least safe (too late I find)

Who trusts it with a foolish wife or friend.

A Dance of Cuckolds.

HORNER. Vain fops but court and dress, and keep a pother,

To pass for women's men with one another;

But he who aims by women to be prized,

First by the men, you see, must be despised. *Exeunt.*

---

[10] A cattle plague; here a curse.

Questions for Discussion

1. To what extent is the theme of the play similar to that of "The Merchant's Tale"? Is the attitude towards marriage in each work the same? To answer this, note the attitudes toward marriage of Sparkish and Mr. Pinchwife in Act III, Scene ii and Alithea and Lucy in Act IV, Scene i.

2. Contrast and compare Pinchwife and January, Mrs. Pinchwife and May, Horner and Damian. Is there any similarity between the ending of the play and the ending of "The Merchant's Tale"?

3. What is the significance of the subplot concerning Alithea and Harcourt? Does it parallel the main plot or contrast with it? In what sense could it be called the moral center of the play?

4. To what extent does Pinchwife deserve being made a fool of by his wife and Horner?

5. Are the switching of the letters and the donning of the disguises only devices to advance the plot or do they serve a further function?

6. Compare the concept of honor held by Sparkish, Dorilant, and Horner with that held by Mrs. Dainty, Mrs. Squeamish, and Lady Fidget. (See Act III, Scene ii and Act V, Scene iv.)

7. Explain Pinchwife's attitude toward his wife at the beginning of Act V.

8. What is significant in the fact that all the characters reveal themselves truthfully in front of Horner?

9. Usually in comedies the principal characters are the same at the end as at the beginning. Is is true of this play? Have any of the characters learned anything they did not already know?

10. In what way does Horner's announcement of his eunuchy expose the hypocrisy of the society in which he lives?

11. How is the contrast between the country and the city used for comic effect? What do they have in common? To what degree are Mrs. Pinchwife and Horner alike?

12. What does Horner mean by calling himself "a Machiavel in Love"?

13. One recent commentator has called the play "nihilistic." Is this judgment in your opinion correct?

14. Choose one scene (such as that between Horner, Sir Jasper Fidget, and Lady Fidget in Act IV, Scene iii) and show how the incongruity in it is the source of the comedy.

George Gordon, Lord Byron (1788-1824)

Don Juan

CANTO I

1

I WANT a hero: an uncommon want,
  When every year and month sends forth a new one,
Till, after cloying the gazettes with cant,
  The age discovers he is not the true one;
Of such as these I should not care to vaunt,
  I'll therefore take our ancient friend Don Juan—
We all have seen him, in the pantomime,
Sent to the Devil somewhat ere his time.

2

Vernon, the butcher Cumberland, Wolfe, Hawke,
  Prince Ferdinand, Granby, Burgoyne, Keppel, Howe,[1] 10
Evil and good, have had their tithe of talk,
  And filled their sign-posts then, like Wellesley now;[2]
Each in their turn like Banquo's monarchs stalk,
  Followers of fame, "nine farrow" of that sow:
France, too, had Buonaparté and Dumourier
Recorded in the Moniteur and Courier.

3

Barnave, Brissot, Condorcet, Mirabeau,
  Petion, Clootz, Danton, Marat, La Fayette[3]
Were French, and famous people, as we know;
  And there were others, scarce forgotten yet, 20
Joubert, Hoche, Marceau, Lannes, Desaix, Moreau,[4]
  With many of the military set,
Exceedingly remarkable at times,
But not at all adapted to my rhymes.

---

[1] Military and naval heroes of the eighteenth century.
[2] Duke of Wellington, the hero of the battle of Waterloo.
[3] French philosophers and politicians active in the French Revolution.
[4] French generals during the Napoleonic wars.

4
Nelson was once Britannia's god of War,
And still should be so, but the tide is turned;
There's no more to be said of Trafalgar,
'T is with our hero quietly inurned;
Because the army's grown more popular,
At which the naval people are concerned; 30
Besides, the Prince is all for the land-service,
Forgetting Duncan, Nelson, Howe, and Jervis.[5]

5
Brave men were living before Agamemnon
And since, exceeding valorous and sage,
A good deal like him too, though quite the same none;
But then they shone not on the poet's page,
And so have been forgotten:—I condemn none,
But can't find any in the present age
Fit for my poem (that is, for my new one);
So, as I said, I'll take my friend Don Juan. 40

6
Most epic poets plunge "*in medias res*"[6]
(Horace makes this the heroic turnpike road),
And then your hero tells, whene'er you please,
What went before—by way of episode,
While seated after dinner at his ease,
Beside his mistress in some soft abode,
Palace, or garden, paradise, or cavern,
Which serves the happy couple for a tavern.

7
That is the usual method, but not mine—
My way is to begin with the beginning; 50
The regularity of my design
Forbids all wandering as the worst of sinning,
And therefore I shall open with a line
(Although it cost me half an hour in spinning),
Narrating somewhat of Don Juan's father,
And also of his mother, if you'd rather.

8
In Seville was he born, a pleasant city,
Famous for oranges and women,—he

---

[5] English admirals prominent in the Napoleonic wars.
[6] "In the middle of things."

Who has not seen it will be much to pity,
  So says the proverb—and I quite agree; 60
Of all the Spanish towns is none more pretty,
  Cadiz perhaps—but that you soon may see;—
Don Juan's parents lived beside the river,
A noble stream, and called the Guadalquivir.

9

His father's name was José—*Don*, of course—
  A true Hidalgo, free from every stain
Of Moor or Hebrew blood, he traced his source
  Through the most Gothic gentleman of Spain;
A better cavalier ne'er mounted horse,
  Or, being mounted, e'er got down again, 70
Than José, who begot our hero, who
Begot—but that's to come—Well, to renew:

10

His mother was a learnéd lady, famed
  For every branch of every science known—
In every Christian language ever named,
  With virtues equalled by her wit alone:
She made the cleverest people quite ashamed,
  And even the good with inward envy groan,
Finding themselves so very much exceeded,
In their own way, by all the things that she did. 80

11

Her memory was a mine: she knew by heart
  All Calderon and greater part of Lopé,[7]
So, that if any actor missed his part,
  She could have served him for the prompter's copy;
For her Feinagle's were a useless art,[8]
  And he himself obliged to shut up shop—he
Could never make a memory so fine as
That which adorned the brain of Donna Inez.

12

Her favourite science was the mathematical,
  Her noblest virtue was her magnanimity, 90

---

7. Calderon de la Barca (1600-1681) and Lope de Vega (1562-1635) were Spanish poets and dramatists.

8 Gregor von Feinagle devised a system for training the mind.

Her wit (she sometimes tried at wit) was Attic all,
Her serious sayings darkened to sublimity;
In short, in all things she was fairly what I call
A prodigy—her morning dress was dimity,
Her evening silk, or, in the summer, muslin,
And other stuffs, with which I won't stay puzzling.

13

She knew the Latin—that is, "the Lord's prayer,"
And Greek—the alphabet—I'm nearly sure;
She read some French romances here and there,
Although her mode of speaking was not pure; 100
For native Spanish she had no great care,
At least her conversation was obscure;
Her thoughts were theorems, her words a problem,
As if she deemed that mystery would ennoble 'em.

14

She liked the English and the Hebrew tongue,
And said there was analogy between 'em;
She proved it somehow out of sacred song,
But I must leave the proofs to those who've seen 'em;
But this I heard her say, and can't be wrong,
And all may think which way their judgments lean 'em, 110
" 'T is strange—the Hebrew noun which means 'I am,'
The English always used to govern d—n."

15

Some women use their tongues—she *looked* a lecture,
Each eye a sermon, and her brow a homily,
An all-in-all sufficient self-director,
Like the lamented late Sir Samuel Romilly[9]
The Law's expounder, and the State's corrector
Whose suicide was almost an anomaly—
One sad example more, that "All is vanity,"—
(The jury brought their verdict in "Insanity!") 120

16

In short, she was a walking calculation,
Miss Edgeworth's novels stepping from their covers,
Or Mrs. Trimmer's books on education,

---

[9] A lawyer who served Byron and then Lady Byron during their separation.

Or "Cœlebs' Wife"[10] set out in quest of lovers,
Morality's prim personification,
In which not Envy's self a flaw discovers;
To others' share let "female errors fall,"
For she had not even one—the worst of all.

17
Oh! she was perfect past all parallel—
Of any modern female saint's comparison; 130
So far above the cunning powers of Hell,
Her Guardian Angel had given up his garrison;
Even her minutest motions went as well
As those of the best time-piece made by Harrison:
In virtues nothing earthly could surpass her
Save thine "incomparable oil," Macassar![11]

18
Perfect she was, but as perfection is
Insipid in this naughty world of ours,
Where our first parents never learned to kiss
Till they were exiled from their earlier bowers, 140
Where all was peace, and innocence, and bliss,
(I wonder how they got through the twelve hours),
Don José, like a lineal son of Eve,
Went plucking various fruit without her leave.

19
He was a mortal of the careless kind,
With no great love for learning, or the learned,
Who chose to go where'er he had a mind,
And never dreamed his lady was concerned;
The world, as usual, wickedly inclined
To see a kingdom or a house o'erturned, 150
Whispered he had a mistress, some said *two*.
But for domestic quarrels *one* will do.

20
Now Donna Inez had, with all her merit,
A great opinion of her own good qualities;
Neglect, indeed, requires a saint to bear it,

---

[10] Hannah More (1745-1833) was a popular novelist of the day. She wrote the didactic tale *Coelebs in Search of a Wife*.
[11] Hair oil.

And such, indeed, she was in her moralities;
But then she had a devil of a spirit,
And sometimes mixed up fancies with realities,
And let few opportunities escape
Of getting her liege lord into a scrape. 160

21
This was an easy matter with a man
Oft in the wrong, and never on his guard;
And even the wisest, do the best they can,
Have moments, hours, and days, so unprepared,
That you might "brain them with their lady's fan";
And sometimes ladies hit exceeding hard,
And fans turn into falchions in fair hands,
And why and wherefore no one understands.

22
'T is pity learnéd virgins ever wed
With persons of no sort of education, 170
Or gentlemen, who, though well born and bred,
Grow tired of scientific conversation:
I don't choose to say much upon this head,
I'm a plain man, and in a single station,
But—Oh! ye lords of ladies intellectual,
Inform us truly, have they not hen-pecked you all?

23
Don José and his lady quarrelled—*why*,
Not any of the many could divine,
Though several thousand people chose to try,
'T was surely no concern of theirs nor mine; 180
I loathe that low vice—curiosity;
But if there's anything in which I shine,
'T is in arranging all my friends' affairs,
Not having, of my own, domestic cares.

24
And so I interfered, and with the best
Intentions, but their treatment was not kind;
I think the foolish people were possessed,
For neither of them could I ever find,
Although their porter afterwards confessed—
But that's no matter, and the worst's behind, 190

For little Juan o'er me threw, down stairs,
A pail of housemaid's water unawares.

25

A little curly-headed, good-for-nothing,
And mischief-making monkey from his birth;
His parents ne'er agreed except in doting
Upon the most unquiet imp on earth;
Instead of quarrelling, had they been but both in
Their senses, they'd have sent young master forth
To school, or had him soundly whipped at home,
To teach him manners for the time to come. 200

26

Don José and the Donna Inez led
For some time an unhappy sort of life,
Wishing each other, not divorced, but dead;
They lived respectably as man and wife,
Their conduct was exceedingly well-bred,
And gave no outward signs of inward strife,
Until at length the smothered fire broke out,
And put the business past all kind of doubt.

27

For Inez called some druggists and physicians,
And tried to prove her loving lord was *mad*, 210
But as he had some lucid intermissions,
She next decided he was only *bad;*
Yet when they asked her for her depositions,
No sort of explanation could be had,
Save that her duty both to man and God
Required this conduct—which seemed very odd.

28

She kept a journal, where his faults were noted,
And opened certain trunks of books and letters,
All which might, if occasion served, be quoted;
And then she had all Seville for abettors, 220
Besides her good old grandmother (who doted);
The hearers of her case became repeaters,
Then advocates, inquisitors, and judges,
Some for amusement, others for old grudges.

29

And then this best and meekest woman bore
With such serenity her husband's woes,

Just as the Spartan ladies did of yore,
Who saw their spouses killed, and nobly chose
Never to say a word about them more—
Calmly she heard each calumny that rose, 230
And saw *his* agonies with such sublimity,
That all the world exclaimed, "What magnanimity!"

30

No doubt this patience, when the world is damning us,
Is philosophic in our former friends;
'T is also pleasant to be deemed magnanimous,
The more so in obtaining our own ends;
And what the lawyers call a "*malus animus*"[12]
Conduct like this by no means comprehends:
Revenge in person's certainly no virtue,
But then 't is not *my* fault, if *others* hurt you. 240

31

And if our quarrels should rip up old stories,
And help them with a lie or two additional,
I'm not to blame, as you well know—no more is
Any one else—they were become traditional;
Besides, their resurrection aids our glories
By contrast, which is what we just were wishing all:
And Science profits by this resurrection—
Dead scandals form good subjects for dissection.

32

Their friends had tried at reconciliation,
Then their relations, who made matters worse. 250
('T were hard to tell upon a like occasion
To whom it may be best to have recourse—
I can't say much for friend or yet relation):
The lawyers did their utmost for divorce,
But scarce a fee was paid on either side
Before, unluckily, Don José died.

33

He died: and most unluckily, because,
According to all hints I could collect
From Counsel learnéd in those kinds of laws,
(Although their talk's obscure and circumspect) 260
His death contrived to spoil a charming cause;

---

[12] "Malice aforethought."

A thousand pities also with respect
To public feeling, which on this occasion
Was manifested in a great sensation.

34

But ah! he died; and buried with him lay
The public feeling and the lawyer's fees:
His house was sold, his servants sent away,
A Jew took one of his two mistresses,
A priest the other—at least so they say:
I asked the doctors after his disease— 270
He died of the slow fever called the tertian,
And left his widow to her own aversion.

35

Yet José was an honourable man,
That I must say, who knew him very well;
Therefore his frailties I'll no further scan,
Indeed there were not many more to tell:
And if his passions now and then outran
Discretion, and were not so peaceable
As Numa's (who was also named Pompilius),[13]
He had been ill brought up, and was born bilious. 280

36

Whate'er might be his worthlessness or worth,
Poor fellow! he had many things to wound him.
Let's own—since it can do no good on earth—
It was a trying moment that which found him
Standing alone beside his desolate hearth,
Where all his household gods lay shivered round him:
No choice was left his feelings or his pride,
Save Death or Doctors' Commons[14]—so he died.

37

Dying intestate, Juan was sole heir
To a chancery suit, and messuages, and lands, 290
Which, with a long minority and care,
Promised to turn out well in proper hands:
Inez became sole guardian, which was fair,

---

[13] The second legendary king of Rome following the death of Romulus. His reign was peaceful, and he was known as a just and wise ruler.
[14] Divorce court.

And answered but to Nature's just demands;
An only son left with an only mother
Is brought up much more wisely than another.

38

Sagest of women, even of widows, she
Resolved that Juan should be quite a paragon,
And worthy of the noblest pedigree,
(His Sire was of Castile, his Dam from Aragon): 300
Then, for accomplishments of chivalry,
In case our Lord the King should go to war again,
He learned the arts of riding, fencing, gunnery,
And how to scale a fortress—or a nunnery.

39

But that which Donna Inez most desired,
And saw into herself each day before all
The learned tutors whom for him she hired,
Was, that this breeding should be strictly moral:
Much into all his studies she inquired,
And so they were submitted first to her, all, 310
Arts, sciences—no branch was made a mystery
To Juan's eyes, excepting natural history.

40

The languages, especially the dead,
The sciences, and most of all the abstruse,
The arts, at least all such as could be said
To be the most remote from common use,
In all these he was much and deeply read:
But not a page of anything that's loose,
Or hints continuation of the species,
Was ever suffered, lest he should grow vicious. 320

41

His classic studies made a little puzzle,
Because of filthy loves of gods and goddesses,
Who in the earlier ages raised a bustle,
But never put on pantaloons or bodices;
His reverend tutors had at times a tussle,
And for their Æneids, Iliads, and Odysseys,
Were forced to make an odd sort of apology,
For Donna Inez dreaded the Mythology.

42

Ovid's a rake, as half his verses show him,
  Anacreon's morals are a still worse sample, 330
Catullus scarcely has a decent poem,
  I don't think Sappho's Ode a good example,
Although Longinus tells us there is no hymn
  Where the Sublime soars forth on wings more ample;
But Virgil's songs are pure, except that horrid one
Beginning with "*Formosum Pastor Corydon.*"[15]

43

Lucretius' irreligion is too strong
  For early stomachs, to prove wholesome food;
I can't help thinking Juvenal[16] was wrong,
  Although no doubt his real intent was good, 340
For speaking out so plainly in his song,
  So much indeed as to be downright rude;
And then what proper person can be partial
To all those nauseous epigrams of Martial?

44

Juan was taught from out the best edition,
  Expurgated by learnéd men, who place,
Judiciously, from out the schoolboy's vision,
  The grosser parts; but, fearful to deface
Too much their modest bard by this omission,
  And pitying sore his mutilated case, 350
They only add them in an appendix,
Which saves, in fact, the trouble of an index;

45

For there we have them all "at one fell swoop,"
  Instead of being scattered through the pages;
They stand forth marshalled in a handsome troop,
  To meet the ingenuous youth of future ages,
Till some less rigid editor shall stoop
  To call them back into their separate cages,
Instead of standing staring all together,
Like garden gods—and not so decent either. 360

---

[15] The beautiful shepherd Corydon. He appears in the 2nd Eclogue of Virgil's *Bucolics*. In the poem he is in love with the boy Alexis.

[16] Roman satirist of the first century A.D. who attacked the corruption of Rome.

46
The Missal too (it was the family Missal)
  Was ornamented in a sort of way
Which ancient mass-books often are, and this all
  Kinds of grotesques illumined; and how they,
Who saw those figures on the margin kiss all,
  Could turn their optics to the text and pray,
Is more than I know—But Don Juan's mother
Kept this herself, and gave her son another.

47
Sermons he read, and lectures he endured,
  And homilies, and lives of all the saints; 370
To Jerome and to Chrysostom[17] inured,
  He did not take such studies for restraints;
But how Faith is acquired, and then insured,
  So well not one of the aforesaid paints
As Saint Augustine in his fine Confessions,
Which make the reader envy his transgressions.

48
This, too, was a sealed book to little Juan—
  I can't but say that his mamma was right,
If such an education was the true one.
  She scarcely trusted him from out her sight; 380
Her maids were old, and if she took a new one,
  You might be sure she was a perfect fright;
She did this during even her husband's life—
I recommend as much to every wife.

49
Young Juan waxed in goodliness and grace;
  At six a charming child, and at eleven
With all the promise of as fine a face
  As e'er to Man's maturer growth was given:
He studied steadily, and grew apace,
  And seemed, at least, in the right road to Heaven, 390
For half his days were passed at church, the other
Between his tutors, confessor, and mother.

50
At six, I said, he was a charming child,
  At twelve he was a fine, but quiet boy;

---

[17] Church fathers of the fourth century.

Although in infancy a little wild,
They tamed him down amongst them: to destroy
His natural spirit not in vain they toiled,
At least it seemed so; and his mother's joy
Was to declare how sage, and still, and steady,
Her young philosopher was grown already. 400

51

I had my doubts, perhaps I have them still,
But what I say is neither here nor there:
I knew his father well, and have some skill
In character—but it would not be fair
From sire to son to augur good or ill:
He and his wife were an ill-sorted pair—
But scandal's my aversion—I protest
Against all evil speaking, even in jest.

52

For my part I say nothing—nothing—but
This I will say—my reasons are my own— 410
That if I had an only son to put
To school (as God be praised that I have none),
'T is not with Donna Inez I would shut
Him up to learn his catechism alone,
No—no—I'd send him out betimes to college,
For there it was I picked up my own knowledge.

53

For there one learns—'t is not for me to boast,
Though I acquired—but I pass over *that*,
As well as all the Greek I since have lost:—
I say that there's the place—but "*Verbum sat*,"[18] 420
I think I picked up too, as well as most,
Knowledge of matters—but no matter *what*—
I never married—but, I think, I know
That sons should not be educated so.

54

Young Juan now was sixteen years of age,
Tall, handsome, slender, but well knit: he seemed
Active, though not so sprightly, as a page;
And everybody but his mother deemed

[18] A word to the wise is sufficient.

Him almost man; but she flew in a rage
  And bit her lips (for else she might have screamed) 430
If any said so—for to be precocious
Was in her eyes a thing the most atrocious.

55
Amongst her numerous acquaintance, all
  Selected for discretion and devotion,
There was the Donna Julia, whom to call
  Pretty were but to give a feeble notion
Of many charms in her as natural
  As sweetness to the flower, or salt to Ocean,
Her zone to Venus, or his bow to Cupid,
(But this last simile is trite and stupid.) 440

56
The darkness of her Oriental eye
  Accorded with her Moorish origin;
(Her blood was not all Spanish; by the by,
  In Spain, you know, this is a sort of sin;)
When proud Granada fell, and, forced to fly,
  Boabdil wept: of Donna Julia's kin[19]
Some went to Africa, some stayed in Spain—
Her great great grandmamma chose to remain.

57
She married (I forget the pedigree)
  With an Hidalgo, who transmitted down 450
His blood less noble than such blood should be;
  At such alliances his sires would frown,
In that point so precise in each degree
  That they bred *in and in*, as might be shown,
Marrying their cousins—nay, their aunts, and nieces,
Which always spoils the breed, if it increases.

58
This heathenish cross restored the breed again,
  Ruined its blood, but much improved its flesh;
For from a root the ugliest in Old Spain
  Sprung up a branch as beautiful as fresh; 460
The sons no more were short, the daughters plain;
  But there's a rumor which I fain would hush,

---

[19] The Moorish leader wept when he surrendered the city of Granada to the Spaniards in 1492.

'T is said that Donna Julia's grandmamma
Produced her Don more heirs at love than law.

59

However this might be, the race went on
Improving still through every generation,
Until it centred in an only son,
Who left an only daughter; my narration
May have suggested that this single one
Could be but Julia (whom on this occasion 470
I shall have much to speak about), and she
Was married, charming, chaste, and twenty-three.

60

Her eye (I'm very fond of handsome eyes)
Was large and dark, suppressing half its fire
Until she spoke, then through its soft disguise
Flashed an expression more of pride than ire,
And love than either; and there would arise
A something in them which was not desire,
But would have been, perhaps, but for the soul
Which struggled through and chastened down the whole. 480

61

Her glossy hair was clustered o'er a brow
Bright with intelligence, and fair, and smooth;
Her eyebrow's shape was like the aërial bow,
Her cheek all purple with the beam of youth,
Mounting, at times, to a transparent glow,
As if her veins ran lightning; she, in sooth,
Possessed an air and grace by no means common:
Her stature tall—I hate a dumpy woman.

62

Wedded she was some years, and to a man
Of fifty, and such husbands are in plenty; 490
And yet, I think, instead of such a ONE
'T were better to have TWO of five-and-twenty,
Especially in countries near the sun:
And now I think on't, "*mi vien in mente*,"[20]
Ladies even of the most uneasy virtue
Prefer a spouse whose age is short of thirty.

---

[20] "It comes to my mind."

63
'T is a sad thing, I cannot choose but say,
And all the fault of that indecent sun,
Who cannot leave alone our helpless clay,
But will keep baking, broiling, burning on, 500
That howsoever people fast and pray,
The flesh is frail, and so the soul undone:
What men call gallantry, and gods adultery,
Is much more common where the climate's sultry.

64
Happy the nations of the moral North!
Where all is virtue, and the winter season
Sends sin, without a rag on, shivering forth
('T was snow that brought St. Anthony to reason);
Where juries cast up what a wife is worth,
By laying whate'er sum, in mulct, they please on 510
The lover, who must pay a handsome price,
Because it is a marketable vice.

65
Alfonso was the name of Julia's lord,
A man well looking for his years, and who
Was neither much beloved nor yet abhorred:
They lived together as most people do,
Suffering each other's foibles by accord,
And not exactly either *one* or *two;*
Yet he was jealous, though he did not show it,
For Jealousy dislikes the world to know it. 520

66
Julia was—yet I never could see why—
With Donna Inez quite a favourite friend;
Between their tastes there was small sympathy,
For not a line had Julia ever penned:
Some people whisper (but, no doubt, they lie,
For Malice still imputes some private end)
That Inez had, ere Don Alfonso's marriage,
Forgot with him her very prudent carriage;

67
And that still keeping up the old connection,
Which Time had lately rendered much more chaste, 530
She took his lady also in affection,

And certainly this course was much the best:
She flattered Julia with her sage protection,
And complimented Don Alfonso's taste;
And if she could not (who can?) silence scandal,
At least she left it a more slender handle.

68

I can't tell whether Julia saw the affair
With other people's eyes, or if her own
Discoveries made, but none could be aware
Of this, at least no symptom e'er was shown; 540
Perhaps she did not know, or did not care,
Indifferent from the first, or callous grown:
I'm really puzzled what to think or say.
She kept her counsel in so close a way.

69

Juan she saw, and, as a pretty child,
Caressed him often—such a thing might be
Quite innocently done, and harmless styled,
When she had twenty years, and thirteen he;
But I am not so sure I should have smiled
When he was sixteen, Julia twenty-three; 550
These few short years make wondrous alterations,
Particularly amongst sun-burnt nations.

70

Whate'er the cause might be, they had become
Changed; for the dame grew distant, the youth shy,
Their looks cast down, their greetings almost dumb.
And much embarrassment in either eye;
There surely will be little doubt with some
That Donna Julia knew the reason why,
But as for Juan, he had no more notion
Than he who never saw the sea, of Ocean. 560

71

Yet Julia's very coldness still was kind,
And tremulously gentle her small hand
Withdrew itself from his, but left behind
A little pressure, thrilling, and so bland
And slight, so very slight, that to the mind
'T was but a doubt; but ne'er magician's wand

Wrought change with all Armida's fairy art[21]
Like what this light touch left on Juan's heart.

72
And if she met him, though she smiled no more,
She looked a sadness sweeter than her smile, 570
As if her heart had deeper thoughts in store
She must not own, but cherished more the while
For that compression in its burning core;
Even Innocence itself has many a wile,
And will not dare to trust itself with truth,
And Love is taught hypocrisy from youth.

73
But Passion most dissembles, yet betrays
Even by its darkness; as the blackest sky
Foretells the heaviest tempest, it displays
Its workings through the vainly guarded eye, 580
And in whatever aspect it arrays
Itself, 't is still the same hypocrisy;
Coldness or Anger, even Disdain or Hate,
Are masks it often wears, and still too late.

74
Then there were sighs, the deeper for suppression,
And stolen glances, sweeter for the theft,
And burning blushes, though for no transgression,
Tremblings when met, and restlessness when left;
All these are little preludes to possession,
Of which young Passion cannot be bereft, 590
And merely tend to show how greatly Love is
Embarrassed at first starting with a novice.

75
Poor Julia's heart was in an awkward state;
She felt it going, and resolved to make
The noblest efforts for herself and mate,
For Honour's, Pride's, Religion's, Virtue's sake:
Her resolutions were most truly great,
And almost might have made a Tarquin quake:[22]
She prayed the Virgin Mary for her grace,
As being the best judge of a lady's case. 600

---

[21] A sorceress in *Jerusalem Delivered* by Tasso (1544-1595).
[22] One of a family of legendary kings of Rome notorious for their violence.

76
She vowed she never would see Juan more,
And next day paid a visit to his mother,
And looked extremely at the opening door,
Which, by the Virgin's grace, let in another;
Grateful she was, and yet a little sore—
Again it opens, it can be no other,
'T is surely Juan now—No! I'm afraid
That night the Virgin was no further prayed.

77
She now determined that a virtuous woman
Should rather face and overcome temptation, 610
That flight was base and dastardly, and no man
Should ever give her heart the least sensation,
That is to say, a thought beyond the common
Preference, that we must feel, upon occasion,
For people who are pleasanter than others,
But then they only seem so many brothers.

78
And even if by chance—and who can tell?
The Devil's so very sly—she should discover
That all within was not so very well,
And, if still free, that such or such a lover 620
Might please perhaps, a virtuous wife can quell
Such thoughts, and be the better when they're over;
And if the man should ask, 't is but denial:
I recommend young ladies to make trial.

79
And, then, there are such things as Love divine,
Bright and immaculate, unmixed and pure,
Such as the angels think so very fine,
And matrons, who would be no less secure,
Platonic, perfect, "just such love as mine;"
Thus Julia said—and thought so, to be sure; 630
And so I'd have her think, were *I* the man
On whom her reveries celestial ran.

80
Such love is innocent, and may exist
Between young persons without any danger.
A hand may first, and then a lip be kissed;

For my part, to such doings I'm a stranger,
But *hear* these freedoms form the utmost list
Of all o'er which such love may be a ranger:
If people go beyond, 't is quite a crime,
But not my fault—I tell them all in time. 640

81

Love, then, but Love within its proper limits,
Was Julia's innocent determination
In young Don Juan's favour, and to him its
Exertion might be useful on occasion;
And, lighted at too pure a shrine to dim its
Ethereal lustre, with what sweet persuasion
He might be taught, by Love and her together—
I really don't know what, nor Julia either.

82

Fraught with this fine intention, and well fenced
In mail of proof—her purity of soul— 650
She, for the future, of her strength convinced,
And that her honour was a rock, or mole,
Exceeding sagely from that hour dispensed
With any kind of troublesome control;
But whether Julia to the task was equal
Is that which must be mentioned in the sequel.

83

Her plan she deemed both innocent and feasible,
And, surely, with a stripling of sixteen
Not Scandal's fangs could fix on much that's seizable,
Or if they did so, satisfied to mean
Nothing but what was good, her breast was peaceable—
A quiet conscience makes one so serene!
Christians have burnt each other, quite persuaded
That all the Apostles would have done as they did.

84

And if in the mean time her husband died,
But Heaven forbid that such a thought should cross
Her brain, though in a dream! (and then she sighed)
Never could she survive that common loss;
But just suppose that moment should betide,
I only say suppose it—*inter nos:* 670

(This should be *entre nous*, for Julia thought
In French, but then the rhyme would go for nought.)

85

I only say, suppose this supposition:
  Juan being then grown up to man's estate
Would fully suit a widow of condition,
  Even seven years hence it would not be too late;
And in the interim (to pursue this vision)
  The mischief, after all, could not be great,
For he would learn the rudiments of Love,
I mean the *seraph* way of those above. 680

86

So much for Julia! Now we'll turn to Juan.
  Poor little fellow! he had no idea
Of his own case, and never hit the true one;
  In feelings quick as Ovid's Miss Medea,
He puzzled over what he found a new one,
  But not as yet imagined it could be a
Thing quite in course, and not at all alarming,
Which, with a little patience, might grow charming.

87

Silent and pensive, idle, restless, slow,
  His home deserted for the lonely wood, 690
Tormented with a wound he could not know,
  His, like all deep grief, plunged in solitude:
I'm fond myself of solitude or so,
  But then, I beg it may be understood,
By solitude I mean a Sultan's (not
A Hermit's), with a haram for a grot.

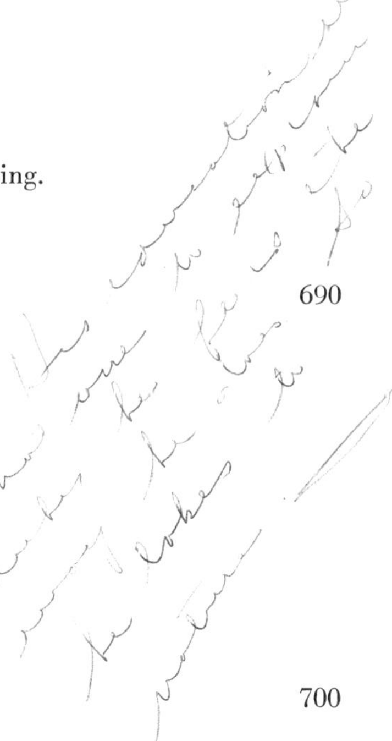

88

"Oh Love! in such a wilderness as this,
  Where Transport and Security entwine,
Here is the Empire of thy perfect bliss,
  And here thou art a God indeed divine." 700
The bard I quote from does not sing amiss,[23]
  With the exception of the second line,
For that same twining "Transport and Security"
Are twisted to a phrase of some obscurity.

---

[23] Thomas Campbell (1777-1844). The lines are quoted from his *Gertrude of Wyoming*.

89
The Poet meant, no doubt, and thus appeals
  To the good sense and senses of mankind,
The very thing which everybody feels,
  As all have found on trial, or may find,
That no one likes to be disturbed at meals
  Or love.—I won't say more about "entwined" 710
Or "Transport," as we knew all that before,
But beg "Security" will bolt the door.

90
Young Juan wandered by the glassy brooks,
  Thinking unutterable things; he threw
Himself at length within the leafy nooks
  Where the wild branch of the cork forest grew;
There poets find materials for their books,
  And every now and then we read them through,
So that their plan and prosody are eligible,
Unless, like Wordsworth, they prove unintelligible. 720

91
He, Juan (and not Wordsworth), so pursued
  His self-communion with his own high soul,
Until his mighty heart, in its great mood,
  Had mitigated part, though not the whole
Of its disease; he did the best he could
  With things not very subject to control,
And turned, without perceiving his condition,
Like Coleridge, into a metaphysician.

92
He thought about himself, and the whole earth
  Of man the wonderful, and of the stars, 730
And how the deuce they ever could have birth;
  And then he thought of earthquakes, and of wars,
How many miles the moon might have in girth,
  Of air-balloons, and of the many bars
To perfect knowledge of the boundless skies;—
And then he thought of Donna Julia's eyes.

93
In thoughts like these true Wisdom may discern
  Longings sublime, and aspirations high,
Which some are born with, but the most part learn

To plague themselves withal, they know not why: 740
'T was strange that one so young should thus concern
His brain about the action of the sky;
If *you* think 't was Philosophy that this did,
I can't help thinking puberty assisted.

94

He pored upon the leaves, and on the flowers,
And heard a voice in all the winds; and then
He thought of wood-nymphs and immortal bowers,
And how the goddesses came down to men:
He missed the pathway, he forgot the hours,
And when he looked upon his watch again, 750
He found how much old Time had been a winner—
He also found that he had lost his dinner.

95

Sometimes he turned to gaze upon his book,
Boscan, or Garcilasso;—by the wind[24]
Even as the page is rustled while we look,
So by the poesy of his own mind
Over the mystic leaf his soul was shook,
As if 't were one whereon magicians bind
Their spells, and give them to the passing gale,
According to some good old woman's tale. 760

96

Thus would he while his lonely hours away
Dissatisfied, not knowing what he wanted;
Nor glowing reverie, nor poet's lay,
Could yield his spirit that for which it panted,
A bosom whereon he his head might lay,
And hear the heart beat with the love it granted,
With—several other things, which I forget,
Or which, at least, I need not mention yet.

97

Those lonely walks, and lengthening reveries,
Could not escape the gentle Julia's eyes; 770
She saw that Juan was not at his ease;
But that which chiefly may, and must surprise,
Is, that the Donna Inez did not tease

[24] Sixteenth century Spanish poets who wrote sonnets modeled after Petrarch.

Her only son with question or surmise;
Whether it was she did not see, or would not,
Or, like all very clever people, could not.

98
This may seem strange, but yet 't is very common;
For instance—gentlemen, whose ladies take
Leave to o'erstep the written rights of Woman,
And break the—Which commandment is't they break? 780
(I have forgot the number, and think no man
Should rashly quote, for fear of a mistake;)
I say, when these same gentlemen are jealous,
They make some blunder, which their ladies tell us.

99
A real husband always is suspicious,
But still no less suspects in the wrong place,
Jealous of some one who had no such wishes,
Or pandering blindly to his own disgrace,
By harbouring some dear friend extremely vicious:
The last indeed's infallibly the case: 790
And when the spouse and friend are gone off wholly,
He wonders at their vice, and not his folly.

100
Thus parents also are at times short-sighted:
Though watchful as the lynx, they ne'er discover,
The while the wicked world beholds delighted,
Young Hopeful's mistress, or Miss Fanny's lover,
Till some confounded escapade has blighted
The plan of twenty years, and all is over;
And then the mother cries, the father swears
And wonders why the devil he got heirs. 800

101
But Inez was so anxious, and so clear
Of sight, that I must think, on this occasion,
She had some other motive much more near
For leaving Juan to this new temptation,
But what that motive was, I shan't say here;
Perhaps to finish Juan's education,
Perhaps to open Don Alfonso's eyes,
In case he thought his wife too great a prize.

102

It was upon a day, a summer's day;—
  Summer's indeed a very dangerous season, 810
And so is spring about the end of May;
  The sun, no doubt, is the prevailing reason;
But whatsoe'er the cause is, one may say,
  And stand convicted of more truth than treason,
That there are months which nature grows more merry in,—
March has its hares, and May must have its heroine.

103

'T was on a summer's day—the sixth of June:
  I like to be particular in dates,
Not only of the age, and year, but moon;
  They are a sort of post-house, where the Fates 820
Change horses, making History change its tune,
  Then spur away o'er empires and o'er states,
Leaving at last not much besides chronology,
Excepting the post-obits of theology.

104

'T was on the sixth of June ,about the hour
  Of half-past six—perhaps still nearer seven—
When Julia sate within as pretty a bower
  As e'er held houri in that heathenish heaven
Described by Mahomet, and Anacreon Moore,[25]
  To whom the lyre and laurels have been given, 830
With all the trophies of triumphant song—
He won them well, and may he wear them long!

105

She sate, but not alone; I know not well
  How this same interview had taken place,
And even if I knew, I shall not tell—
  People should hold their tongues in any case;
No matter how or why the thing befell,
  But there were she and Juan, face to face—
When two such faces are so, 't would be wise,
But very difficult, to shut their eyes. 840

106

How beautiful she looked! her conscious heart
  Glowed in her cheek, and yet she felt no wrong:

[25] Thomas Moore (1779-1852) translated the Greek poet, Anacreon. The allusion is to the tale of "Paradise and the Peri" in his poem *Lalla Rookh* (1817).

Oh Love! how perfect is thy mystic art,
  Strengthening the weak, and trampling on the strong!
How self-deceitful is the sagest part
  Of mortals whom thy lure hath led along!—
The precipice she stood on was immense,
So was her creed in her own innocence.

107
She thought of her own strength, and Juan's youth,
  And of the folly of all prudish fears, 850
Victorious Virtue, and domestic Truth,
  And then of Don Alfonso's fifty years:
I wish these last had not occurred, in sooth,
  Because that number rarely much endears,
And through all climes, the snowy and the sunny,
Sounds ill in love, whate'er it may in money.

108
When people say, "I've told you *fifty* times,"
  They mean to scold, and very often do;
When poets say, "I've written *fifty* rhymes,"
  They make you dread that they'll recite them too; 860
In gangs of *fifty*, thieves commit their crimes;
  At *fifty* love for love is rare, 't is true,
But then, no doubt, it equally as true is,
A good deal may be bought for *fifty* Louis.

109
Julia had honour, virtue, truth, and love
  For Don Alfonso; and she inly swore,
By all the vows below to Powers above,
  She never would disgrace the ring she wore,
Nor leave a wish which wisdom might reprove;
  And while she pondered this, besides much more, 870
One hand on Juan's carelessly was thrown,
Quite by mistake—she thought it was her own;

110
Unconsciously she leaned upon the other,
  Which played within the tangles of her hair;
And to contend with thoughts she could not smother
  She seemed by the distraction of her air.
'T was surely very wrong in Juan's mother
  To leave together this imprudent pair,

She who for many years had watched her son so—
I'm very certain *mine* would not have done so. 880

111
The hand which still held Juan's, by degrees
  Gently, but palpably confirmed its grasp,
As if it said, "Detain me, if you please;"
  Yet there's no doubt she only meant to clasp
His fingers with a pure Platonic squeeze;
  She would have shrunk as from a toad, or asp,
Had she imagined such a thing could rouse
A feeling dangerous to a prudent spouse.

112
I cannot know what Juan thought of this,
  But what he did, is much what you would do; 890
His young lip thanked it with a grateful kiss,
  And then, abashed at its own joy, withdrew
In deep despair, lest he had done amiss,—
  Love is so very timed when 't is new:
She blushed, and frowned not, but she strove to speak,
And held her tongue, her voice was grown so weak.

113
The sun set, and up rose the yellow moon:
  The Devil's in the moon for mischief; they
Who called her CHASTE, methinks, began too soon
  Their nomenclature; there is not a day, 900
The longest, not the twenty-first of June,
  Sees half the business in a wicked way,
On which three single hours of moonshine smile—
And then she looks so modest all the while!

114
There is a dangerous silence in that hour,
  A stillness, which leaves room for the full soul
To open all itself, without the power
  Of calling wholly back its self-control;
The silver light which, hallowing tree and tower,
  Sheds beauty and deep softness o'er the whole, 910
Breathes also to the heart, and o'er it throws
A loving languor, which is not repose.

115
And Julia sate with Juan, half embraced
  And half retiring from the glowing arm,

Which trembled like the bosom where 't was placed;
  Yet still she must have thought there was no harm,
Or else 't were easy to withdraw her waist;
  But then the situation had its charm,
And then—God knows what next—I can't go on;
I'm almost sorry that I e'er begun. 920

116

Oh Plato! Plato! you have paved the way,
  With your confounded fantasies, to more
Immoral conduct by the fancied sway
  Your system feigns o'er the controlless core
Of human hearts, than all the long array
  Of poets and romancers:—You're a bore,
A charlatan, a coxcomb—and have been,
At best, no better than a go-between.

117

And Julia's voice was lost, except in sighs,
  Until too late for useful conversation; 930
The tears were gushing from her gentle eyes,
  I wish, indeed, they had not had occasion;
But who, alas! can love, and then be wise?
  Not that Remorse did not oppose Temptation;
A little still she strove, and much repented,
And whispering "I will ne'er consent"—consented.

118

'T is said that Xerxes offered a reward
  To those who could invent him a new pleasure:
Methinks the requisition 's rather hard,
  And must have cost his Majesty a treasure: 940
For my part, I'm a moderate-minded bard,
  Fond of a little love (which I call leisure);
I care not for new pleasures, as the old
Are quite enough for me, so they but hold.

119

Oh Pleasure! you're indeed a pleasant thing,
  Although one must be damned for you, no doubt:
I make a resolution every spring
  Of reformation, ere the year run out,
But somehow, this my vestal vow takes wing,
  Yet still, I trust, it may be kept throughout: 950

I'm very sorry, very much ashamed,
And mean, next winter, to be quite reclaimed.

120

Here my chaste Muse a liberty must take—
  Start not! still chaster reader—she'll be nice hence-
Forward, and there is no great cause to quake;
  This liberty is a poetic licence,
Which some irregularity may make
  In the design, and as I have a high sense
Of Aristotle and the Rules, 't is fit
To beg his pardon when I err a bit. 960

121

This licence is to hope the reader will
  Suppose from June the sixth (the fatal day,
Without whose epoch my poetic skill
  For want of facts would all be thrown away),
But keeping Julia and Don Juan still
  In sight, that several months have passed; we'll say
'T was in November, but I'm not so sure
About the day—the era's more obscure.

122

We'll talk of that anon.—'T is sweet to hear
  At midnight on the blue and moonlit deep 970
The song and oar of Adria's[26] gondolier,
  By distance mellowed, o'er the waters sweep;
'T is sweet to see the evening star appear;
  'T is sweet to listen as the night-winds creep
From leaf to leaf; 't is sweet to view on high
The rainbow, based on ocean, span the sky.

123

'T is sweet to hear the watch-dog's honest bark
  Bay deep-mouthed welcome as we draw near home;
'T is sweet to know there is an eye will mark
  Our coming, and look brighter when we come; 980
'T is sweet to be awakened by the lark,
  Or lulled by falling waters; sweet the hum
Of bees, the voice of girls, the song of birds,
The lisp of children, and their earliest words.

---

[26] Venice on the Adriatic Sea.

124
Sweet is the vintage, when the showering grapes
In Bacchanal profusion reel to earth,
Purple and gushing: sweet are our escapes
From civic revelry to rural mirth;
Sweet to the miser are his glittering heaps,
Sweet to the father is his first-born's birth, 990
Sweet is revenge—especially to women—
Pillage to soldiers, prize-money to seamen.

125
Sweet is a legacy, and passing sweet
The unexpected death of some old lady,
Or gentleman of seventy years complete,
Who've made "us youth" wait too—too long already,
For an estate, or cash, or country seat,
Still breaking, but with stamina so steady,
That all the Israelites are fit to mob its
Next owner for their double-damned post-obits. 1000

126
'T is sweet to win, no matter how, one's laurels,
By blood or ink, 't is sweet to put an end
To strife; 't is sometimes sweet to have our quarrels,
Particularly with a tiresome friend:
Sweet is old wine in bottles, ale in barrels;
Dear is the helpless creature we defend
Against the world; and dear the schoolboy spot
We ne'er forget, though there we are forgot.

127
But sweeter still than this, than these, than all,
Is first and passionate Love—it stands alone, 1010
Like Adam's recollection of his fall;
The Tree of Knowledge has been plucked—all's known—
And Life yields nothing further to recall
Worthy of this ambrosial sin, so shown,
No doubt in fable, as the unforgiven
Fire which Prometheus filched for us from Heaven.

128
Man's a strange animal, and makes strange use
Of his own nature, and the various arts,
And likes particularly to produce

Some new experiment to show his parts, 1020
This is the age of oddities let loose,
Where different talents find their different marts;
You'd best begin with truth, and when you've lost your
Labour, there's a sure market for imposture.

129

What opposite discoveries we have seen!
(Signs of true genius, and of empty pockets.)
One makes new noses, one a guillotine,
One breaks your bones, one sets them in their sockets;
But Vaccination certainly has been
A kind antithesis to Congreve's rockets,[27] 1030
With which the Doctor paid off an old pox,
By borrowing a new one from an ox.

130

Bread has been made (indifferent) from potatoes:
And Galvanism has set some corpses grinning,[28]
But has not answered like the apparatus
Of the Humane Society's beginning,
By which men are unsuffocated gratis:
What wondrous new machines have late been spinning!
I said the small-pox has gone out of late;
Perhaps it may be followed by the great. 1040

131

'T is said the great came from America,
Perhaps it may set out on its return,—
The population there so spreads, they say
'T is grown high time to thin it in its turn,
With war, or plague, or famine—any way,
So that civilisation they may learn;
And which in ravage the more loathsome evil is—
Their real *lues*, or our pseudo-syphillis?

132

This is the patent age of new inventions
For killing bodies, and for saving souls, 1050
All propagated with the best intentions;
Sir Humphry Davy's lantern, by which coals

---

[27] Sir William Congreve (1772-1828) invented an explosive rocket.
[28] Experiments in shooting electricity through the body of a corpse.

Are safely mined for in the mode he mentions,
  Tombuctoo travels, voyages to the Poles
Are ways to benefit mankind, as true,
Perhaps, as shooting them at Waterloo.

133
Man's a phenomenon, one knows not what,
  And wonderful beyond all wondrous measure;
'T is pity though, in this sublime world, that
  Pleasure's a sin, and sometimes Sin's a pleasure; 1060
Few mortals know what end they would be at,
  But whether Glory, Power, or Love, or Treasure,
The path is through perplexing ways, and when
The goal is gained, we die, you know—and then—

134
What then?—I do not know, no more do you—
  And so good night.—Return we to our story:
'T was in November, when fine days are few,
  And the far mountains wax a little hoary,
And clap a white cape on their mantles blue;
  And the sea dashes round the promontory, 1070
And the loud breaker boils against the rock,
And sober suns must set at five o'clock.

135
'T was, as the watchmen say, a cloudy night;
  No moon, no stars, the wind was low or loud
By gusts, and many a sparkling hearth was bright
  With the piled wood, round which the family crowd;
There's something cheerful in that sort of light,
  Even as a summer sky's without a cloud:
I'm fond of fire, and crickets, and all that,
A lobster salad, and champagne, and chat. 1080

136
'T was midnight—Donna Julia was in bed,
  Sleeping, most probably,—when at her door
Arose a clatter might awake the dead,
  If they had never been awoke before,
And that they have been so we all have read,
  And are to be so, at the least, once more;—
The door was fastened, but with voice and fist
First knocks were heard, then "Madam—Madam—hist!

137

"For God's sake, Madam—Madam—here's my master,
With more than half the city at his back— 1090
Was ever heard of such a curst disaster!
'T is not my fault—I kept good watch—Alack!
Do pray undo the bolt a little faster—
They're on the stair just now, and in a crack
Will all be here; perhaps he yet may fly—
Surely the window's not so *very* high!"

138

By this time Don Alfonso was arrived,
With torches, friends, and servants in great number;
The major part of them had long been wived,
And therefore paused not to disturb the slumber 1100
Of any wicked woman, who contrived
By stealth her husband's temples to encumber.
Examples of this kind are so contagious,
Were *one* not punished, *all* would be outrageous.

139

I can't tell how, or why, or what suspicion
Could enter into Don Alfonso's head;
But for a cavalier of his condition
It surely was exceedingly ill-bred,
Without a word of previous admonition,
To hold a levee round his lady's bed, 1110
And summon lackeys, armed with fire and sword,
To prove himself the thing he most abhorred.

140

Poor Donna Julia! starting as from sleep,
(Mind—that I do not say—she had not slept),
Began at once to scream, and yawn, and weep;
Her maid, Antonia, who was an adept,
Contrived to fling the bed-clothes in a heap,
As if she had just now from out them crept:
I can't tell why she should take all this trouble
To prove her mistress had been sleeping double. 1120

141

But Julia mistress, and Antonia maid,
Appeared like two poor harmless women who
Of goblins, but still more of men afraid,

Had thought one man might be deterred by two,
And therefore side by side were gently laid,
Until the hours of absence should run through,
And truant husband should return, and say,
"My dear,—I was the first who came away."

142
Now Julia found at length a voice, and cried,
"In Heaven's name, Don Alfonso, what d' ye mean? 1130
Has madness seized you? would that I had died
Ere such a monster's victim I had been!
What may this midnight violence betide,
A sudden fit of drunkenness or spleen?
Dare you suspect me, whom the thought would kill?
Search, then, the room!"—Alfonso said, "I will."

143
He searched, *they* searched, and rummaged everywhere,
Closet and clothes' press, chest and window-seat,
And found much linen, lace, and several pair
Of stockings, slippers, brushes, combs, complete 1140
With other articles of ladies fair,
To keep them beautiful, or leave them neat:
Arras they pricked and curtains with their swords,
And wounded several shutters, and some boards.

144
Under the bed they searched, and there they found—
No matter what—it was not that they sought;
They opened windows, gazing if the ground
Had signs of footmarks, but the earth said nought;
And then they stared each others' faces round:
'T is odd, not one of all these seekers thought, 1150
And seems to me almost a sort of blunder,
Of looking *in* the bed as well as under.

145
During this inquisition Julia's tongue
Was not asleep—"Yes, search and search," she cried,
"Insult on insult heap, and wrong on wrong!
It was for this that I became a bride!
For this in silence I have suffered long
A husband like Alfonso at my side;

But now I'll bear no more, nor here remain,
If there be law or lawyers in all Spain. 1160

146
"Yes, Don Alfonso! husband now no more,
If ever you indeed deserved the name,
Is't worthy of your years?—you have threescore—
Fifty, or sixty, it is all the same—
Is't wise or fitting, causeless to explore
For facts against a virtuous woman's fame?
Ungrateful, perjured, barbarous Don Alfonso,
How dare you think your lady would go on so?

147
"Is it for this I have disdained to hold
The common privileges of my sex? 1170
That I have chosen a confessor so old
And deaf, that any other it would vex,
And never once he has had cause to scold,
But found my very innocence perplex
So much, he always doubted I was married—
How sorry you will be when I've miscarried!

148
"Was it for this that no Cortejo e'er[29]
I yet have chosen from out the youth of Seville?
Is it for this I scarce went anywhere,
Except to bull-fights, mass, play, rout, and revel? 1180
Is it for this, whate'er my suitors were,
I favoured none—nay, was almost uncivil?
Is is for this that General Count O'Reilly,[30]
Who took Algiers, declares I used him vilely?

149
"Did not the Italian *Musico* Cazzani
Sing at my heart six months at least in vain?
Did not his countryman, Count Corniani,
Call me the only virtuous wife in Spain?
Were there not also Russians, English, many?

---

[29] Lover.

[30] General Alexander O'Reilly (1722-1794) was a Spaniard of Irish birth. He was disastrously defeated in an attempt to capture Algiers in 1775.

The Count Strongstroganoff I put in pain, 1190
And Lord Mount Coffeehouse, the Irish peer,
Who killed himself for love (with wine) last year.

150
"Have I not had two bishops at my feet?
The Duke of Ichar, and Don Fernan Nunez;
And is it thus a faithful wife you treat?
I wonder in what quarter now the moon is:
I praise your vast forbearance not to beat
Me also, since the time so opportune is—
Oh, valiant man! with sword drawn and cocked trigger,
Now, tell me, don't you cut a pretty figure? 1200

151
"Was it for this you took your sudden journey,
Under pretence of business indispensable
With that sublime of rascals your attorney,
Whom I see standing there, and looking sensible
Of having played the fool? though both I spurn, he
Deserves the worst, his conduct's less defensible,
Because, no doubt, 't was for his dirty fee,
And not from any love to you nor me.

152
"If he comes here to take a deposition,
By all means let the gentleman proceed; 1210
You've made the apartment in a fit condition;—
There's pen and ink for you, sir, when you need—
Let everything be noted with precision,
I would not you for nothing should be fee'd—
But, as my maid's undressed, pray turn your spies out."
"Oh!" sobbed Antonia, "I could tear their eyes out."

153
"There is the closet, there the toilet, there
The antechamber—search them under, over;
There is the sofa, there the great arm-chair,
The chimney—which would really hold a lover. 1220
I wish to sleep, and beg you will take care
And make no further noise, till you discover
The secret cavern of this lurking treasure—
And when 't is found, let me, too, have that pleasure.

154
"And now, Hidalgo! now that you have thrown
Doubt upon me, confusion over all,
Pray have the courtesy to make it known
Who is the man you search for? how d' ye call
Him? what's his lineage? let him but be shown—
I hope he's young and handsome—is he tall? 1230
Tell me—and be assured, that since you stain
My honour thus, it shall not be in vain.

155
"At least, perhaps, he has not sixty years,
At that age he would be too old for slaughter,
Or for so young a husband's jealous fears—
(Antonia! let me have a glass of water.)
I am ashamed of having shed these tears,
They are unworthy of my father's daughter;
My mother dreamed not in my natal hour,
That I should fall into a monster's power. 1240

156
"Perhaps 't is of Antonia you are jealous,
You saw that she was sleeping by my side,
When you broke in upon us with your fellows:
Look where you please—we've nothing, sir, to hide;
Only another time, I trust you'll tell us,
Or for the sake of decency abide
A moment at the door, that we may be
Dressed to receive so much good company.

157
"And now, sir, I have done, and say no more;
The little I have said may serve to show 1250
The guileless heart in silence may grieve o'er
The wrongs to whose exposure it is slow:—
I leave you to your conscience as before,
'T will one day ask you *why* you used me so?
God grant you feel not then the bitterest grief!—
Antonia! where's my pocket-handkerchief?"

158
She ceased, and turned upon her pillow; pale
She lay, her dark eyes flashing through their tears,
Like skies that rain and lighten; as a veil,

Waved and o'ershading her wan cheek, appears 1260
Her streaming hair; the black curls strive, but fail
To hide the glossy shoulder, which uprears
Its snow through all;—her soft lips lie apart,
And louder than her breathing beats her heart.

159

The Senhor Don Alfonso stood confused;
Antonia bustled round the ransacked room,
And, turning up her nose, with looks abused
Her master, and his myrmidons, of whom
Not one, except the attorney, was amused;
He, like Achates, faithful to the tomb,[31] 1270
So there were quarrels, cared not for the cause,
Knowing they must be settled by the laws.

160

With prying snub-nose, and small eyes, he stood,
Following Antonia's motions here and there,
With much suspicion in his attitude;
For reputations he had little care;
So that a suit or action were made good,
Small pity had he for the young and fair,
And ne'er believed in negatives, till these
Were proved by competent false witnesses. 1280

161

But Don Alfonso stood with downcast looks,
And, truth to say, he made a foolish figure;
When, after searching in five hundred nooks,
And treating a young wife with so much rigour,
He gained no point, except some self-rebukes,
Added to those his lady with such vigour
Had poured upon him for the last half-hour,
Quick, thick, and heavy—as a thunder-shower.

162

At first he tried to hammer an excuse,
To which the sole reply was tears, and sobs, 1290
And indications of hysterics, whose
Prologue is always certain throes, and throbs,

---

[31] Achates was a faithful friend of Aeneas during his journey from Troy to Rome in Virgil's *Aeneid.*

Gasps, and whatever else the owners choose;
  Alfonso saw his wife, and thought of Job's;
He saw too, in perspective, her relations,
And then he tried to muster all his patience.

163
He stood in act to speak, or rather stammer,
  But sage Antonia cut him short before
The anvil of his speech received the hammer,
  With "Pray, sir, leave the room, and say no more, 1300
Or madam dies."—Alfonso muttered, "D—n her,"
  But nothing else, the time of words was o'er;
He cast a rueful look or two, and did,
He knew not wherefore, that which he was bid.

164
With him retired his "*posse comitatus*,"[32]
  The attorney last, who lingered near the door
Reluctantly, still tarrying there as late as
  Antonia let him—not a little sore
At this most strange and unexplained "*hiatus*"
  In Don Alfonso's facts, which just now wore 1310
An awkward look; as he revolved the case,
The door was fastened in his legal face.

165
No sooner was it bolted, than—Oh Shame!
  Oh Sin! Oh Sorrow! and Oh Womankind!
How can you do such things and keep your fame,
  Unless this world, and t' other too, be blind?
Nothing so dear as an unfilched good name!
  But to proceed—for there is more behind:
With much heartfelt reluctance be it said,
Young Juan slipped, half-smothered, from the bed. 1320

166
He had been hid—I don't pretend to say
  How, nor can I indeed describe the where—
Young, slender, and packed easily, he lay,
  No doubt, in little compass, round or square;
But pity him I neither must nor may

---

[32] "Power of the county." The form of the word "posse" meaning citizens called by a sheriff to maintain order in the county.

His suffocation by that pretty pair;
'T were better, sure, to die so, than be shut
With maudlin Clarence in his Malmsey butt.

167
And, secondly, I pity not, because
He had no business to commit a sin, 1330
Forbid by heavenly, fined by human laws;—
At least 't was rather early to begin,
But at sixteen the conscience rarely gnaws
So much as when we call our old debts in
At sixty years, and draw the accompts of evil,
And find a deuced balance with the Devil.

168
Of his position I can give no notion:
'T is written in the Hebrew Chronicle,
How the physicians, leaving pill and potion,
Prescribed, by way of blister, a young belle, 1340
When old King David's blood grew dull in motion,
And that the medicine answered very well;
Perhaps 't was in a different way applied,
For David lived, but Juan nearly died.

169
What's to be done? Alfonso will be back
The moment he has sent his fools away.
Antonia's skill was put upon the rack,
But no device could be brought into play—
And how to parry the renewed attack?
Besides, it wanted but few hours of day: 1350
Antonia puzzled; Julia did not speak,
But pressed her bloodless lips to Juan's cheek.

170
He turned his lips to hers, and with his hand
Called back the tangles of her wandering hair;
Even then their love they could not all command,
And half forgot their danger and despair:
Antonia's patience now was at a stand—
"Come, come, 't is no time for fooling there."
She whispered, in great wrath—"I must deposit
This pretty gentleman within the closet: 1360

171
"Pray, keep your nonsense for some luckier night—
  Who can have put my master in this mood?
What will become on 't—I'm in such a fright,
  The Devil's in the urchin, and no good—
Is this a time for giggling? this a plight?
  Why don't you know that it may end in blood?
You'll lose your life, and I shall lose my place,
My mistress all, for that half-girlish face.

172
"Had it but been for a stout cavalier
  Of twenty-five or thirty—(come, make haste) 1370
But for a child, what piece of work is here!
  I really, madam, wonder at your taste—
(Come, sir, get in)—my master must be near:
  There, for the present, at the least, he's fast,
And if we can but till the morning keep
Our counsel—(Juan, mind, you must not sleep.)"

173
Now, Don Alfonso entering, but alone,
  Closed the oration of the trusty maid:
She loitered, and he told her to be gone,
  An order somewhat sullenly obeyed; 1380
However, present remedy was none,
  And no great good seemed answered if she staid:
Regarding both with slow and sidelong view,
She snuffed the candle, curtsied, and withdrew.

174
Alfonso paused a minute—then begun
  Some strange excuse for his late proceeding;
He would not justify what he had done,
  To say the best, it was extremely ill-breeding;
But there were ample reasons for it, none
  Of which he specified in this his pleading: 1390
His speech was a fine sample, on the whole,
Of rhetoric, which the learned called "*rigmarole*."

175
Julia said nought; though all the while there rose
  A ready answer, which at once enables
A matron, who her husband's foibles knows,

By a few timely words to turn the tables,
Which, if it does not silence, still must pose,—
Even if it should comprise a pack of fables;
'T is to retort with firmness, and when he
Suspects with *one*, do you reproach with *three*. 1400

176
Julia, in fact, had tolerable grounds,—
Alfonso's loves with Inez were well known;
But whether 't was that one's own guilt confounds—
But that can't be, as has been often shown,
A lady with apologies abounds;—
It might be that her silence sprang alone
From delicacy to Don Juan's ear,
To whom she knew his mother's fame was dear.

177
There might be one more motive, which makes two;
Alfonso ne'er to Juan had alluded,— 1410
Mentioned his jealousy, but never who
Had been the happy lover, he concluded,
Concealed amongst his premises; 't is true,
His mind the more o'er this its mystery brooded;
To speak of Inez now were, one may say,
Like throwing Juan in Alfonso's way.

178
A hint, in tender cases, is enough;
Silence is best: besides, there is a *tact*—
(That modern phrase appears to me sad stuff,
But it will serve to keep my verse compact)— 1420
Which keeps, when pushed by questions rather rough,
A lady always distant from the fact:
The charming creatures lie with such a grace,
There's nothing so becoming to the face.

179
They blush, and we believe them; at least I
Have always done so: 't is of no great use,
In any case, attempting a reply,
For then their eloquence grows quite profuse;
And when at length they're out of breath, they sigh,
And cast their languid eyes down, and let loose 1430
A tear or two, and then we make it up;
And then—and then—and then—sit down and sup.

180
Alfonso closed his speech, and begged her pardon,
Which Julia half withheld, and then half granted,
And laid conditions he thought very hard on,
Denying several little things he wanted:
He stood like Adam lingering near his garden,
With useless penitence perplexed and haunted;
Beseeching she no further would refuse,
When, lo! he stumbled o'er a pair of shoes. 1440

181
A pair of shoes!—what then? not much, if they
Are such as fit with ladies' feet, but these
(No one can tell how much I grieve to say)
Were masculine; to see them, and to seize,
Was but a moment's act.—Ah! well-a-day!
My teeth begin to chatter, my veins freeze!
Alfonso first examined well their fashion,
And then flew out into another passion.

182
He left the room for his relinquished sword,
And Julia instant to the closet flew. 1450
"Fly, Juan, fly! for Heaven's sake—not a word—
The door is open—you may yet slip through
The passage you so often have explored—
Here is the garden-key—Fly—fly—Adieu!
Haste—haste! I hear Alfonso's hurrying feet
Day has not broke—there's no one in the street."

183
None can say that this was not good advice,
The only mischief was, it came too late;
Of all experience 't is the usual price,
A sort of income-tax laid on by fate: 1460
Juan had reached the room-door in a trice,
And might have done so by the garden-gate,
But met Alfonso in his dressing-gown,
Who threatened death—so Juan knocked him down.

184
Dire was the scuffle, and out went the light;
Antonia cried out "Rape!" and Julia "Fire!"
But not a servant stirred to aid the fight.

Alfonso, pommelled to his heart's desire,
Swore lustily he'd be revenged this night;
And Juan, too, blasphemed an octave higher; 1470
His blood was up: though young, he was a Tartar.
And not at all disposed to prove a martyr.

185
Alfonso's sword had dropped ere he could draw it,
And they continued battling hand in hand,
For Juan very luckily ne'er saw it;
His temper not being under great command,
If at that moment he had chanced to claw it,
Alfonso's days had not been in the land
Much longer.—Think of husbands', lovers' lives!
And how ye may be doubly widows—wives! 1480

186
Alfonso grappled to detain the foe,
And Juan throttled him to get away,
And blood ('t was from the nose) began to flow;
At last, as they more faintly wrestling lay,
Juan contrived to give an awkward blow,
And then his only garment quite gave way;
He fled, like Joseph,[33] leaving it; but there,
I doubt, all likeness ends between the pair.

187
Lights came at length, and men, and maids, who found
An awkward spectacle their eyes before; 1490
Antonia in hysterics, Julia swooned,
Alfonso leaning, breathless by the door;
Some half-torn drapery scattered on the ground,
Some blood, and several footsteps, but no more:
Juan the gate gained, turned the key about,
And liking not the inside, locked the out.

188
Here ends this canto.—Need I sing, or say,
How Juan, naked, favoured by the night,
Who favours what she should not, found his way,
And reached his home in an unseemly plight? 1500
The pleasant scandal which arose next day,

[33] Joseph fled the enticing wife of Potiphar, part of his garments in her hand.

The nine days' wonder which was brought to light,
And how Alfonso sued for a divorce,
Were in the English newspapers, of course.

189
If you would like to see the whole proceedings,
The depositions, and the Cause at full,
The names of all the witnesses, the pleadings
Of Counsel to nonsuit, or to annul,
There's more than one edition, and the readings
Are various, but they none of them are dull: 1510
The best is that in short-hand ta'en by Gurney,
Who to Madrid on purpose made a journey.

190
But Donna Inez, to divert the train
Of one of the most circulating scandals
That had for centuries been known in Spain,
At least since the retirement of the Vandals,
First vowed (and never had she vowed in vain)
To Virgin Mary several pounds of candles;
And then, by the advice of some old ladies,
She sent her son to be shipped off from Cadiz. 1520

191
She had resolved that he should travel through
All European climes, by land and sea,
To mend his former morals, and get new,
Especially in France and Italy—
(At least this is the thing most people do.)
Julia was sent into a convent—she
Grieved—but, perhaps, her feelings may be better
Shown in the following copy of her Letter:

192
"They tell me 't is decided you depart:
'T is wise—'t is well, but not the less a pain; 1530
I have no further claim on your young heart,
Mine is the victim, and would be again:
To love too much has been the only art
I used;—I write in haste, and if a stain
Be on this sheet, 't is not what it appears;
My eyeballs burn and throb, but have no tears.

193
"I loved, I love you, for this love has lost
State, station, Heaven, Mankind's my own esteem,
And yet can not regret what it hath cost,
So dear is still the memory of that dream; 1540
Yet, if I name my guilt, 't is not to boast,
None can deem harshlier of me than I deem:
I trace this scrawl because I cannot rest—
I've nothing to reproach, or to request.

194
"Man's love is of man's life a thing apart,
'T is a Woman's whole existence; Man may range
The Court, Camp, Church, the Vessel, and the Mart;
Sword, Gown, Gain, Glory offer, in exchange
Pride, Fame, Ambition, to fill up his heart,
And few there are whom these can not estrange; 1550
Men have all these resources, We but one—
To love again, and be again undone.

195
"You will proceed in pleasure, and in pride,
Beloved and loving many; all is o'er
For me on earth, except some years to hide
My shame and sorrow deep in my heart's core:
These I could bear, but cannot cast aside
The passion which still rages as before,—
And so farewell—forgive me, love me—No,
That word is idle now—but let it go. 1560

196
"My breast has been all weakness, is so yet;
But still I think I can collect my mind;
My blood still rushes where my spirit's set,
As roll the waves before the settled wind;
My heart is feminine, nor can forget—
To all, except one image, madly blind;
So shakes the needle, and so stands the pole,
As vibrates my fond heart to my fixed soul.

197
"I have no more to say, but linger still,
And dare not set my seal upon this sheet, 1570

And yet I may as well the task fulfil,
  My misery can scarce be more complete;
I had not lived till now, could sorrow kill;
  Death shuns the wretch who fain the blow would meet,
And I must even survive this last adieu,
And bear with life, to love and pray for you!"

198

This note was written upon gilt-edged paper
  With a neat little crow-quill, slight and new;
Her small white hand could hardly reach the taper,
  It trembled as magnetic needles do, 1580
And yet she did not let one tear escape her;
  The seal a sun-flower; "*Elle vous suit partout,*"[34]
The motto cut upon a white cornelian;
The wax was superfine, its hue vermilion.

199

This was Don Juan's earliest scrape; but whether
  I shall proceed with his adventures is
Dependent on the public altogether;
  We'll see, however, what they say to this:
Their favour in an author's caps's a feather,
  And no great mischief's done by their caprice; 1590
And if their approbation we experience,
Perhaps they'll have some more about a year hence.

200

My poem's epic, and is meant to be
  Divided in twelve books; each book containing,
With Love, and War, a heavy gale at sea,
  A list of ships, and captains, and kings reigning,
New characters; the episodes are three:
  A panoramic view of Hell's in training.
After the style of Virgil and of Homer,
So that my name of Epic's no misnomer. 1600

201

All these things will be specified in time,
  With strict regard to Aristotle's rules,
The *Vade Mecum*[35] of the true sublime,

[34] "She follows you everywhere."
[35] Guidebook ("go with me"). Byron is mocking those who use Aristotle's *Poetics* as a guidebook for tragedy and the epic.

Which makes so many poets, and some fools:
Prose poets like blank-verse, I'm fond of rhyme,
Good workmen never quarrel with their tools;
I've got new mythological machinery,
And very handsome supernatural scenery.

202
There's only one slight difference between
Me and my epic brethren gone before, 1610
And here the advantage is my own, I ween,
(Not that I have not several merits more,
But this will more peculiarly be seen);
They so embellish, that 't is quite a bore
Their labyrinth of fables to thread through,
Whereas this story's actually true.

203
If any person doubt it, I appeal
To History, Tradition, and to Facts,
To newspapers, whose truth all know and feel,
To plays in five, and operas in three acts; 1620
All these confirm my statement a good deal,
But that which more completely faith exacts
Is, that myself, and several now in Seville,
Saw Juan's last elopement with the Devil.

204
If ever I should condescend to prose,
I'll write poetical commandments, which
Shall supersede beyond all doubt all those
That went before; in these I shall enrich
My text with many things that no one knows,
And carry precept to the highest pitch: 1630
I'll call the work "Longinus o'er a Bottle,
Or, Every Poet his *own* Aristotle."

205
Thou shalt believe in Milton, Dryden, Pope;
Thou shalt not set up Wordsworth, Coleridge, Southey;
Because the first is crazed beyond all hope,
The second drunk, the third so quaint and mouthy:
With Crabbe it may be difficult to cope,
And Campbell's Hippocrene is somewhat drouthy:

Thou shalt not steal from Samuel Rogers, nor
Commit—flirtation with the muse of Moore. 1640

206

Thou shalt not covet Mr. Sotheby's Muse,[36]
His Pagasus, nor anything that's his;
Thou shalt not bear false witness like "the Blues"—
(There's *one*, at least, is very fond of this);
Thou shalt not write, in short, but what I choose:
This is true criticism, and you may kiss—
Exactly as you please, or not,—the rod;
But if you don't, I'll lay it on, by G—d!

207

If any person should presume to assert
This story is not moral, first, I pray, 1650
That they will not cry out before they're hurt,
Then that they'll read it o'er again, and say
(But, doubtless, nobody will be so pert),
That this is not a moral tale, though gay:
Besides, in Canto Twelfth, I mean to show
The very place where wicked people go.

208

If, after all, there should be some so blind
To their own good this warning to despise,
Led by some tortuosity of mind,
Not to believe my verse and their own eyes, 1660
And cry that they "the moral cannot find,"
I tell him, if a clergyman, he lies;
Should captains the remark, or critics, make,
They also lie too—under a mistake.

209

The public approbation I expect,
And beg they'll take my word about the moral,
Which I with their amusement will connect
(So children cutting teeth receive a coral);
Meantime they'll doubtless please to recollect
My epical pretensions to the laurel: 1670
For fear some prudish readers should grow skittish,
I've bribed my Grandmother's Review—the British.

[36] William Sotheby (1757-1833), a translator and minor poet, satirized by Byron in his earlier poetry.

210
I sent it in a letter to the Editor,
  Who thanked me duly by return of post—
I'm for a handsome article his creditor;
  Yet, if my gentle Muse he please to roast,
And break a promise after having made it her,
  Denying the receipt of what it cost,
And smear his page with gall instead of honey,
All I can say is—that he had the money. 1680

211
I think that with this holy *new* alliance
  I may ensure the public, and defy
All other magazines of art or science,
  Daily, or monthly, or three monthly, I
Have not essayed to multiply their clients,
  Because they tell me 't were in vain to try,
And that the Edinburgh Review and Quarterly
Treat a dissenting author very martyrly.

212
"*Non ego hoc ferrem calidus juventâ*[37]
  Consule Planco," Horace said, and so 1690
Say I; by which quotation there is meant a
  Hint that some six or seven good years ago
(Long ere I dreamt of dating from the Brenta
  I was most ready to return a blow,
And would not brook at all this sort of thing
In my hot youth—when George the Third was King.

213
But now at thirty years my hair is grey—
  (I wonder what it will be like at forty?
I thought of a peruke the other day—)
  My heart is not much greener; and, in short, I 1700
Have squandered my whole summer while 't was May,
  And feel no more the spirit to retort; I
Have spent my life, both interest and principal,
And deem not, what I deemed—my soul invincible.

214
No more—no more—Oh! never more on me

---

[37] "I should not have endured this in the heat of youth when Plancus was Consul." Horace, *Odes*, III, 14:27-28.

The freshness of the heart can fall like dew,
Which out of all the lovely things we see
Extracts emotions beautiful and new,
Hived in our bosoms like the bag o' the bee.
Think'st thou the honey with those objects grew? 1710
Alas! 't was not in them, but in thy power
To double even the sweetness of a flower.

215

No more—no more—Oh! never more, my heart,
Canst thou be my sole world, my universe!
Once all in all, but now a thing apart,
Thou canst not be my blessing or my curse:
The illusion's gone for ever, and thou art
Insensible, I trust, but none the worse,
And in thy stead I've got a deal of judgment,
Though Heaven knows how it ever found a lodgment. 1720

216

My days of love are over; me no more
The charms of maid, wife, and still less of widow,
Can make the fool of which they made before,—
In short, I must not lead the life I did do;
The credulous hope of mutual minds is o'er,
The copious use of claret is forbid too,
So for a good old-gentlemanly vice,
I think I must take up with avarice.

217

Ambition was my idol, which was broken
Before the shrines of Sorrow, and of Pleasure; 1730
And the two last have left me many a token
O'er which reflection may be made at leisure:
Now, like Friar Bacon's Brazen Head, I've spoken,[38]
"Time is, Time was, Time's past:"—a chymic treasure
Is glittering Youth, which I have spent betimes—
My heart in passion, and my head on rhymes.

218

What is the end of fame? 't is but to fill
A certain portion of uncertain paper:
Some liken it to climbing up a hill,
Whose summit, like all hills, is lost in vapour; 1740

[38] See Robert Greene, *Friar Bacon and Friar Bungay*, Act IV, scene 1.

For this men write, speak, preach, and heroes kill,
  And bards burn what they call their "midnight taper,"
To have, when the original is dust,
A name, a wretched picture and worse bust.

219
What are the hopes of man? Old Egypt's King
  Cheops erected the first Pyramid
And largest, thinking it was just the thing
  To keep his memory whole, and mummy hid;
But somebody or other rummaging,
  Burglariously broke his coffin's lid: 1750
Let not a monument give you or me hopes,
Since not a pinch of dust remains of Cheops.

220
But I, being fond of true philosophy,
  Say very often to myself, "Alas!
All things that have been born were born to die,
  And flesh (which Death mows down to hay) is grass;
You've passed your youth not so unpleasantly,
  And if you had it o'er again—'t would pass—
So thank your stars that matters are no worse,
And read your Bible, Sir, and mind your purse." 1760

221
But for the present, gentle reader! and
  Still gentler purchaser! the Bard—that's I—
Must with permission, shake you by the hand,
  And so—"your humble servant, and Good-bye!"
We meet again, if we should understand
  Each other; and if not, I shall not try
Your patience further than by this short sample—
'T were well if others followed my example.

222
"Go, little Book, from this my solitude!
  I cast thee on the waters—go thy ways! 1770
And if—as I believe, thy vein be good,
  The World will find thee after many days."
When Southey's read, and Wordsworth understood,
  I can't help putting in my claim to praise—
The four first rhymes are Southey's every line:
For God's sake, reader! take them not for mine.

Questions for Discussion

1. Define the kind of comic poem Byron is writing by examining stanzas 1-7 and 200-204.

2. Describe the narrator of the poem, indicating his fitness for the role of comic story-teller. What is the purpose of his digressions such as those found in stanzas 22, 52, and 205-222?

3. How similar is the idea of marriage in the poem to that found in "The Merchant's Tale" and *The Country Wife?* In particular compare the triangle beginning with stanza 62 with that found in Chaucer's story and Wycherley's play. Are there any similarities in the [illegible]

4. How does Byron present different kinds of love (Platonic, romantic, and realistic) in a comic manner?

5. What aspects of Don Juan make him appropriate for the role of a comic hero?

6. Is Don Juan the only comic figure in the canto? What others described might fit the role and why might they be called comic?

7. Compare the pear tree scene in "The Merchant's Tale," the fake marriage scene between Horner and Mrs. Pinchwife in Act V of *The Country Wife,* and the bedroom scene in *Don Juan* beginning with stanza 136. What characteristics of comedy do they all share?

8. What do you think Byron meant when he said that in *Don Juan* he was "a little quietly facetious upon everything"?

Triangles in the Story - Sex is Too Serious

Recognize there is great [illegible] attracted to sex - [illegible] People can be attracted to other people. Two men of 25 better than 1 of 52.

Marriage as the Foundation of Comedy Wycherly

Marriage is a sacred institution, it means I don't [illegible] something. Some believe [illegible] understand things. [illegible]

Nikolai Gogol (1809-1852)

The Nose

I

An incredible thing happened in Petersburg on March 25th. Ivan Yakovlevich, the barber on Voznesensky Avenue (his last name has been lost and does not even figure on the signboard bearing a picture of a gentleman with a soapy cheek and the inscription WE ALSO LET BLOOD HERE), woke up rather early and detected a smell of newly baked bread. He raised himself a little and saw that his wife, a quite respectable woman and one extremely fond of coffee, was taking fresh rolls out of the oven.

"Praskovia Osipovna," he said to his wife, "no coffee for me this morning. I'll have a hot roll with onions instead."

Actually Ivan Yakovlevich would have liked both but he knew his wife frowned on such whims. And, sure enough, she thought:

"It's fine with me if the fool wants bread. That'll leave me another cup of coffee."

And she tossed a roll onto the table.

Mindful of his manners, Ivan Yakovlevich put his frock coat on over his nightshirt, seated himself at the table, poured some salt, got a couple of onions, took a knife and, assuming a dignified expression, proceeded to cut the roll in two.

Suddenly he stopped, surprised. There was something whitish in the middle of the roll. He poked at it with his knife, then felt it with his finger.

"It's quite compact . . ." he muttered under his breath. "Whatever can it be? . . ."

"The Nose," from *The Diary of a Madman and Other Stories* by Nikolai Gogol, translated by Andrew R. MacAndrew.

He thrust in two fingers this time and pulled it out. It was a nose.

He almost fell off his chair. Then he rubbed his eyes and felt the thing again. It was a nose all right, no doubt about it. And, what's more, a nose that had something familiar about it. His features expressed intense horror.

But the intensity of the barber's horror was nothing compared with the intensity of his wife's indignation.

"Where," she screamed, "did you lop off that nose, you beast? You crook," she shouted, "you drunkard! I'll report you to the police myself, you thug! Three customers have complained to me before this about the way you keep pulling their noses when you shave them, so that it's a wonder they manage to stay on at all."

But Ivan Yakovlevich, at that moment more dead than alive, was immune to her attack. He had remembered where he had seen the nose before and it was on none other than Collegiate Assessor Kovalev, whom he shaved regularly each Wednesday and Sunday.

"Wait, my dear, I'll wrap it in a rag and put it away somewhere in a corner. Let it stay there for a while, then I'll take it away."

"I won't even listen to you! Do you really imagine that I'll allow a cut-off nose to remain in my place, you old crumb! All you can do is strop your damn razor and when it comes to your duties, you're no good. You stupid, lousy, skirt-chasing scum! So you want me to get into trouble with the police for your sake? Is that it, you dirty mug? You're a stupid log, you know. Get it out of here. Do what you like with it, you hear me, but don't let me ever see it here again."

The barber stood there dumfounded. He thought and thought but couldn't think of anything.

"I'll be damned if I know how it happened," he said in the end, scratching behind his ear. "Was I drunk last night when I came home? I'm not sure. Anyway, it all sounds quite mad: bread is a baked product while a nose is something else again. Makes no sense to me. . . ."

So he fell silent. The thought that the police would find the nose on him and accuse him drove him to despair. He could already see the beautiful silver-braided, scarlet collars of the police and started trembling all over.

Still, in the end he stirred and went to get his trousers and his boots. He pulled on these sorry garments, wrapped the nose in a rag, and left under Praskovia Osipovna's unendearing barrage of recriminations.

He wanted to get rid of the nose, to leave it under a seat, stick it in a doorway, or just drop it as if by accident and then rush down a side street. But he kept meeting acquaintances who immediately proceeded to inquire where he was going or whom he was planning to shave so early in the morning, and he missed every opportunity. At one point he actually dropped the nose, but a watchman pointed to it with his halberd and informed him that he'd lost something. And Ivan Yakovlevich had to pick up the nose and stuff it back into his pocket. Things began to look completely hopeless for him when the stores began opening and the streets became more and more crowded.

Then he decided to try throwing the nose into the Neva from the Isakievsky Bridge. . . .

But, at this point, we should say a few words about Ivan Yakovlevich, a man who had a number of good points.

Like every self-respecting Russian tradesman, Ivan Yakovlevich was a terrible drunkard. And although he shaved other people's chins every day, his own looked permanently unshaven. His frock coat (he never wore an ordinary coat) was piebald. That is to say, it had been black originally but now it was studded with yellowish-brown and gray spots. His collar was shiny and three threads dangling from his coat indicated where the missing buttons should have been. Ivan Yakovlevich was a terrible cynic.

While being shaved the collegiate assessor often complained:

"Your hands always stink, Ivan Yakovlevich!"

He would answer: "How can they stink?"

"I don't know how, man, but they stink!" the other would say.

In answer Ivan Yakovlevich would take a pinch of snuff and proceed to soap Kovalev's cheeks and under his nose and behind his ears and under his chin, in fact, anywhere he felt like.

By and by, this worthy citizen reached the Isakievsky Bridge. He glanced around and then, leaning over the parapet, peered under the bridge as if to ascertain the whereabouts of some fish. But actually he discreetly dropped the rag containing the nose. He felt as if a three-hundred-pound weight had been taken off his back. He let out a little laugh and, instead of going back to shave the chins of government employees, he decided he had to recuperate. He was setting out for an establishment which operated under the sign MEALS AND TEA, to treat himself to a glass of punch, when all of a sudden he saw a police inspector of most imposing appearance—handlebar mustache, three-cornered hat, saber and all. He froze in his tracks. The policeman beckoned to him and said:

"Just step over here, fellow!"

Having great respect for this particular uniform, Ivan Yakovlevich pulled off his cap while he was still a good distance away, trotted toward the policeman and said:

"Good morning officer."

"Instead of good morning, you'd better tell me what you were doing in the middle of the bridge over there."

"I was on my way to shave people, officer, and I wanted to see whether the current was fast——"

"You're lying, man. You won't get away with it. You'd better answer my question."

"Officer, I'll give you two . . . no, three free shaves every week . . . what do you say, officer?" said Ivan Yakovlevich.

"Not a chance. I have three barbers to shave me as it is. And they consider it a great honor, too. So you get on with it and explain what you were doing."

Ivan Yakovlevich turned ashen. . . . But here the incident becomes befogged and it is completely unknown what happened after this point.

II

That morning Collegiate Assessor[1] Kovalev had awakened rather early. He went brrr . . . brrr with his lips as he always did upon waking, although he himself could not explain why. He stretched himself and asked his man for the small mirror that stood on his dressing table. He needed it to examine a pimple that had broken out on his nose the day before. But he was bewildered to find that instead of his nose there was nothing but a bare smooth surface. Horrified, he asked for water and rubbed his eyes with a towel. There was no doubt about it: his nose was not there. He felt himself all over to make sure he was not asleep. It seemed he wasn't. Collegiate Assessor Kovalev jumped up then and shook himself. Still no nose. He called for his clothes and rushed directly to the police inspector.

But, in the meantime, a few things should be said about Kovalev to show what sort of collegiate assessor he was. Collegiate assessors who reach their positions by obtaining academic degrees cannot be compared with the collegiate assessors that used to be appointed in the Caucasus. They are two completely unrelated species. The collegiate assessors equipped with learning . . .

But Russia is a strange place and if we say something about one collegiate assessor, all of them, from Riga to Kamchatka, will take it personally. The same is true of all vocations and ranks.

Kovalev was a Caucasus-made collegiate assessor. Moreover, he had been a collegiate assessor for only two years. In order to feel distinguished and important he never referred to himself as a collegiate assessor but employed the equivalent military rank of major.

"Look here, my good woman," he used to say when he met a woman selling shirt fronts in the street, "I want you to deliver them to my place.

---

[1] There were fourteen ranks in Russian civil service established by Peter the Great. The Collegiate Assessor was the eighth rank. Although military titles were attached to the ranks, only those in the upper echelon such as generals used them.

I live on Sadovaya Street. Just ask for Major Kovalev's, anybody'll show you."

And if he met someone pretty, he would whisper to her discreetly: "You just ask for Major Kovalev's apartment, deary."

As a rule, Major Kovalev went out for a daily walk along Nevsky Avenue. The collar of his shirt was always clean and well starched. He had whiskers such as are still to be found on provincial surveyors, and architects if they happen to be Russian, among persons performing various police functions, and, in general, on men who have full faces, ruddy cheeks, and play a strong hand at certain games of chance. Whiskers of this type flow straight across the middle of the cheek up to the very nostrils.

Major Kovalev always carried with him a great quantity of seals, both seals engraved with coats of arms and others on which were carved WEDNESDAY, THURSDAY, MONDAY, and that sort of thing. He had come to Petersburg on business, namely, to find a position commensurate with his rank. He hoped, if lucky, to get a Vice-Governorship; otherwise, he would consider a post as executive in some administration. Nor was Major Kovalev averse to matrimony, as long as the bride happened to have a capital of about two hundred thousand rubles.

And now that all this has been said about the major, it can be imagined how he felt when, instead of a quite acceptable-looking, medium-sized nose, he found an absurd, smooth flatness.

And, to make things worse, there was not a cab to be seen in the street and he was forced to walk all the way wrapped in his cloak, his face covered with a handkerchief, pretending he was bleeding, and repeating to himself:

"Maybe it's just imagination. How could I possibly have lost my nose so stupidly? . . ."

He entered a tearoom simply to have a look in a mirror. Fortunately the place was empty except for waiters sweeping the floor and moving chairs around and some others who, with sleepy eyes, were carrying trays with hot buns somewhere. Yesterday's newspapers spotted with coffee were strewn around on tables and chairs.

"Well, thank heaven there's no one here," he said. "I'll be able to have a look."

Gingerly he approached the mirror and looked.

"Filth," he said, spitting, "goddammit. If only there was something to take the nose's place! But it's completely blank!"

He bit his lip in anger and, leaving the tearoom, decided that, contrary to his usual custom, he wouldn't look at the people he met or smile at anyone. Suddenly he stopped dead near the entrance door of a house. An incredible sequence of events unrolled before his eyes. A carriage stopped at the house entrance. Its door opened. A uniformed gentleman appeared.

Stooping, he jumped out of the carriage, ran up the steps and entered the house. A combination of horror and amazement swept over Kovalev when he recognized the stranger as his own nose. At this eerie sight, everything swayed before his eyes. But although he could hardly stand on his feet, he felt compelled to wait until the nose returned to the carriage. He waited, shaking as though he had malaria.

After two minutes or so, the nose emerged from the house. He wore a gold-braided, brightly colored uniform, buckskin breeches, a three-cornered hat, and a saber. The plumes on his hat indicated the rank of state councilor. From everything else it could be inferred that he was setting off on some sort of official visit. He looked left, then right, called out to the coachman to bring the carriage up to the very door, got in and was off.

This almost drove poor Kovalev insane. He could no longer think coherently about the whole affair. No, really, how was it possible that the nose, until yesterday on his face, utterly incapable of walking or driving around, should show up like this today and, what's more, wearing a uniform! And Kovalev ran after the carriage, which, luckily for him, did not have far to go. It stopped before Kazan Cathedral.

Kovalev reached the spot and, rushing after the nose, had to elbow his way through a throng of old beggar-women who used to make him laugh because of the way they kept their faces completely wrapped in rags, leaving only slits for their eyes. He entered the cathedral. There were a few worshipers around, all standing near the entrance. Kovalev was in such a depressed state that he could not possibly muster the strength to pray and instead his eyes scrutinized every recess in search of the gentleman. Finally he discovered him standing in a corner. The nose's face was completely concealed by his high, stand-up collar and he was praying with an expression of the utmost piety.

"How shall I address him?" Kovalev wondered. "From his uniform, his hat, everything about him, he must be a state councilor. Damned if I know what to do. . . ."

He approached and cleared his throat. But the nose never even changed his pious posture and remained absorbed in his worship.

"Excuse me, sir . . ." Kovalev said, scraping up all his courage.

"Yes?" the nose said, turning around.

"I don't know how to put it, sir . . . I would say . . . it seems . . . it seems you ought to know where you belong, and where do I find you? Of all places, in church. You must surely agree——"

"Pardon me, but I can make neither head nor tail of what you're saying. Just what do you want?"

Kovalev tried to think how he could explain to the nose what he had in mind and, taking a deep breath, said:

"Of course, sir, for my part . . . but, after all, I am a major, you know, and it's most improper, in my position to walk around without a nose. Some old woman selling peeled oranges by the Voskresensky Bridge might be able to get along without a nose. But for someone who is almost certain of a high administrative appointment . . . you can judge for yourself, sir. I really fail to understand . . ." At this point Kovalev shrugged. "You'll excuse me, but if this affair were handled according to the code of honor and duty . . . You can see for yourself——"

"I don't see anything," the nose said. "Kindly come to the point."

"Sir," Kovalev said with dignity, "I don't know how to interpret your words. The matter is quite clear, I believe. Unless you are trying . . . Don't you realize that you are my nose?"

The nose looked at the major and frowned slightly.

"You're mistaken, sir. I'm all on my own. Moreover, there couldn't possibly have been close relations between us. Judging by your dress, you must be employed by the Senate, or possibly by the Ministry of Justice, whereas my field is science."

And having said this, the nose turned away and resumed his prayers.

Kovalev was now completely at a loss. Then he heard the pleasant rustle of a feminine dress. He saw a middle-aged lady covered with lace and, with her, a pretty, slender thing in a white dress which set off a very moving waistline, and with a straw hat as light as whipped cream. Behind them walked a tall man with side whiskers and a very complicated collar.

Kovalev worked his way toward them, pulled up the spotless collar of his shirt front to make sure it showed, straightened the seals that hung on a golden chain, and concentrated his attention on the young lady who, like a spring blossom, raised her white hand with its half-transparent fingers to her forehead. And Kovalev's smile spread twice as wide when, under the hat, he made out a chin of a tender whiteness and a cheek touched by the early spring coloring of a rose. But then he jumped back as though burned. He had remembered that instead of a nose he had absolutely nothing, and the tears sprang to his eyes.

He turned to the gentleman dressed as a state councilor to tell him that he was nothing but a fraud and a crook, nothing but his, Kovalev's, personally owned nose.

But the nose was nowhere to be seen. He must have driven off on another official visit.

Kovalev was in despair. He retraced his steps, stopped for a while under the colonnade, and looked intently around him in the hope of catching sight of the nose. He remembered that the nose had had a plumed hat and a gold-braided uniform, but he hadn't noticed his greatcoat, or the color of his carriage, or his horses, or even whether he had had a footman up behind him and, if so, what livery he wore. And then there were so many carriages rushing back and forth, all going so fast that he would have had difficulty in picking one out and no way of stopping it anyway. It was a lovely sunny day. Nevsky Avenue was thronged with people; from the central police station to Anichkin Bridge, ladies poured over the sidewalks in a colorful cascade. There went an acquaintance of his, a court councilor, whom he addressed as Lieutenant-Colonel, especially in the presence of outsiders. Then Kovalev saw Yaryzhkin, head clerk in the Senate, a good friend who always lost whenever they played cards together. And there was another major, another Caucasus-made collegiate assessor, beckoning . . .

"Goddammit," Kovalev said, "what the hell does he want from me? Cabbie! To the police commissioner's!"

He got into the cab and kept exhorting the cabbie again and again: "Come on, let's go! Quick! Now turn into Ivanovskaya Street."

"Is the Commissioner in?" he called out, as soon as he entered the house.

"No, sir," the doorman answered. "He left only a minute ago."

"That's really too much [illegible]"

"Yes, sir," the doorman said. "If you'd come a minute earlier, you'd have caught him."

Kovalev, still holding his handkerchief to his face, got back into the cab and shouted in a desperate voice:

"Get going."

"Where to?"

"Straight ahead."

"Straight ahead? But this is a dead end. Shall I go right or left?"

Kovalev was caught off balance and forced to give the matter some thought. In his position, he ought first to go to the National Security Administration, not because it was directly connected with the police, but because its orders would be acted on more rapidly than those of others.

Certainly it was no use taking his grievance to the scientific department where the nose claimed to have a post. At best, it would be unwise, since, judging by his statement that he had never seen Kovalev before, it was obvious that he held nothing sacred and he might lie whenever he found it convenient. So Kovalev was about to tell the cabman to drive him to the National Security Administration when it occurred to him that the crook and impostor, who had just behaved so unscrupulously toward him, might very well try to slip out of town, in which case finding him would be quite hopeless or would take, God forbid, a whole month perhaps. Finally, he had what seemed like a divine inspiration. He decided to go straight to the Press Building to have an advertisement put in the papers with a detailed description of the nose in all his aspects, so that anyone who met him could turn him over to Kovalev, or at least inform him of the nose's whereabouts.

So, having decided this, he told the cabman to take him to the Press Building and, during the entire ride, he kept pommeling him on the back with his fist and shouting:

"Faster, damn you! Faster!"

"Really, sir!" the cabman said, shaking his head and flicking the reins at his horse, which had hair as long as a lap dog's.

At last the cab came to a stop, and Kovalev, panting, burst into the small outer office where a gray-haired, bespectacled employee in an ancient frock coat was seated at a table, his pen clenched between his teeth, counting out the change someone had paid in.

"Who handles advertisements here?" shouted Kovalev. "Ah," he said, "good morning!"

"Good morning, sir," the gray-haired employee said, raising his eyes for a moment and lowering them again to the little piles of coins before him.

"I want to insert—"

"Excuse me. Would you mind waiting just a moment, please," the employee said, writing down a figure with his right hand while his left hand moved two beads on his abacus.

A footman, whose gold-braided livery and whole appearance testified to his service in an aristocratic house, stood by the old employee holding a piece of paper in his hand and, to prove his worldliness, started chattering away:

"Believe me, I'm quite sure the mutt isn't worth eighty kopeks. In fact, I wouldn't give eight kopeks, if you ask me. But the Countess loves that cur—she has to if she's willing to give a hundred rubles to the person who finds it. Since we are among people who understand, I'll tell you one thing: it's all a matter of taste. I can understand a dog lover. But then, go and get a deerhound or maybe a poodle. Then, if you want to spend five hundred or a thousand on it, it's only natural. But, in my opinion, when you pay you are entitled to a *real* dog. . . ."

The elderly employee was listening to this spech with an important expression and was counting the number of letters in the text of the advertisement the manservant had handed him. The room was full of old women, shopkeepers, and doormen, all holding pieces of paper on which advertisements had been written out. In one a coachman, sober and dependable, was for hire; another announced that a carriage with very little mileage, brought from Paris in 1814, was for sale; a nineteen year old girl, a washerwoman's assistant, but suitable for other work too, wanted employment; also for sale were an excellent hansom cab (one spring missing) and a young, seventeen-year-old, dappled-gray horse, as well as a consignment of turnip and radish seeds straight from London, a summer house with a two-carriage coach house and a piece of land very suitable for planting a lovely birch wood.

Another advertisement invited persons desirous of buying secondhand shoe soles to present themselves in a certain salesroom between 8 A.M. and 3 P.M.

The reception room in which all these people waited was quite small and the air was getting stuffy. But the smell didn't bother Collegiate Assessor Kovalev because he kept his face covered with a handkerchief and also because his nose happened to be God knew where.

"Excuse me, sir . . . I don't want to bother you, but this is an emergency," he said impatiently at last.

"Wait, wait . . . two rubles, forty-three kopeks, please. One minute, please! . . . One ruble, sixty-four, over there . . ." the old employee said, shoving sheets of paper under the noses of porters and old women. "Now, what can I do for you?" he said finally, turning to Kovalev.

"I wanted," Kovalev said, "to ask you to . . . a fraud, or perhaps a theft, has been committed. I'm still not clear. I want you to run an advertisement simply saying that whoever delivers that robber to me will get a handsome reward."

"Your name, please."

"My name? What for? I can't tell you my name. I have too many acquaintances, such as Mrs. Chekhtareva, the wife of a civil servant, and Palageya Grigorievna Podtochina, who's married to Captain Podtochin, an officer on the Army General Staff. . . . Suppose they found out, God forbid. Write simply 'a collegiate assessor' or, better still, 'a major.' "

"And the runaway, was he a household serf?"

"A household serf. That wouldn't be half so vicious a crime. The runaway is my nose . . . yes, my own nose. . . ."

"Hm . . . odd name. And now may I inquire the sum, the amount, of which this Mr. Nose has defrauded you?"

"No, no, you don't understand. I said nose. My own nose, which has disappeared God knows where. I am the victim of some foul joke. . . ."

"But how could it disappear? I still don't understand, sir."

"Well, I can't explain how, but the main thing is that he mustn't go all over town impersonating a state councilor. That's why I want you to advertise that anyone who catches him should contact me as quickly as possible. Besides, imagine how I feel with such a conspicuous part of my body missing. It's not just a matter of, say, a toe. You could simply stick your foot into your shoe and no one would be the wiser. On Thursdays, I usually visit Mrs. Chekhtareva, the wife of a state councilor. . . . And Mrs. Podtochina, the wife of the staff officer, has an extremely pretty daughter. They are close friends of mine, you see, and now tell me, what am I to do? . . . How can I show myself to them?"

The employee was thinking hard, as could be seen from his tightly pressed lips.

"I am sorry, sir, but I cannot accept your advertisement," he said, after a long silence.

"What's that! Why?"

"I just can't. A newspaper could lose its good name if everybody started advertising vagrant noses. . . . No, sir, as it is, too many absurdities and unfounded rumors manage to slip into print."

"Why is it absurd? I don't see anything so unusual about it."

"It may look that way to you. But just let me tell you . . . Last week, for instance, a government employee came to see me just as you have now. I even remember that his advertisement came to two rubles, seventy-three kopeks. But what it all boiled down to was that a black poodle had run away. You'd think there was nothing to it, wouldn't you? But wait. Turned out to be deliberate libel because the poodle in question happened to be the treasurer of I can't recall exactly what."

"But listen, I'm not advertising about a poodle but about my own nose which is the same as myself."

"Sorry, I can't accept the advertisement."

"But I have lost my nose!"

"If you have, it is a matter for a doctor. I've heard that there are specialists who can fit you with any sort of nose you want. But I'm beginning to think that you are one of these cheerful people who likes to have his little joke."

"But I swear to you by all that's holy! And if it comes to that, I'll show you."

"Why take the trouble," the employee said, taking a pinch of snuff. "But then, after all, if you really don't mind," he added, making a slight movement indicating curiosity, "why, I wouldn't mind having a look."

Kovalev removed the handkerchief from his face.

"My! It *is* strange!" the employee said. "Why, it's as flat as a fresh-cooked pancake, incredibly smooth!"

"Well, now you won't refuse to run my advertisement, will you? It simply must be published. I will be very much obliged to you, and I'm very happy that this accident has given me a chance to make your acquaintance. . . ."

The major, it can be seen, had decided that he'd better make up to him a bit.

"Certainly, running it is no great problem," the employee said, "but I don't see that it would do you any good. However, if you absolutely want to see it in print, why not entrust it to someone who can really write and ask him to present it as a rare natural phenomenon and have it published in the *Northern Bee*"[2]—here he took another pinch of snuff—"for the edification

[2] A reactionary Petersburg journal which supported Nicholas I and which criticized Gogol.

of the young"—here he wiped his nose—"or just as a matter of general interest."

The collegiate assessor was taken aback. He lowered his eyes and his glance happened to fall on the theatrical announcements at the bottom of the page of a newspaper. His face was just about to break into a smile at the sight of the name of a very pretty actress and his hand had already plunged into his pocket to see whether he had a five-ruble bill on him, since, in his opinion, an officer of his rank should sit in the stalls, when he remembered the nose and everything was ruined.

The employee, too, seemed touched by Kovalev's awkward position. To alleviate his distress, he thought it would be appropriate to express his sympathy in a few words:

"I'm very sorry that such a painful thing should have happened to you. Perhaps you'd feel better if you took a pinch of snuff. It eases people's headaches and cheers them up. It's even good for hemorrhoids."[3]

As he said this, the employee offered Kovalev his snuffbox, rather deftly folding back the lid which had a picture on it of some lady in a hat.

At this unintentional provocation, Kovalev's patience snapped.

"I simply don't understand how you can make a joke of it," he said angrily. "Can't you see that I am missing just what I would need to take a pinch of snuff with? You know what you can do with your snuff! I can't even look at it now, especially not at your cheap Berezinsky brand. You might at least have offered me something better. . . ."

Incensed, he rushed out of the Press Building. He decided to take his case to the borough Police Commissioner.

At the moment when Kovalev entered the office of the Commissioner, the latter had just finished stretching himself and reflecting:

"I might as well treat myself to a nap. A couple of hours or so."

Thus it would have been easy to predict that the major's visit was rather poorly timed. Incidentally, the Commissioner, though a great lover of the arts and of commerce, still preferred a bill put in circulation by the Imperial Russian Bank over anything else. His opinion on the matter was as follows:

"It has everything: it doesn't have to be fed, it doesn't take up much room, and, in any case, can always be fitted into a pocket. If you drop it, it doesn't break."

The Commissioner was rather cold with Kovalev. Right after a meal, he said, was not the proper time for investigations. Nature itself, he said, dictated rest when one's belly was full. From this, the collegiate assessor was

---

[3] They were called "the Petersburg disease" because of their prevalence among government clerks and officials.

able to gather that the Commissioner was rather familiar with the maxims of the wise men of antiquity.

"Moreover," the Commisioner said, "they don't tear noses off decent citizens' faces."

Bull's-eye! We must note here that Kovalev was quick to take offense. He could forgive anything that was said about himself personally, but he couldn't stand anything that he considered a slur on his rank and position. He even held the view that, in dramatic works, while a disparaging reference to subaltern ranks was permissible, it became intolerable when applied to officers above the rank of captain. He was so disconcerted by the reception given him by the Commissioner that he shook his head slightly, shrugged, and on his way out, said in a dignified tone:

"Well, I must say . . . after your offensive remarks I have nothing further to add."

He reached home hardly able to feel his feet beneath him. It was getting dark. After his futile search, his place looked sad and repulsive. As he walked in, he saw Ivan, his manservant, lying on his back on the old leather divan in the entrance hall spitting at the ceiling—very successfully it must be said. Ivan was hitting the same spot again and again. But such indifference enraged Kovalev. He hit him on the head with his hat and said bitterly:

"Swine! You think of nothing but trivialities."

Ivan jumped up and started anxiously to help Kovalev off with his coat.

The major went into his room and let himself fall into an armchair, sad and exhausted. He let out a few sighs, after which he said:

"Good heavens! Why is all this happening to *me?* What have *I* done wrong? It would have been better to have lost an arm or a leg. It would have been bad enough without ears, yet still bearable. But without a nose a man is not a man but God knows what—neither fish nor fowl. He can't even be a proper citizen any more. If only I had had it lopped off during a war or in a duel or if *I* had been responsible for the loss. But I lost it for no reason and for nothing; I haven't even got a kopek out of it! No, it's impossible," he added after a pause, "it is impossible that the nose could have disappeared. Incredible! It is probably a dream or just a hallucination . . . maybe, by mistake, I drank a glassful of the vodka with which I rub my face after shaving? That fool Ivan must have forgotten to put it away and I must have swallowed it inadvertently."

To prove to himself that he was really drunk, the major pinched himself so hard that he let out a moan. The pain convinced him that he was quite sober. Then, slowly, as though stalking something, he approached the mirror, his eyes half closed, in the vague hope that, who knows, perhaps the nose would be in its proper place. But immediately he jumped away.

"What a slanderous sight!"

It was really quite bewildering. Many things get lost: a button, a silver spoon, a watch, or some such object. But to disappear just like that. . . . And what's more, in his own apartment! Having weighed the matter, Major Kovalev came to what seemed to be the most likely explanation: the culprit behind it all was Mrs. Podtochina, who wanted him to marry her daughter. He rather enjoyed the girl's company himself but he was just not ready for a final decision. And when Mrs. Podtochina had told him plainly that she wanted him to marry her daughter, he had quietly beaten a polite retreat, saying that he was still very young and that he ought to devote another five years or so to his career, after which he would be at least forty-two. So, probably, that was when Mrs. Podtochina had decided to maim him and had hired witches or something for the purpose, because by no stretch of the imagination could it be assumed that the nose had been cut off; no one had entered his bedroom; Ivan Yakovlevich, the barber, hadn't shaved him since Wednesday and during the rest of that day and even on Thursday, his nose, all in one piece, had been on his face. He was absolutely certain of it. Moreover, had the nose been cut off he would have felt pain and the wound could never have healed so fast and become as smooth as a pancake. . . .

All sorts of plans clashed in his head: should he take the lady to court or would it be better to go directly to her and denounce her to her face? But his thoughts were interrupted by light seeping in through the cracks in the door, indicating that Ivan had lit a candle in the entrance hall. Soon Ivan appeared carrying the candle high above his head, lighting up the entire room. Kovalev's first thought was to grab the handkerchief and cover the place where, only yesterday, the nose had sat, so that this stupid man should not stand there gaping, noticing the peculiar state of his master's face.

But no sooner had Ivan left than he heard an unknown voice coming from the apartment door ask:

"Does Collegiate Assessor Kovalev live here?"

"Come in. Major Kovalev is in," Kovalev shouted, jumping up and rushing into the hall.

It was a police officer, a quite handsome man with whiskers neither too light nor too dark and with rather full cheeks. In fact it was the same one who, at the beginning of this story, had been standing by the Isakievsky Bridge.

"Did you happen to lose your nose, sir?"

"Yes, I did."

"It has been found."

"Is it possible?"

Joy paralyzed the major's tongue. He stared at the police officer standing in front of him, the reflection of the candlelight shining on his damp, full lips.

"How did it happen?" he managed to say at last.

"By sheer coincidence. Your nose was caught as he was getting on the stagecoach for Riga. He had a passport made out in the name of a government official and the strange thing is that, at first, I myself took him for a gentleman. But luckily I had my glasses with me, so I put them on and recognized immediately that he was a nose. The thing is, I am very shortsighted, sir, and with you standing right in front of me there, I can make out your face but I can't discern your beard, or your nose, or anything else. My mother-in-law, that's the mother of my wife, can't see a thing either."

Kovalev was beside himself with excitement.

"Where is he? Where? I'll run over there now. . . ."

"Don't trouble, sir. I thought you might need it, so I brought it along. But you know, the funny part about it is that the main suspect in the affair is the barber from Voznesensky Avenue, a crook who's now being held at the police station. I've had my eye on him for some time because I suspected him of being a thief and a drunkard. As a matter of fact, he lifted a box of buttons in a store the other day. By the way, your nose is exactly as before, sir."

Saying this, the police officer put his hand in his pocket and extracted the nose wrapped in a piece of paper.

"That's it! That's it!" Kovalev shouted. "No doubt about it! Do come in and have some tea with me, won't you?"

"It would be a great honor, sir, but I am afraid I can't. I must stop over at the house of correction—prices are going up, sir. . . . My mother-in-law, I mean the wife's mother, is living with me . . . we have children too. The eldest son is particularly promising, a very clever boy, but we have no money for his education. . . ."

When the police officer had left, the collegiate assessor remained for some minutes in an indeterminate state, just barely able to see and feel. It was his immense joy that had plunged him into his halfconsciousness. Very carefully he held his just-recovered nose in his cupped hands and once again looked it over.

"Yes, that's it, that's it all right. And here, on the left side, is the pimple that sprang up the other day."

The major almost shouted with pleasure.

But there is nothing long-lived in this world and one's joy in the minute that follows the first is no longer as vivid. It further weakens during the third and finally dissolves into one's everyday state just as the circles produced on the surface of a pond by the fall of a pebble dissolve into the smooth surface. Kovalev began to ponder and realized that his troubles were not quite over: the nose had been found. That was fine; but it still had to be put back, fixed in its old place.

"And what if it doesn't stick?"

As he asked himself this question, the major turned white.

With inexpressible anxiety he leapt toward his dressing table and pulled the mirror closer, fearing that he would stick the nose on crooked. His hands trembled. Finally, with infinite hesitations and precautions he pressed the nose into place. Oh, horror! It wouldn't stick! He brought it close to his mouth and warmed it slightly with his breath. Then he placed it again on top of the smooth area between his two cheeks. But the nose would not stay on.

"Come on! Come on now! Stick—you fool!" Kovalev told the nose again and again. But the nose felt as if it were made of wood and kept falling off. And as it hit the dressing table it produced a queer light sound, like a cork. The major's face twisted spasmodically. Panic pervaded him.

"Can it possibly *not* stick?"

He repeatedly pressed the nose against the approximate spot, but his efforts were futile. Then he decided to send Ivan to fetch the doctor who occupied the best apartment in the house where the major lived.

The doctor was a fine figure of a man. He had pitch-black whiskers and a quite fresh and healthy wife. Furthermore, he ate fresh apples in the morning and kept his mouth in a state of incredible cleanliness, rinsing it for about three-quarters of an hour at a time and then brushing his teeth with five different kinds of toothbrush.

The doctor arrived within the minute. Having asked the major how long ago the misfortune had struck, he grabbed him by the chin and tweaked him so hard on the former site of his nose that Kovalev recoiled violently and banged the back of his head against the wall. The doctor said that it was quite all right and, advising him to move a bit further away from the wall, ordered him to bend his head to the right, felt the spot vacated by the nose with his fingers and said, "Hmmm . . ." Then he asked him to bend his head to the left, touched the spot again and said, "Hmmm. . . ." Finally the doctor delivered another tweak with his thumb and forefinger, making Kovalev toss up his head like a horse whose teeth are being inspected.

Having thus completed his examination, the doctor shook his head and declared:

"No. Can't be done. You'd better stay as you are or your condition might deteriorate even further. Of course, it is possible to stick it on. I could have stuck it on now. But, take my advice, that would make it worse for you."

"That's fine! And how can I stay without a nose? And how could I be worse off than I am? It is absolutely disgusting! And where can I show myself in this obscene condition? I have an active social life. Why, even today I was invited to two important parties. And I have many connections . . . Mrs. Chekhtareva, the wife of a state councilor, Mrs. Podtochina, the wife of a senior army officer . . . although after this business I don't want to have anything to do with her, except through the police. . . ."

And Kovalev added imploringly:

"Do me a great favor, Doctor, can't you think of a way? Make it stick somehow. It doesn't matter if it doesn't hold too well—just as long as it stays on somehow. I could even support it with my hand in case of emergency. I don't even dance, you know, and so couldn't jeopardize it by some inadvertent jerk. As to my appreciation of your services, please rest assured that in the measure of my resources . . ."

"Believe it or not," the doctor said neither too loudly nor too softly but with persuasiveness and magnetic force, "I never dispense my services out of material considerations. It would be contrary to my principles and to professional ethics. True, I do charge for my visits but only in order not to offend people by refusing to accept a fee. Of course I could stick your nose back on, but I assure you, on my honor, if you won't take my simple word for it, that it will be much worse. You're better off letting things take their natural course. Wash often with cold water and I assure you that you'll feel just as healthy without a nose as you felt with one. As to the nose, you can put it in a jar of alcohol or, better still, add two soupspoonfuls of vodka and warmed-up vinegar to it. I'll bet you could make money out of it. In fact, I'd purchase it myself if it weren't too expensive."

"No, no! I'll never sell it," shouted the desolate major, "I'd rather it disappeared again!"

"Forgive me," the doctor said, "I was simply trying to help. Well, I can do no more. At least you see that I tried."

The doctor departed with dignity. Kovalev had not even looked at his face, dazed as he was, he was only aware of the spotless white cuffs sticking out of the black sleeves of the doctor's frock coat.

The next day Kovalev decided to write to Mrs. Podtochina asking her to restore to him voluntarily what was rightfully his and saying that otherwise he would be forced to lodge a complaint. The letter he composed read as follows:

Dear Madam,

I am at a loss to understand your strange action. Rest assured that you will achieve nothing by acting this way, and you certainly won't force me to marry your daughter. Please believe me, Madam, that I am fully aware of exactly what happened to my nose as well as of the fact that you, and nobody else, are the prime instigator of this affair. Its sudden detachment from its assigned place, its desertion, and its masquerading first as a state councilor and then in its natural shape is nothing but the result of witchcraft practiced by you or by those specialized in such pursuits. For my part, I deem it my duty to warn you that if the above-mentioned nose is not back in its proper place this very day, I shall be forced to avail myself of my rights and ask for the protection of the law.

I remain,
Faithfully yours,
Platon Kovalev.

To which the lady sent an immediate reply:

My dear Platon,

I was very surprised by your letter. To be perfectly frank, I never expected anything of this kind from you, especially your unfair reproaches. For your information, I have never received the state councilor you mention at my house, either in disguise or in his natural shape. However, I did receive Philip Ivanovich, but, despite the fact that he asked me for my daughter's hand and was a man of irreproachable character, sober habits, and great learning, I never held out any hopes for him. You also mention your nose. If you mean it symbolically, that I wanted you to stop nosing around my daughter, i.e., that I had decided to refuse you her hand, I am surprised at your saying such things when you are fully aware of my feelings on the subject, namely that, if you asked for her hand formally tomorrow, I would be prepared to grant your request forthwith, since it has always been in agreement with my wishes and in hope of which,

I remain,
Always at your service,
Alexandra Podtochina.

"She," Kovalev said, after he had read the letter, "is certainly not involved. Someone guilty of a crime couldn't write such a letter."

And the collegiate assessor knew what he was talking about because he had taken part in several judicial investigations back in the Caucasus.

"But then, how the devil did it happen, after all? How'll I ever get it straight?" he said, dropping his arms to his sides.

In the meantime, rumors about the extraordinary occurrence spread all over the capital and, as was to be expected, not without all sorts of embellishments. At that time people were prone to fall for supernatural things: only a short time before, experiments with magnetism had caused a sensation. Also, the story about the dancing chairs of Stables Street[4] was still fresh, and people soon began to repeat that Collegiate Assessor Kovalev's nose was to be seen taking a daily walk on Nevsky Avenue at 3:00 P.M. sharp. And every day a multitude of the curious gathered there. Then someone said that the nose was in Junker's Department Store, and, as a result, such a melee developed there that the police had to interfere. A shady character with side whiskers, who nevertheless looked very respectable, and who sold all sorts of dry cakes at the entrance to the theater, got hold of some special wooden benches, perfectly safe to stand on, and invited the curious to do so for a fee of eighty kopeks per person. A highly respected colonel, who had left his home especially early for this purpose, managed to make his way through the dense throng with great difficulty only to see in the display window not a nose but an ordinary woollen sweater and a lithograph of a girl pulling up her stocking with a well-dressed gentleman wearing a waistcoat with lapels and a small beard, a lithograph that had rested there, in the identical spot, for more than ten years. As the colonel left, he declared:

"It shouldn't be allowed—befuddling people with such stupid and improbable rumors!"

Then a rumor spread that Major Kovalev's nose was taking promenades, not on Nevsky Avenue, but in the Tavrichesky Gardens, and that it had been doing so for some time now. In fact, even when Khosrov Mirza lived there he used to marvel at this freak of nature. Students from the School of Surgeons went there. One socially prominent lady wrote a special letter to the director of the park suggesting that he show this rare object to children, if possible with explanations and instructions that would edify the younger generation.

All this was quite welcome to those who never miss a party and like to display their wit before the ladies; without it topics of conversation would have been exhausted. But there was also a dissatisfied and displeased minority among respectable people. One gentleman said he could not understand how it was possible in our enlightened age for such preposterous lies to be believed and that he was flabbergasted at the passivity of the authorities. Apparently this gentleman was one of those who desire the government to interfere in everything, including his daily fights with his wife.

Following these events . . . but here again, things become beclouded and what followed these events has remained completely unknown.

---

[4] There were rumors throughout Petersburg in December, 1833, of dancing chairs over the royal stables.

III

The world is full of absolute nonsense. Sometimes it is really unbelievable. Suddenly, the very nose that used to go around as a state councilor and caused such a stir all over the city turned up, as though nothing had happened, in its proper place, namely between the cheeks of Major Kovalev. This happened on April 7. Waking up and chancing to glance in the mirror, what did he see but his nose! He grabbed it with his hand—no doubt about it—it was his nose, all right!

"Aha!" Kovalev said.

And in his infinite joy he would have performed a jig, barefoot as he was, had not Ivan come in at that moment. He ordered Ivan to bring him some water to wash with and, while washing, looked again into the mirror: he had his nose. Drying himself with his towel, he looked again—the nose was as still there!

"Here, Ivan, look, I think I have a pimple on my nose," he said, all the while thinking anxiously: "Wouldn't it be terrible if Ivan came out with something like, 'No, sir, not only is there no pimple on your nose, there is no nose on your face.' "

But Ivan simply said:

"Nothing, sir, I see no pimple, the nose is clear."

"Feels good, dammit!" the major said to himself and snapped his fingers gaily.

At that moment, through the partly opened door, there appeared the head of Ivan Yakovlevich, the barber, wearing the expression of a cat that had just been smacked for the theft of a piece of suet.

"Your hands clean?" Kovalev shouted out to him.

"They're clean, sir."

"Liar!"

"I swear they're clean."

"You know, they'd better be."

Kovalev sat down. The barber wrapped a towel around his neck and in one instant transformed the major's whiskers and a part of his cheek into whipped cream of the kind that is likely to be served at a birthday party in the house of a rich merchant.

"Well, I'll be damned!" Ivan Yakovlevich muttered under his breath, looking at the nose. Then he turned the major's head and looked at the nose from the other side and muttered. "Well, well, well . . . who would have thought . . ." and he stared at the nose for a moment.

Then, with a daintiness that can only be imagined, he lifted two fingers to catch the nose by its tip. Such was Ivan Yakovlevich's shaving style.

"Look out, look out, careful!" Kovalev shouted and IvanYakovlevich dropped his hand and stood there frozen and embarrassed as never before. Finally he snapped out of it and started carefully tickling the major under his chin with the razor. And although it felt quite awkward and unusual for him to shave someone without holding him by the olfactory organ of the human body, he managed, somehow, by resting his rough thumb on Kovalev's cheek, then on his lower gum, to overcome all the obstacles and complete the shaving operation.

When he was through being shaved Kovalev hurried to get dressed, rushed out, took a cab and drove to the tearoom. Before even sitting down, he shouted: "Waiter, a cup of chocolate!" then rushed over to the mirror: the nose was there. Happy, he glanced around the room and twisted his face into a sarcastic expression by slightly screwing up his eyes, when he saw two army officers, one of whom had a nose about the size of a waistcoat button. Then he left for the department through which he was trying to get the vice-gubernatorial post or, failing that, a position in the administration. Walking through the reception room, he glanced in the mirror: the nose was in its place.

Then he drove to see another collegiate assessor, that is, a major like himself. This major was a biting wit, and, parrying his digs, Kovalev would often say to him:

"Oh, I see through you clearly, you needler!"

On his way there, Kovalev thought: "Now, if the major does not split his sides with laughter when he sees me, that will be a sure sign that whatever I may have is sitting in its proper place."

And when the other collegiate assessor showed no signs of hilarity, Kovalev thought:

"Fine! It feels good, it feels good, dammit!"

In the street he met Mrs. Podtochina and her daughter and was greeted with joyful exclamations which went to show that they did not find he was missing anything. He had a very long talk with them and, on purpose, took out his snuffbox and filled his nose with great deliberation, through both orifices, muttering under his breath:

"Here, look and admire, you hens! But still, I won't marry the daughter, just *par amour* as they say, but nothing more. . . ."

And from then on, Major Kovalev could be seen on Nevsky Avenue, in theaters, everywhere. And the nose was there, sitting on his face, as though nothing had happened. And after that, Major Kovalev was always in good spirits, smiling, pursuing absolutely every pretty lady without exception and even stopping one day in front of a small shop and purchasing some sort of ribbon for his lapel, although his reason for doing so remained a mystery because he had never been made a knight of any order.

So that's what happened in the northern capital of our vast country. Only now, on further thought, do we see that there is much that is improbable in it. Without even mentioning the strangeness of such a supernatural severance of the nose and its appearance in various places in the form of a state councilor, how could Kovalev have failed to understand that he could not go and advertise about a nose in the press? I don't mean that I think that an advertisement would have cost too much, that would be nonsense and I'm not stingy; but it's not decent, it's not clever, and it's not proper! And then too, how could the nose have got into the roll of bread, and how could Ivan Yakovlevich himself? . . . Now, that I cannot understand. It's absolutely beyond me. But strangest of all, the most incomprehensible thing, is that there are authors who can choose such subjects to write about. This, I confess, is completely inexplicable, it's like . . . no, no I can't understand it at all. In the first place there is absolutely no advantage in it for our mother country. Secondly . . . well, what advantage is there in it at all? I simply cannot understand what it is. . . .

However, when all is said and done, and although, of course, we conceive the possibility, one and the other and maybe even . . . Well, but then what exists without inconsistencies? And still, if you give it a thought, there *is* something to it. Whatever you may say, such things *do* happen—seldom, but they do.

Questions for Discussion

1. How is Kovalev's discovery of the loss of his nose similar to the barber's discovery of the nose in his morning roll?
2. Why does Kovalev feel out of place without his nose? Does he think of it as an abnormal situation?
3. Is Kovalev simply made fun of by Gogol or does the author intend something more serious by him?
4. Why does Kovalev see nothing unusual about advertising for a "vagrant nose"?
5. How is the return of the nose ironical?
6. How are the specific rumors of the nose throughout the capital related to the political and social themes of the story?
7. What is the narrator's attitude toward his story, the characters, and the society he describes?
8. Is the story realistic or fantastic in its handling of the comic or a combination of the two? In the first version of the story Gogol ended with the hero waking to realize the whole thing "was only a dream." Why do you think he deleted this ending?
9. The story has been called a "savage joke on ordinary life." How much truth do you think there is to such an interpretation?
10. One of the features of Gogol's humor is his emphasis on realistic details that are absurdly exaggerated such as the doctor with "five different kinds of toothbrush." What is the purpose of such details and how do they suit this particular story?

James Joyce (1882-1941)

The Boarding House

Mrs. Mooney was a butcher's daughter. She was a woman who was quite able to keep things to herself: a determined woman. She had married her father's foreman and opened a butcher's shop near Spring Gardens. But as soon as his father-in-law was dead Mr. Mooney began to go to the devil. He drank, plundered the till, ran head-long into debt. It was no use making him take the pledge: he was sure to break out again a few days after. By fighting his wife in the presence of customers and by buying bad meat he ruined his business. One night he went for his wife with the cleaver and she had to sleep in a neighbour's house.

After that they lived apart. She went to the priest and got a separation from him with care of the children. She would give him neither money nor food nor house-room; and so he was obliged to enlist himself as a sheriff's man. He was a shabby stooped little drunkard with a white face and a white moustache and white eyebrows, pencilled above his little eyes, which were pink-veined and raw; and all day long he sat in the bailiff's room, waiting to be put on a job. Mrs. Mooney, who had taken what remained of her money out of the butcher business and set up a boarding house in Hardwicke Street, was a big imposing woman. Her house had a floating population made up of tourists from Liverpool and the Isle of Man and, occasionally *artistes* from the music halls. Its resident population was made up of clerks from the city. She governed the house cunningly and firmly, knew when to give credit, when to be stern and when to let things pass. All the resident young men spoke of her as *The Madam.*

Mrs. Mooney's young men paid fifteen shillings a week for board and

---

lodgings (beer or stout at dinner excluded). They shared in common tastes and occupations and for this reason they were very chummy with one another. They discussed with one another the chances of favourites and outsiders. Jack Mooney, the Madam's son, who was clerk to a commission agent in Fleet Street, had the reputation of being a hard case. He was fond of using soldiers' obscenities: usually he came home in the small hours. When he met his friends he had always a good one to tell them and he was always sure to be on to a good thing—that is to say, a likely horse or a likely *artiste*. He was also handy with the mits and sang comic songs. On Sunday nights there would often be a reunion in Mrs. Mooney's front drawing-room The music-hall *artistes* would oblige; and Sheridan played waltzes and polkas and vamped accompaniments. Polly Mooney, the Madam's daughter, would also sing. She sang:

> *"I'm a . . . naughty girl.*
> *You needn't sham:*
> *You know I am."*

Polly was a slim girl of nineteen; she had light soft hair and a small full mouth. Her eyes, which were grey with a shade of green through them, had a habit of glancing upwards when she spoke with anyone, which made her look like a little perverse madonna. Mrs. Mooney had first sent her daughter to be a typist in a corn-factor's office but, as a disreputable sheriff's man used to come every other day to the office, asking to be allowed to say a word to his daughter, she had taken her daughter home again and set her to do housework. As Polly was very lively the intention was to give her the run of the young men. Besides, young men like to feel that there is a young woman not very far away. Polly, of course, flirted with the young men but Mrs. Mooney, who was a shrewd judge, knew that the young men were only passing the time away: none of them meant business. Things went on so for a long time and Mrs. Mooney began to think of sending Polly back to typewriting when she noticed that something was going on between Polly and one of the young men. She watched the pair and kept her own counsel.

Polly knew that she was being watched, but still her mother's persistent silence could not be misunderstood. There had been no open complicity between mother and daughter, no open understanding but, though people in the house began to talk of the affair, still Mrs. Mooney did not intervene. Polly began to grow a little strange in her manner and the young man was evidently perturbed. At last, when she judged it to be the right moment, Mrs. Mooney intervened. She dealt with moral problems as a cleaver deals with meat: and in this case she had made up her mind.

It was a bright Sunday morning of early summer, promising heat, but with a fresh breeze blowing. All the windows of the boarding house were open and the lace curtains ballooned gently towards the street beneath the raised sashes. The belfry of George's Church sent out constant peals and worshippers, singly or in groups, traversed the little circus before the church, revealing their purpose by their self-contained demeanour no less than by the little volumes in their gloved hands. Breakfast was over in the boarding house and the table of the breakfast-room was covered with plates on which lay yellow streaks of eggs with morsels of bacon-fat and bacon-rind. Mrs. Mooney sat in the straw arm-chair and watched the servant Mary remove the breakfast things. She made Mary collect the crusts and pieces of broken bread to help to make Tuesday's bread-pudding. When the table was cleared, the broken bread collected, the sugar and butter safe under lock and key, she began to reconstruct the interview which she had had the night before with Polly. Things were as she had suspected: she had been frank in her questions and Polly had been frank in her answers. Both had been somewhat awkward, of course. She had been made awkward by her not wishing to receive the news in too cavalier a fashion or to seem to have connived and Polly had been made awkward not merely because allusions of that kind always made her awkward but also because she did not wish it to be thought that in her wise innocence she had divined the intention behind her mother's tolerance.

Mrs. Mooney glanced instinctively at the little gilt clock on the mantelpiece as soon as she had become aware through her revery that the bells of George's Church had stopped ringing. It was seventeen minutes past eleven: she would have lots of time to have the matter out with Mr. Doran and then catch short twelve at Marlborough Street. She was sure she would win. To begin with she had all the weight of social opinion on her side: she was an outraged mother. She had allowed him to live beneath her roof, assuming that he was a man of honour, and he had simply abused her hospitality. He was thirty-four or thirty-five years of age, so that youth could not be pleaded as his excuse; nor could ignorance be his excuse since he was a man who had seen something of the world. He had simply taken advantage of Polly's youth and inexperience: that was evident. The question was: What reparation would he make?

There must be reparation made in such case. It is all very well for the man: he can go his ways as if nothing had happened, having had his moment of pleasure, but the girl has to bear the brunt. Some mothers would be content to patch up such an affair for a sum of money; she had known cases of it. But she would not do so. For her only one reparation could make up for the loss of her daughter's honour: marriage.

She counted all her cards again before sending Mary up to Mr. Doran's room to say that she wished to speak with him. She felt sure she would win. He was a serious young man, not rakish or loud-voiced like the others. If it had been Mr. Sheridan or Mr. Meade or Bantam Lyons her task would have been much harder. She did not think he would face publicity. All the lodgers in the house knew something of the affair; details had been invented by some. Besides, he had been employed for thirteen years in a great Catholic wine-merchant's office and publicity would mean for him, perhaps, the loss of his job. Whereas if he agreed all might be well. She knew he had a good screw for one thing and she suspected he had a bit of stuff put by.

Nearly the half-hour! She stood up and surveyed herself in the pier-glass. The decisive expression of her great florid face satisfied her and she thought of some mothers she knew who could not get their daughters off their hands.

Mr. Doran was very anxious indeed this Sunday morning. He had made two attempts to shave but his hand had been so unsteady that he had been obliged to desist. Three days' reddish beard fringed his jaws and every two or three minutes a mist gathered on his glasses so that he had to take them off and polish them with his pocket-handkerchief. The recollection of his confession of the night before was a cause of acute pain to him, the priest had drawn out every ridiculous detail of the affair and in the end had so magnified his sin that he was almost thankful at being afforded a loophole of reparation. The harm was done. What could he do now but marry her or run away? He could not brazen it out. The affair would be sure to be talked of and his employer would be certain to hear of it. Dublin is such a small city: everyone knows everyone else's business. He felt his heart leap warmly in his throat as he heard in his excited imagination old Mr. Leonard calling out in his rasping voice: "Send Mr. Doran here, please."

All his long years of service gone for nothing! All his industry and diligence thrown away! As a young man he had sown his wild oats, of course; he had boasted of his free-thinking and denied the existence of God to his companions in public-houses. But that was all passed and done with . . . nearly. He still bought a copy of *Reynolds's Newspaper* every week but he attended to his religious duties and for nine-tenths of the year lived a regular life. He had money enough to settle down on; it was not that. But the family would look down on her. First of all there was her disreputable father and then her mother's boarding house was beginning to get a certain fame. He had a notion that he was being had. He could imagine his friends talking of the affair and laughing. She *was* a little vulgar; sometimes she said "I seen" and "if I had've known." But what would grammar matter if he really loved her? He could not make up his mind whether to like her or despise her for what she had done. Of course he had done it too. His instinct urged him to remain free, not to marry. Once you are married you are done for, it said.

While he was sitting helplessly on the side of the bed in shirt and trousers she tapped lightly at his door and entered. She told him all, that she had made a clean breast of it to her mother and that her mother would speak with him that morning. She cried and threw her arms round his neck, saying:

"O Bob! Bob! What am I to do? What am I to do at all?"

She would put an end to herself, she said.

He comforted her feebly, telling her not to cry, that it would be all right, never fear. He felt against his shirt the agitation of her bosom.

It was not altogether his fault that it had happened. He remembered well, with the curious patient memory of the celibate, the first casual caresses her dress, her breath, her fingers had given him. Then late one night as he was undressing for bed she had tapped at his door, timidly. She wanted to relight her candle at his for hers had been blown out by a gust. It was her bath night. She wore a loose open combing jacket of printed flannel. Her white instep shone in the opening of her furry slippers and the blood glowed warmly behind her perfumed skin. From her hands and wrists too as she lit and steadied her candle a faint perfume arose.

On nights when he came in very late it was she who warmed up his dinner. He scarcely knew what he was eating feeling her beside him alone, at night, in the sleeping house. And her thoughtfulness! If the night was anyway cold or wet or windy there was sure to be a little tumbler of punch ready for him. Perhaps they could be happy together. . . .

They used to go upstairs together on tiptoe, each with a candle, and on the third landing exchange reluctant good-nights. They used to kiss. He remembered well her eyes, the touch of her hand and his delirium. . . .

But delirium passes. He echoed her phrase, applying it to himself: "*What am I to do?*" The instinct of the celibate warned him to hold back. But the sin was there; even his sense of honour told him that reparation must be made for such a sin.

While he was sitting with her on the side of the bed Mary came to the door and said that the missus wanted to see him in the parlour. He stood up to put on his coat and waistcoat, more helpless than ever. When he was dressed he went over to her to comfort her. It would be all right, never fear. He left her crying on the bed and moaning softly: "*O my God!*"

Going down the stairs his glasses became so dimmed with moisture that he had to take them off and polish them. He longed to ascend through the roof and fly away to another country where he would never hear again of his trouble, and yet a force pushed him downstairs step by step. The implacable faces of his employer and of the Madam stared upon his discomfiture. On the last flight of stairs he passed Jack Mooney who was coming up from the pantry nursing two bottles of *Bass*. They saluted coldly; and the lover's eyes rested for a second or two on a thick bulldog face and a pair of thick short arms. When he reached the foot of the staircase he glanced up and saw Jack regarding him from the door of the return-room.

Suddenly he remembered the night when one of the music-hall *artistes*, a little blond Londoner, had made a rather free allusion to Polly. The reunion had been almost broken up on account of Jack's violence. Everyone tried to quiet him. The music-hall *artiste*, a little paler than usual, kept smiling and saying that there was no harm meant: but Jack kept shouting at him that if any fellow tried that sort of a game on with his sister he'd bloody well put his teeth down his throat, so he would.

* * *

Polly sat for a little time on the side of the bed, crying. Then she dried her eyes and went over to the looking-glass. She dipped the end of the towel in the water-jug and refreshed her eyes with the cool water. She looked at herself in profile and readjusted a hairpin above her ear. Then she went back to the bed again and sat at the foot. She regarded the pillows for a long time and the sight of them awakened in her mind secret, amiable memories. She rested the nape of her neck against the cool iron bed-rail and fell into a revery. There was no longer any perturbation visible on her face.

She waited on patiently, almost cheerfully, without alarm, her memories gradually giving place to hopes and visions of the future. Her hopes and visions were so intricate that she no longer saw the white pillows on which her gaze was fixed or remembered that she was waiting for anything.

At last she heard her mother calling. She started to her feet and ran to the banisters.

"Polly! Polly!"

"Yes, mamma?"

"Come down, dear. Mr. Doran wants to speak to you."

Then she remembered what she had been waiting for.

Questions for Discussion

1. How does the concept of marriage in the story differ from that found in "The Merchant's Tale" and *Don Juan?*

2. Although the situation is basically a serious one, how does the author's treatment of it bring out the humorous aspects?

3. Who is the central figure—Mrs. Mooney or Mr. Doran? How are they contrasted? In particular compare their methods of handling moral problems.

4. What seems to be the narrator's view of the characters? What effect does he achieve through this view?

5. Is Polly a sentimental, a scheming, or a naive person? Does the author use her for comic effect?

Aldous Huxley (1894-1963)

Nuns at Luncheon

"What have I been doing since you saw me last?" Miss Penny repeated my question in her loud, emphatic voice. "Well, when did you see me last?"

"It must have been June," I computed.

"Was that after I'd been proposed to by the Russian General?"

"Yes; I remember hearing about the Russian General."

Miss Penny threw back her head and laughed. Her long earrings swung and rattled—corpses hanging in chains: an agreeably literary simile. And her laughter was like brass, but that had been said before.

"That was an uproarious incident. It's sad you should have heard of it. I love my Russian General story. '*Vos yeux me rendent fou.*' "[1] She laughed again.

Vos yeux—she had eyes like a hare's, flush with her head and very bright with a superficial and expressionless brightness. What a formidable woman. I felt sorry for the Russian General.

" '*Sans cœur et sans entrailles,*' "[2] she went on, quoting the poor devil's words. "Such a delightful motto, don't you think? Like '*Sans peur et sans reproche.*'[3] But let me think; what have I been doing since then?" Thoughtfully she bit into the crust of her bread with long, sharp, white teeth.

"Two mixed grills," I said parenthetically to the waiter.

"But of course," exclaimed Miss Penny suddenly. "I haven't seen you since my German trip. All sorts of adventures. My appendicitis; my nun."

"Your nun?"

---

[1] "Your eyes drive me mad."

[2] "Without heart and without guts."

[3] "Without fear and without reproach."

"My marvellous nun. I must tell you all about her."

"Do." Miss Penny's anecdotes were always curious. I looked forward to an entertaining luncheon.

"You knew I'd been in Germany this autumn?"

"Well, I didn't, as a matter of fact. But still——"

"I was just wandering round." Miss Penny described a circle in the air with her gaudily jewelled hand. She always twinkled with massive and improbable jewellery. "Wandering round, living on three pounds a week, partly amusing myself, partly collecting materials for a few little articles. 'What it Feels Like to be a Conquered Nation'—sob-stuff for the Liberal press, you know—and 'How the Hun is Trying to Wriggle out of the Indemnity,' for the other fellows. One has to make the best of all possible worlds, don't you find? But we mustn't talk shop. Well, I was wandering round, and very pleasant I found it. Berlin, Dresden, Leipzig. Then down to Munich and all over the place. One fine day I got to Grauburg. You know Grauburg? It's one of those picture-book German towns with a castle on a hill, hanging beer-gardens, a Gothic church, an old university, a river, a pretty bridge, and forests all round. Charming. But I hadn't much opportunity to appreciate the beauties of the place. The day after I arrived there—bang!—I went down with appendicitis—screaming, I may add."

"But how appalling!"

"They whisked me off to hospital, and cut me open before you could say knife. Excellent surgeon, highly efficient Sisters of Charity to nurse me—I couldn't have been in better hands. But it was a bore being tied there by the leg for four weeks—a great bore. Still, the thing had its compensations. There was my nun, for example. Ah, here's the food, thank Heaven!"

The mixed grill proved to be excellent. Miss Penny's description of the nun came to me in scraps and snatches. A round, pink, pretty face in a winged coif; blue eyes and regular features; teeth altogether too perfect—false, in fact; but the general effect extremely pleasing. A youthful Teutonic twenty-eight.

"She wasn't my nurse," Miss Penny explained. "But I used to see her quite often when she came in to have a look at the *tolle Engländerin.*[4] Her name was Sister Agatha. During the war, they told me, she had converted any number of wounded soldiers to the true faith—which wasn't surprising, considering how pretty she was."

"Did she try and convert you?" I asked.

"She wasn't such a fool." Miss Penny laughed, and rattled the miniature gallows of her ears.

I amused myself for a moment with the thought of Miss Penny's conver-

[4] Crazy Englishwoman.

sion—Miss Penny confronting a vast assembly of Fathers of the Church, rattling her earrings at their discourses on the Trinity, laughing her appalling laugh at the doctrine of the Immaculate Conception, meeting the stern look of the Grand Inquisitor with a flash of her bright, emotionless hare's eyes. What was the secret of the woman's formidableness?

But I was missing the story. What had happened? Ah yes, the gist of it was that Sister Agatha had appeared one morning, after two or three days' absence, dressed, not as a nun, but in the overalls of a hospital charwoman, with a handkerchief instead of a winged coif on her shaven head.

"Dead," said Miss Penny; "she looked as though she were dead. A walking corpse, that's what she was. It was a shocking sight. I shouldn't have thought it possible for anyone to change so much in so short a time. She walked painfully, as though she had been ill for months, and she had great burnt rings round her eyes and deep lines in her face. And the general expression of unhappiness—that was something quite appalling."

She leaned out into the gangway between the two rows of tables, and caught the passing waiter by the end of one of his coat-tails. The little Italian looked round with an expression of surprise that deepened into terror on his face.

"Half a pint of Guinness," ordered Miss Penny. "And, after this, bring me some jam roll."

"No jam roll to-day, madam."

"Damn!" said Miss Penny. "Bring me what you like, then."

She let go of the waiter's tail, and resumed her narrative.

"Where was I? Yes, I remember. She came into my room, I was telling you, with a bucket of water and a brush, dressed like a charwoman. Naturally I was rather surprised. 'What on earth are you doing, Sister Agatha?' I asked. No answer. She just shook her head, and began to scrub the floor. When she'd finished, she left the room without so much as looking at me again. 'What's happened to Sister Agatha?' I asked my nurse when she next came in. 'Can't say.'—'Won't say,' I said. No answer. It took me nearly a week to find out what really had happened. Nobody dared tell me; it was *strengst verboten*,[5] as they used to say in the good old days. But I wormed it out in the long run. My nurse, the doctor, the charwomen—I got something out of all of them. I always get what I want in the end." Miss Penny laughed like a horse.

"I'm sure you do," I said politely.

"Much obliged," acknowledged Miss Penny. "But to proceed. My information came to me in fragmentary whispers. 'Sister Agatha ran away with a man.'—Dear me!—'One of the patients.'—You don't say so.—'A criminal

[5] Strictly forbidden.

out of the jail.'—The plot thickens.—'He ran away from her.'—It seems to grow thinner again.—'They brought her back here; she's been disgraced. There's been a funeral service for her in the chapel—coffin and all. She had to be present at it—her own funeral. She isn't a nun any more. She has to do charwoman's work now, the roughest in the hospital. She's not allowed to speak to anybody, and nobody's allowed to speak to her. She's regarded as dead.' " Miss Penny paused to signal to the harassed little Italian. "My small 'Guinness,' " she called out.

"Coming, coming," and the foreign voice cried "Guinness" down the lift, and from below another voice echoed, "Guinness."

"I filled in the details bit by bit. There was our hero, to begin with; I had to bring him into the picture, which was rather difficult, as I had never seen him. But I got a photograph of him. The police circulated one when he got away; I don't suppose they ever caught him." Miss Penny opened her bag. "Here it is," she said. "I always carry it about with me; it's become a superstition. For years, I remember, I used to carry a little bit of heather tied up with string. Beautiful, isn't it? There's a sort of Renaissance look about it, don't you think? He was half-Italian, you know."

Italian. Ah, that explained it. I had been wondering how Bavaria could have produced this thin-faced creature with the big dark eyes, the finely modelled nose and chin, and the flashy lips so royally and sensually curved.

"He's certainly very superb," I said, handing back the picture.

Miss Penny put it carefully away in her bag. "Isn't he?" she said. "Quite marvellous. But his character and his mind were even better. I see him as one of those innocent, childlike monsters of iniquity who are simply unaware of the existence of right and wrong. And he had genius—the real Italian genius for engineering, for dominating and exploiting nature. A true son of the Roman aqueduct builders he was, and a brother of the electrical engineers. Only Kuno—that was his name—didn't work in water; he worked in women. He knew how to harness the natural energy of passion; he made devotion drive his mills. The commercial exploitation of love-power, that was his specialty. I sometimes wonder," Miss Penny added in a different tone, "whether I shall ever be exploited, when I get a little more middle-aged and celibate, by one of these young engineers of the passions. It would be humiliating, particularly as I've done so little exploiting from my side."

She frowned and was silent for a moment. No, decidedly, Miss Penny was not beautiful; you could not even honestly say that she had charm or was attractive. That high Scotch colouring, those hare's eyes, the voice, the terrifying laugh, and the size of her, the general formidableness of the woman. No, no, no.

"You said he had been in prison," I said. The silence, with all its implications, was becoming embarrassing.

Miss Penny sighed, looked up, and nodded. "He was fool enough," she said, "to leave the straight and certain road of female exploitation for the dangerous courses of burglary. We all have our occasional accesses of folly. They gave him a heavy sentence, but he succeeded in getting pneumonia, I think it was, a week after entering jail. He was transferred to the hospital. Sister Agatha, with her known talent for saving souls, was given him as his particular attendant. But it was he, I'm afraid, who did the converting."

Miss Penny finished off the last mouthful of the ginger pudding which the waiter had brought in lieu of jam roll.

"I suppose you don't smoke cheroots," I said, as I opened my cigar-case.

"Well, as a matter of fact, I do," Miss Penny replied. She looked sharply round the restaurant. "I must just see if there are any of those horrible little gossip paragraphers here to-day. One doesn't want to figure in the social and personal column to-morrow morning: 'A fact which is not so generally known as it ought to be, is that Miss Penny, the well-known woman journalist, always ends her luncheon with a six-inch Burma cheroot. I saw her yesterday in a restaurant—not a hundred miles from Carmelite Street—smoking like a house on fire.' You know the touch. But the coast seems to be clear, thank goodness."

She took a cheroot from the case, lit it at my proffered match, and went on talking.

"Yes, it was young Kuno who did the converting. Sister Agatha was converted back into the worldly Melpomene Fugger she had been before she became the bride of holiness."

"Melpomene Fugger?"

"That was her name. I had her history from my old doctor. He had seen all Grauburg, living and dying and propagating, for generations. Melpomene Fugger—why, he had brought little Melpel into the world, little Melpchen. Her father was Professor Fugger, the great Professor Fugger, the *berühmter Geolog.*[6] Oh yes, of course, I know the name. So well . . . He was the man who wrote the standard work on Lemuria—you know, the hypothetical continent where the lemurs come from. I showed due respect. Liberal-minded he was, a disciple of Herder, a world-burgher, as they beautifully call it over there. Anglophile, too, and always ate porridge for breakfast—up till August 1914. Then, on the radiant morning of the fifth, he renounced it for ever, solemnly and with tears in his eyes. The national food of a people who had betrayed culture and civilization—how could he go on eating it? It would stick in his throat. In future he would have a lightly boiled egg. He sounded, I thought, altogether charming. And his daughter, Melpomene—she sounded charming, too; and such thick, yellow pigtails when she was young! Her

[6] Famous geologist.

mother was dead, and a sister of the great Professor's ruled the house with an iron rod. Aunt Bertha was her name. Well, Melpomene grew up, very plump and appetizing. When she was seventeen, something very odious and disagreeable happened to her. Even the doctor didn't know exactly what it was; but he wouldn't have been surprised if it had had something to do with the then Professor of Latin, an old friend of the family's, who combined, it seems, great erudition with a horrid fondness for very young ladies."

Miss Penny knocked half an inch of cigar ash into her empty glass.

"If I wrote short stories," she went on reflectively "(but it's too much bother), I should make this anecdote into a sort of potted life history, beginning with a scene immediately after this disagreeable event in Melpomene's life. I see the scene so clearly. Poor little Melpel is leaning over the bastions of Brauburg Castle, weeping into the June night and the mulberry trees in the gardens thirty feet below. She is besieged by the memory of what happened this dreadful afternoon. Professor Engelmann, her father's old friend, with the magnificent red Assyrian beard . . . Too awful—too awful! But then, as I was saying, short stories are really too much bother; or perhaps I'm too stupid to write them. I bequeath it to you. You know how to tick these things off."

"You're generous."

"Not at all," said Miss Penny. "My terms are a ten per cent commission on the American sale. Incidentally there won't be an American sale. Poor Melpchen's history is not for the chaste public of Those States. But let me hear what you propose to do with Melpomene now you've got her on the castle bastions."

"That's simple," I said. "I know all about German university towns and castles on hills. I shall make her look into the June night, as you suggest, into the violet night with its points of golden flame. There will be the black silhouette of the castle, with its sharp roofs and hooded turrets, behind her. From the hanging beer-gardens in the town below the voices of the students, singing in perfect four-part harmony, will float up through the dark-blue spaces. '*Röslein, Röslein, Röslein rot*'[7] and '*Das Ringlein sprang in zwei*'[8]—the heart-rendingly sweet old songs will make her cry all the more. Her tears will patter like rain among the leaves of the mulberry trees in the garden below. Does that seem to you adequate?"

"Very nice," said Miss Penny. "But how are you going to bring the sex problem and all its horrors into your landscape?"

"Well, let me think." I called to memory those distant foreign summers when I was completing my education. "I know. I shall suddenly bring a

[7] "Little Rose . . . . Red" by Johann Wolfgang Goethe (1749-1832).

[8] "The Little Ring broke in two" by Joseph Freiherr von Eichendorff (1788-1857), German poet, dramatist, and novelist.

swarm of moving candles and Chinese lanterns under the mulberry trees. You imagine the rich lights and shadows, the jewel-bright leafage, the faces and moving limbs of men and women, seen for an instant and gone again. They are students and girls of the town come out to dance, this windless, blue June night, under the mulberry trees. And now they begin, thumping round and round in a ring, to the music of their own singing:

'Wir können spielen
Vio-vio-vio-lin,
Wir können spielen
Vi-o-lin.'[9]

Now the rhythm changes, quickens:

'Und wir können tanzen Bumstarara,
Bumstarara, Bumstarara,
Und wir können tanzen Bumstarara,
Bumstarara rara.'[10]

The dance becomes a rush, an elephantine prancing on the dry lawn under the mulberry trees. And from the bastion Melpomene looks down and perceives, suddenly and apocalyptically, that everything in the world is sex, sex, sex. Men and women, male and female—always the same, and all, in the light of the horror of the afternoon, disgusting. That's how I should do it, Miss Penny."

"And very nice, too. But I wish you could find a place to bring in my conversation with the doctor. I shall never forget the way he cleared his throat and coughed before embarking on the delicate subject. 'You may know, ahem, gracious Miss,' he began—'you may know that religious phenomena are often, ahem, closely connected with sexual causes.' I replied that I had heard rumours which might justify me in believing this to be true among Roman Catholics, but that in the Church of England—and I for one was a practitioner of Anglicanismus—it was very different. That might be, said the doctor; he had had no opportunity in the course of his long medical career of personally studying Anglicanismus. But he could vouch for the fact that among his patients, here in Grauburg, mysticismus was very often mixed up with the *Geschlechtsleben*.[11] Melpomene was a case in point. After that hateful afternoon she had become extremely religious; the Professor of Latin had diverted her emotions out of their normal channels. She rebelled against the placid Agnosticismus of her father, and at night, in secret, when

[9] "We can play the violin . . ."
[10] "And we can dance Bumstarara . . ." "Bumstarara" is a sound imitation of a dance beat.
[11] Sex life.

Aunt Bertha's dragon eyes were closed, she would read such forbidden books as *The Life of St Theresa*, *The Little Flowers of St Francis*, *The Imitation of Christ*, and the horribly enthralling *Book of Martyrs*. Aunt Bertha confiscated these works whenever she came upon them; she considered them more pernicious than the novels of Marcel Prévost. The character of a good potential housewife might be completely undermined by reading of this kind. It was rather a relief for Melpomene when Aunt Bertha shuffled off, in the summer of 1911, this mortal coil. She was one of those indispensables of whom one makes the discovery, when they are gone, that one can get on quite as well without them. Poor Aunt Bertha!"

"One can imagine Melpomene trying to believe she was sorry, and horribly ashamed to find that she was really, in secret, almost glad." The suggestion seemed to me ingenious, but Miss Penny accepted it as obvious.

"Precisely," she said; "and the emotion would only further confirm and give new force to the tendencies which her aunt's death left her free to indulge as much as she liked. Remorse, contrition—they would lead to the idea of doing penance. And for one who was now wallowing in the martyrology, penance was the mortification of the flesh. She used to kneel for hours, at night, in the cold; she ate too little, and when her teeth ached, which they often did,—for she had a set, the doctor told me, which had given trouble from the very first,—she would not go and see the dentist, but lay awake at night, savouring to the full her excruciations, and feeling triumphantly that they must, in some strange way, be pleasing to the Mysterious Powers. She went on like that for two or three years, till she was poisoned through and through. In the end she went down with gastric ulcer. It was three months before she came out of hospital, well for the first time in a long space of years, and with a brand new set of imperishable teeth, all gold and ivory. And in mind, too, she was changed—for the better, I suppose. The nuns who nursed her had made her see that in mortifying herself she had acted supererogatively and through spiritual pride; instead of doing right, she had sinned. The only road to salvation, they told her, lay in discipline, in the orderliness of established religion, in obedience to authority. Secretly, so as not to distress her poor father, whose Agnosticismus was extremely dogmatic, for all its unobtrusiveness, Melpomene became a Roman Catholic. She was twenty-two. Only a few months later came the war and Professor Fugger's eternal renunciation of porridge. He did not long survive the making of that patriotic gesture. In the autumn of 1914 he caught a fatal influenza. Melpomene was alone in the world. In the spring of 1915 there was a new and very conscientious Sister of Charity at work among the wounded in the hospital of Grauburg. Here," explained Miss Penny, jabbing the air with her forefinger, "you put a line of asterisks or dots to signify a six years' gulf in the narrative. And you begin again right in the middle of a dialogue between Sister Agatha and the newly convalescent Kuno."

"What's their dialogue to be about?" I asked.

"Oh, that's easy enough," said Miss Penny. "Almost anything would do. What about this, for example? You explain that the fever has just abated; for the first time for days the young man is fully conscious. He feels himself to be well, reborn, as it were, in a new world—a world so bright and novel and jolly that he can't help laughing at the sight of it. He looks about him; the flies on the ceiling strike him as being extremely comic. How do they manage to walk upside down? They have suckers on their feet, says Sister Agatha, and wonders if her natural history is quite sound. Suckers on their feet—ha, ha! What an uproarious notion! Suckers on their feet—that's good that's damned good! You can say charming, pathetic, positively tender things about the irrelevant mirth of convalescents—the more so in this particular case, where the mirth is expressed by a young man who is to be taken back to jail as soon as he can stand firmly on his legs. Ha, ha! Laugh on, unhappy boy! It is the quacking of the Fates, the Parcæ, the Norns!"

Miss Penny gave an exaggerated imitation of her own brassy laughter. At the sound of it the few lunchers who still lingered at the other tables looked up, startled.

"You can write pages about Destiny and its ironic quacking. It's tremendously impressive, and there's money in every line."

"You may be sure I shall."

"Good! Then I can get on with my story. The days pass and the first hilarity of convalescence fades away. The young man remembers, and grows sullen; his strength comes back to him, and with it a sense of despair. His mind broods incessantly on the hateful future. As for the consolations of religion, he won't listen to them. Sister Agatha perseveres—oh, with what anxious solicitude!—in the attempt to make him understand and believe and be comforted. It is all so tremendously important, and in this case, somehow, more important than in any other. And now you see the *Geschlechtsleben* working yeastily and obscurely, and once again the quacking of the Norns is audible. By the way," said Miss Penny, changing her tone and leaning confidentially across the table, "I wish you'd tell me something. Do you really —honestly, I mean—do you seriously believe in literature?"

"Believe in literature?"

"I was thinking," Miss Penny explained, "of Ironic Fate and the quacking of the Norns and all that."

" 'M yes."

"And then there's this psychology and introspection business; and construction and good narrative and word pictures and *le mot juste* and verbal magic and striking metaphors."

I remembered that I had compared Miss Penny's tinkling earrings to skeletons hanging in chains.

"And then, finally, and to begin with—Alpha and Omega—there's ourselves: two professionals gloating, with an absolute lack of sympathy, over a seduced nun, and speculating on the best method of turning her misfortunes into cash. It's all very curious, isn't it?—when one begins to think about it dispassionately."

"Very curious," I agreed. "But, then, so is everything else if you look at it like that."

"No, no," said Miss Penny. "Nothing's so curious as our business. But I shall never get to the end of my story if I get started on first principles."

Miss Penny continued her narrative. I was still thinking of literature. Do you believe in it? Seriously? Ah! Luckily the question was quite meaningless. The story came to me rather vaguely, but it seemed that the young man was getting better; in a few more days, the doctor had said, he would be well—well enough to go back to jail. No, no. The question was meaningless. I would think about it no more. I concentrated my attention again.

"Sister Agatha," I heard Miss Penny saying, "prayed, exhorted, indoctrinated. Whenever she had half a minute to spare from her other duties she would come running into the young man's room. 'I wonder if you fully realize the importance of prayer?' she would ask, and, before he had time to answer, she would give him a breathless account of the uses and virtues of regular and patient supplication. Or else it was: 'May I tell you about St Theresa?' or 'St Stephen, the first martyr—you know about him, don't you?' Kuno simply wouldn't listen at first. It seemed so fantastically irrelevant, such an absurd interruption to his thoughts, his serious, despairing thoughts about the future. Prison was real, imminent, and this woman buzzed about him with her ridiculous fairy-tales. Then, suddenly, one day he began to listen, he showed signs of contrition and conversion. Sister Agatha announced her triumph to the other nuns, and there was rejoicing over the one lost sheep. Melpomene had never felt so happy in her life, and Kuno, looking at her radiant face, must have wondered how he could have been such a fool as not to see from the first what was now so obvious. The woman had lost her head about him. And he had only four days now—four days in which to tap the tumultuous love power, to canalize it, to set it working for his escape. Why hadn't he started a week ago? He could have made certain of it then. But now? There was no knowing. Four days was a horribly short time."

"How did he do it?" I asked, for Miss Penny had paused.

"That's for you to say," she replied, and shook her earrings at me. "I don't know. Nobody knows, I imagine, except the two parties concerned and perhaps Sister Agatha's confessor. But one can reconstruct the crime, as they say. How would you have done it? You're a man, you ought to be familiar with the processes of amorous engineering."

"You flatter me," I answered. "Do you seriously suppose——" I extended my arms. Miss Penny laughed like a horse. "No. But, seriously, it's a problem. The case is a very special one. The person, a nun; the place, a hospital; the opportunities, few. There could be no favourable circumstances—no moonlight, no distant music; and any form of direct attack would be sure to fail. That audacious confidence which is your amorist's best weapon would be useless here."

"Obviously," said Miss Penny. "But there are surely other methods. There is the approach through pity and the maternal instincts. And there's the approach through Higher Things, through the soul. Kuno must have worked on those lines, don't you think? One can imagine him letting himself be converted, praying with her, and at the same time appealing for her sympathy and even threatening—with a great air of seriousness—to kill himself rather than go back to jail. You can write that up easily and convincingly enough. But it's the sort of thing that bores me so frightfully to do. That's why I can never bring myself to write fiction. What is the point of it all? And the way you literary men think yourselves so important—particularly if you write tragedies. It's all very queer, very queer indeed."

I made no comment. Miss Penny changed her tone and went on with the narrative.

"Well," she said, "whatever the means employed, the engineering process was perfectly successful. Love was made to find out a way. On the afternoon before Kuno was to go back to prison, two Sisters of Charity walked out of the hospital gates, crossed the square in front of it, glided down the narrow streets towards the river, boarded a tram at the bridge, and did not descend till the car had reached its terminus in the farther suburbs. They began to walk briskly along the high road out into the country. 'Look!' said one of them, when they were clear of the houses; and with the gesture of a conjurer produced from nowhere a red leather purse. 'Where did it come from?' asked the other, opening her eyes. Memories of Elisha and the ravens, of the widow's cruse, of the loaves and fishes, must have floated through the radiant fog in poor Melpomene's mind. 'The old lady I was sitting next to in the tram left her bag open. Nothing could have been simpler.' 'Kuno! You don't mean to say you stole it?' Kuno swore horribly. He had opened the purse. 'Only sixty marks. Who'd have thought that an old camel, all dressed up in silk and furs, would only have sixty marks in her purse. And I must have a thousand at least to get away.' It's easy to reconstruct the rest of the conversation down to the inevitable, 'For God's sake, shut up,' with which Kuno put an end to Melpomene's dismayed moralizing. They trudge on in silence. Kuno thinks desperately. Only sixty marks; he can do nothing with that. If only he had something to sell, a piece of jewellery, some gold or silver—anything, anything. He knows such a good place for selling things. Is he to be caught again for lack of a few marks? Melpomene is also thinking. Evil must often be done that good may follow. After all, had not she herself stolen Sister Mary of the Purification's clothes when she was asleep after night duty? Had not she run away from the convent, broken her vows? And yet how convinced she was that she was doing rightly! The mysterious Powers emphatically approved; she felt sure of it. And now there was the red purse. But what was a red purse in comparison with a saved soul—and, after all, what was she doing but saving Kuno's soul?" Miss Penny, who had adopted the voice and gestures of a debater asking rhetorical questions, brought her hand with a slap on to the table. "Lord, what a bore this sort of stuff is!" she exclaimed. "Let's get to the end of this dingy anecdote as quickly as possible. By this time, you must imagine, the shades of night were falling fast—the chill November twilight, and so on; but I leave the natural descriptions to you. Kuno gets into the ditch at the roadside and takes off his robes. One imagines that he would feel himself safer in trousers, more capable of acting with decision in a crisis. They tramp on for miles. Late in the evening they leave the high road and strike up through the fields towards the forest. At the fringe of the wood they find one of those wheeled huts where the shepherds sleep in the lambing season."

"The real 'Maison du Berger.' "[12]

"Precisely," said Miss Penny, and she began to recite:

> *'Si ton cœur gémissant du poids de notre vie*
> *Se traîne et se débat comme un aigle blessé. . . .'*[13]

How does it go on? I used to adore it all so much when I was a girl:

> *'Le seuil est parfumé, l'alcôve est large et sombre,*
> *Et là parmi les fleurs, nous trouverons dans l'ombre,*
> *Pour nos cheveux unis un lit silencieux.'*[14]

I could go on like this indefinitely."

"Do," I said.

"No, no. No, no. I'm determined to finish this wretched story. Kuno broke the padlock of the door. They entered. What happened in that little hut?" Miss Penny leaned forward at me. Her large hare's eyes glittered, the long earrings swung and faintly tinkled. "Imagine the emotions of a virgin of thirty, and a nun at that, in the terrifying presence of desire. Imagine the easy, familiar brutalities of the young man. Oh, there's pages to be made

---

[12] "La Maison du Berger," ("The House of the Shepherd") by Alfred de Vigny (1797-1863).

[13] "If your heart laments the weight of our life, crawling and fighting like a wounded eagle. . . ."

[14] "The threshold is perfumed, the alcove is large and somber, and there among the flowers we shall find in the shade a silent bed for our mingled hair."

out of this—the absolutely impenetrable darkness, the smell of straw, the voices, the strangled crying, the movements! And one likes to fancy that the emotions pulsing about in that confined space made palpable vibrations like a deep sound that shakes the air. Why, it's ready-made literature, this scene. In the morning," Miss Penny went on, after a pause, "two woodcutters on their way to work noticed that the door of the hut was ajar. They approached the hut cautiously, their axes raised and ready for a blow if there should be need of it. Peeping in, they saw a woman in a black dress lying face downwards in the straw. Dead? No; she moved, she moaned. 'What's the matter?' A blubbered face, smeared with streaks of tear-clotted grey dust, is lifted towards them. 'What's the matter?'—'He's gone!' What a queer, indistinct utterance. The woodcutters regard one another. What does she say? She's a foreigner, perhaps. 'What's the matter?' they repeat once more. The woman bursts out violently crying. 'Gone, gone! He's gone,' she sobs out in her vague, inarticulate way. 'Oh, gone. That's what she says. Who's gone?'—'He's left me.'—'What?'—'Left me . . .'—'What the devil . . . ? Speak a little more distinctly.'—'I can't,' she wails; 'he's taken my teeth.'—'Your what?'—'My teeth!'—and the shrill voice breaks into a scream, and she falls back sobbing into the straw. The woodcutters look significantly at one another. They nod. One of them applies a thick yellow-nailed forefinger to his forehead."

Miss Penny looked at her watch.

"Good heavens!" she said, "it's nearly half-past three. I must fly. Don't forget about the funeral service," she added, as she put on her coat. "The tapers, the black coffin in the middle of the aisle, the nuns in their white-winged coifs, the gloomy chanting, and the poor cowering creature without any teeth, her face all caved in like an old woman's, wondering whether she wasn't really and in fact dead—wondering whether she wasn't already in hell. Good-bye."

Questions for Discussion

1. What is comically incongruous about Penny?

2. From the standpoint of comedy why is Penny an appropriate teller for the tale she unfolds? Does the story she narrates reveal anything about her own nature?

3. How does the nun, though potentially a tragic figure, heighten the comedy?

4. How does the narrator make comedy out of sex? Why does Penny not do it? What is her attitude toward sex? What is the narrator's attitude toward the story he hears?

5. To what extent is Penny in telling the story poking fun at literature in a way similar to that of the narrator in *Don Juan?*

6. How is religion made amusing?

7. Whom does Penny sympathize with in the story she tells, Sister Agatha or Kuno? Explain.

8. In what way is the surprise ending of Sister Agatha's story anticipated? Does the nun "die"?

Ring Lardner (1885-1933)

Some Like Them Cold

N. Y., Aug. 3.

Dear Miss Gillespie: How about our bet now as you bet me I would forget all about you the minute I hit the big town and would never write you a letter. Well girlie it looks like you lose so pay me. Seriously we will call all bets off as I am not the kind that bet on a sure thing and it sure was a sure thing that I would not forget a girlie like you and all that is worrying me is whether it may not be the other way round and you are wondering who this fresh guy is that is writeing you this letter. I bet you are so will try and refreshen your memory.

Well girlie I am the handsome young man that was wondering round the Lasalle st. station Monday and "happened" to sit down beside of a mighty pretty girlie who was waiting to meet her sister from Toledo and the train was late and I am glad of it because if it had not of been that little girlie and I would never of met. So for once I was a lucky guy but still I guess it was time I had some luck as it was certainly tough luck for you and I to both be liveing in Chi all that time and never get together till a half hour before I was leaveing town for good.

Still "better late than never" you know and maybe we can make up for lost time though it looks like we would have to do our makeing up at long distants unless you make good on your threat and come to N. Y. I wish you would do that little thing girlie as it looks like that was the only way we would get a chance to play around together as it looks like they was little or no chance of me comeing back to Chi as my whole future is in the big town. N. Y. is the only spot and specially for a man that expects to make my liveing in the song writeing game as here is the Mecca for that line of work and no matter how good a man may be they don't get no recognition unless they live in N. Y.

Well girlie you asked me to tell you all about my trip. Well I remember you saying that you would give anything to be makeing it yourself but as far as the trip itself was conserned you ought to be thankfull you did not have to make it as you would of sweat your head off. I know I did specially wile going through Ind. Monday P.M. but Monday night was the worst of all trying to sleep and finely I give it up and just layed there with the prespiration rolling off of me though I was laying on top of the covers and nothing on but my underwear.

Yesterday was not so bad as it rained most of the A.M. comeing through N. Y. state and in the P.M. we road along side of the Hudson all P.M. Some river girlie and just looking at it makes a man forget all about the heat and everything else except a certain girlie who I seen for the first time Monday and then only for a half hour but she is the kind of a girlie that a man don't need to see her only once and they would be no danger of forgetting her. There I guess I better lay off that subject or you will think I am a "fresh guy."

Well that is about all to tell you about the trip only they was one amuseing incidence that come off yesterday which I will tell you. Well they was a dame got on the train at Toledo Monday and had the birth opp. mine but I did not see nothing of her that night as I was out smokeing till late and she hit the hay early but yesterday A.M. she come in the dinner and sit at the same table with me and tried to make me and it was so raw that the dinge waiter seen it and give me the wink and of course I paid no tension and I waited till she got through so as they would be no danger of her folling me out but she stopped on the way out to get a tooth pick and when I come out she was out on the platform with it so I tried to brush right by but she spoke up and asked me what time it was and I told her and she said she guessed her watch was slow so I said maybe it just seem slow on acct. of the company it was in.

I don't know if she got what I was driveing at or not but any way she give up trying to make me and got off at Albany. She was a good looker but I have no time for gals that tries to make strangers on a train.

Well if I don't quit you will think I am writeing a book but will expect a long letter in answer to this letter and we will see if you can keep your promise like I have kept mine. Don't dissapoint me girlie as I am all alone in a large city and hearing from you will keep me from getting home sick for old Chi though I never thought so much of the old town till I found out you lived there. Don't think that is kidding girlie as I mean it.

You can address me at this hotel as it looks like I will be here right along as it is on 47th st. right off of old Broadway and handy to everything and am only paying $21 per wk. for my rm. and could of got one for $16 but without bath but am glad to pay the differents as am lost without my bath in the A.M. and sometimes at night too.

Tomorrow I expect to commence fighting the "battle of Broadway" and will let you know how I come out that is if you answer this letter. In the mean wile girlie au reservoir and don't do nothing I would not do.

Your new friend (?)
Chas. F. Lewis.

Chicago, Ill., Aug. 6.

My Dear Mr. Lewis: Well, that certainly was a "surprise party" getting your letter and you are certainly a "wonder man" to keep your word as I am afraid most men of your sex are gay deceivers but maybe you are "different." Anyway it sure was a surprise and will gladly pay the bet if you will just tell me what it was we bet. Hope it was not money as I am a "working girl" but if it was not more than a dollar or two will try to dig it up even if I have to "beg, borrow or steal."

Suppose you will think me a "case" to make a bet and then forget what it was, but you must remember, Mr. Man, that I had just met you and was "dazzled." Joking aside I was rather "fussed" and will tell you why. Well, Mr. Lewis, I suppose you see lots of girls like the one you told me about that you saw on the train who tried to "get acquainted" but I want to assure you that I am not one of those kind and sincerely hope you will believe me when I tell you that you was the first man I ever spoke to meeting them like that and my friends and the people who know me would simply faint if they knew I ever spoke to a man without a "proper introduction."

Believe me, Mr. Lewis, I am not that kind and I don't know now why I did it only that you was so "different" looking if you know what I mean and not at all like the kind of men that usually try to force their attentions on every pretty girl they see. Lots of times I act on impulse and let my feelings run away from me and sometimes I do things on the impulse of the moment which I regret them later on, and that is what I did this time, but hope you won't give me cause to regret it and I know you won't as I know you are not that kind of a man a specially after what you told me about the girl on the train. But any way as I say, I was in a "daze" so can't remember what it was we bet, but will try and pay it if it does not "break" me.

Sis's train got in about ten minutes after yours had gone and when she saw me what do you think was the first thing she said? Well, Mr. Lewis, she said: "Why Mibs (That is a pet name some of my friends have given me) what has happened to you? I never seen you have as much color." So I passed it off with some remark about the heat and changed the subject as I certainly was not going to tell her that I had just been talking to a man who I had never met or she would of dropped dead from the shock. Either that or she would not of believed me as it would be hard for a person who knows me well to imagine me doing a thing like that as I have quite a reputation for "squelching" men who try to act fresh. I don't mean anything personal by that, Mr. Lewis, as am a good judge of character and could tell without you telling me that you are not that kind.

Well, Sis and I have been on the "go" ever since she arrived as I took yesterday and today off so I could show her the "sights" though she says she would be perfectly satisfied to just sit in the apartment and listen to me "rattle on." Am afraid I am a great talker, Mr. Lewis, but Sis says it is as good as a show to hear me talk as I tell things in such a different way as I cannot help from seeing the humorous side of everything and she says she never gets tired of listening to me, but of course she is my sister and thinks the world of me, but she really does laugh like she enjoyed my craziness.

Maybe I told you that I have a tiny little apartment which a girl friend of mine and I have together and it is hardly big enough to turn round in, but still it is "home" and I am a great home girl and hardly ever care to go out evenings except occasionally to the theatre or dance. But even if our "nest" is small we are proud of it and Sis complimented us on how cozy it is and how "homey" it looks and she said she did not see how we could afford to have everything so nice and Edith (my girl friend) said: "Mibs deserves all the credit for that. I never knew a girl who could make a little money go a long ways like she can." Well, of course she is my best friend and always saying nice things about me, but I do try and I hope I get results. Have always said that good taste and being careful is a whole lot more important than lots of money though it is nice to have it.

You must write and tell me how you are getting along in the "battle of Broadway" (I laughed when I read that) and whether the publishers like your songs though I know they will. Am crazy to hear them and hear you play the piano as I love good jazz music even better than classical, though I suppose it is terrible to say such a thing. But I usually say just what I think though sometimes I wish afterwards I had not of. But still I believe it is better for a girl to be her own self and natural instead of always acting. But am afraid I will never have a chance to hear you play unless you come back to Chi and pay us a visit as my "threat" to come to New York was just a "threat" and I don't see any hope of ever getting there unless some rich New Yorker should fall in love with me and take me there to live. Fine chance for poor little me, eh Mr. Lewis?

Well, I guess I have "rattled on" long enough and you will think I am writing a book unless I quit and besides, Sis has asked me as a special favor to make her a pie for dinner. Maybe you don't know it, Mr. Man, but I am quite famous for my pie and pastry, but I don't suppose a "genius" is interested in common things like that.

Well, be sure and write soon and tell me what N. Y. is like and all about it and don't forget the little girlie who was "bad" and spoke to a strange man in the station and have been blushing over it ever since.

Your friend (?)
Mabelle Gillespie.

N. Y., Aug. 10.

Dear Girlie: I bet you will think I am a fresh guy commenceing that way but Miss Gillespie is too cold and a man can not do nothing cold in this kind of weather specially in this man's town which is the hottest place I ever been in and I guess maybe the reason why New Yorkers is so bad is because they think they are all ready in H—— and can not go no worse place no matter how they behave themselves. Honest girlie I certainly envy you being where there is a breeze off the old Lake and Chi may be dirty but I never heard of nobody dying because they was dirty but four people died here yesterday on acct. of the heat and I seen two different women flop right on Broadway and had to be taken away in the ambulance and it could not of been because they was dressed too warm because it would be impossible for the women here to leave off any more cloths.

Well have not had much luck yet in the battle of Broadway as all the heads of the big music publishers is out of town on their vacation and the big boys is the only ones I will do business with as it would be silly for a man with the stuff I have got to waste my time on somebody that is just on the staff and have not got the final say. But I did play a couple of my numbers for the people up to Levy's and Goebel's and they went crazy over them in both places. So it looks like all I have to do is wait for the big boys to get back and then play my numbers for them and I will be all set. What I want is to get taken on the staff of one of the big firms as that gives a man the inside and they will plug your numbers more if you are on the staff. In the mean wile have not got nothing to worry me but am just seeing the sights of the big town as have saved up enough money to play round for a wile and any way a man that can play piano like I can don't never have to worry about starveing. Can certainly make the old music box talk girlie and am always good for a $75 or $100 job.

Well have been here a week now and on the go every minute and I thought I would be lonesome down here but no chance of that as I have been treated fine by the people I have met and have sure met a bunch of them. One of the boys liveing in the hotel is a vaudeville actor and he is a member of the Friars club and took me over there to dinner the other night and some way another the bunch got wise that I could play the piano so of course I had to sit down and give them some of my numbers and everybody went crazy over them. One of the boys I met there was Paul Sears the song writer but he just writes the lyrics and has wrote a bunch of hits and when he heard some of my melodies he called me over to one side and said he would like to work with me on some numbers. How is that girlie as he is one of the biggest hit writers in N. Y.

N. Y. has got some mighty pretty girlies and I guess it would not be hard to get acquainted with them and in fact several of them has tried to make me since I been here but I always figure that a girl must be something wrong with her if she tries to make a man that she don't know nothing about so I pass them all up. But I did meet a couple of pips that a man here in the hotel went up on Riverside Drive to see them and insisted on me going along and they got on some way that I could make a piano talk so they was nothing but I must play for them so I sit down and played some of my own stuff and they went crazy over it.

One of the girls wanted I should come up and see her again, and I said I might but I think I better keep away as she acted like she wanted to vamp me and I am not the kind that likes to play round with a gal just for their company and dance with them etc. but when I see the right gal that will be a different thing and she won't have to beg me to come and see her as I will camp right on her trail till she says yes. And it won't be none of these N. Y. fly by nights neither. They are all right to look at but a man would be a sucker to get serious with them as they might take you up and next thing you know you would have a wife on your hands that don't know a dish rag from a waffle iron.

Well girlie will quit and call it a day as it is too hot to write any more and I guess I will turn on the cold water and lay in the tub a wile and then turn in. Don't forget to write to

Your friend,
Chas. F. Lewis.

Chicago, Ill., Aug. 13.

Dear Mr. Man: Hope you won't think me a "silly Billy" for starting my letter that way but "Mr. Lewis" is so formal and "Charles" is too much the other way and any way I would not dare call a man by their first name after only knowing them only two weeks. Though I may as well confess that Charles is my favorite name for a man and have always been crazy about it as it was my father's name. Poor old dad, he died of cancer three years ago, but left enough insurance so that mother and we girls were well provided for and do not have to do anything to support ourselves though I have been earning my own living for two years to make things easier for mother and also because I simply can't bear to be doing nothing as I feel like a "drone." So I flew away from the "home nest" though mother felt bad about it as I was her favorite and she always said I was such a comfort to her as when I was in the house she never had to worry about how things would go.

But there I go gossiping about my domestic affairs just like you would be interested in them though I don't see how you could be though personally I always like to know all about my friends, but I know men are different so will try and not bore you any longer. Poor Man, I certainly feel sorry for you if New York is as hot as all that. I guess it has been very hot in Chi, too, at least everybody has been complaining about how terrible it is. Suppose you will wonder why I say "I guess" and you will think I ought to know if it is hot. Well, sir, the reason I say "I guess" is because I don't feel the heat like others do or at least I don't let myself feel it. That sounds crazy I know, but don't you think there is a good deal in mental suggestion and not letting yourself feel things? I believe that if a person simply won't allow themselves to be affected by disagreeable things, why such things won't bother them near as much. I know it works with me and that is the reason why I am never cross when things go wrong and "keep smiling" no matter what happens and as far as the heat is concerned, why I just don't let myself feel it and my friends say I don't even look hot no matter if the weather is boiling and Edith, my girl friend, often says that I am like a breeze and it cools her off just to have me come in the room. Poor Edie suffers terribly during the hot weather and says it almost makes her mad at me to see how cool and unruffled I look when everybody else is perspiring and have red faces etc.

I laughed when I read what you said about New York being so hot that people thought it was the "other place." I can appreciate a joke, Mr. Man, and that one did not go "over my head." Am still laughing at some of the things you said in the station though they probably struck me funnier than they would most girls as I always see the funny side and sometimes something is said and I laugh and the others wonder what I am laughing at as they cannot see anything in it themselves, but it is just the way I look at things so of course I cannot explain to them why I laughed and they think I am crazy. But I had rather part with almost anything rather than my sense of humour as it helps me over a great many rough spots.

Sis has gone back home though I would of liked to of kept her here much longer, but she had to go though she said she would of liked nothing better than to stay with me and just listen to me "rattle on." She always says it is just like a show to hear me talk as I always put things in such a funny way and for weeks after she has been visiting me she thinks of some of the things I said and laughs over them. Since she left Edith and I have been pretty quiet though poor Edie wants to be on the "go" all the time and tries to make me go out with her every evening to the pictures and scolds me when I say I had rather stay home and read and calls me a "bookworm." Well, it is true that I had rather stay home with a good book than go to some crazy old picture and the last two nights I have been reading myself to sleep with Robert W. Service's poems. Don't you love Service or don't you care for "highbrow" writings?

Personally there is nothing I love more than to just sit and read a good book or sit and listen to somebody play the piano, I mean if they can really play and I really believe I like popular music better than the classical though I suppose that is a terrible thing to confess, but I love all kinds of music but a specially the piano when it is played by somebody who can really play.

Am glad you have not "fallen" for the "ladies" who have tried to make your acquaintance in New York. You are right in thinking there must be something wrong with girls who try to "pick up" strange men as no girl with self respect would do such a thing and when I say that, Mr. Man, I know you will think it is a funny thing for me to say on account of the way our friendship started, but I mean it and I assure you that was the first time I ever done such a thing in my life and would never of thought of doing it had I not known you were the right kind of a man as I flatter myself that I am a good judge of character and can tell pretty well what a person is like by just looking at them and I assure you I had made up my mind what kind of a man you were before I allowed myself to answer your opening remark. Otherwise, I am the last girl in the world that would allow myself to speak to a person without being introduced to them.

When you write again you must tell me all about the girl on Riverside Drive and what she looks like and if you went to see her again and all about her. Suppose you will think I am a little old "curiosity shop" for asking all those questions and will wonder why I want to know. Well, sir, I won't tell you why, so there, but I insist on you answering all questions and will scold you if you don't. Maybe you will think that the reason why I am so curious is because I am "jealous" of the lady in question. Well, sir, I won't tell you whether I am or not, but will keep you "guessing." Now, don't you wish you knew?

Must close or you will think I am going to "rattle on" forever or maybe you have all ready become disgusted and torn my letter up. If so all I can say is poor little me—she was a nice little girl and meant well, but the man did not appreciate her.

There! Will stop or you will think I am crazy if you do not all ready.

Yours (?)
Mabelle.

N. Y., Aug. 20.

Dear Girlie: Well girlie I suppose you thought I was never going to answer your letter but have been busier than a one armed paper hanger the last week as have been working on a number with Paul Sears who is one of the best lyric writers in N. Y. and has turned out as many hits as Berlin or Davis or any of them. And believe me girlie he has turned out another hit this time that is he and I have done it together. It is all done now and we are just waiting for the best chance to place it but will not place it nowheres unless we get the right kind of a deal but maybe will publish it ourselves.

The song is bound to go over big as Sears has wrote a great lyric and I have give it a great tune or at least every body that has heard it goes crazy over it and it looks like it would go over bigger than any song since Mammy and would not be surprised to see it come out the hit of the year. If it is handled right we will make a bbl. of money and Sears says it is a cinch we will clean up as much as $25000 apiece which is pretty fair for one song but this one is not like the most of them but has got a great lyric and I have wrote a melody that will knock them out of their seats. I only wish you could hear it girlie and hear it the way I play it. I had to play it over and over about 50 times at the Friars last night.

I will copy down the lyric of the chorus so you can see what it is like and get the idea of the song though of course you can't tell much about it unless you hear it played and sang. The title of the song is When They're Like You and here is the chorus:

> "Some like them hot, some like them cold.
> Some like them when they're not too darn old.
> Some like them fat, some like them lean.
> Some like them only at sweet sixteen.
> Some like them dark, some like them light.
> Some like them in the park, late at night.
> Some like them fickle, some like them true,
> But the time I like them is when they're like you."

How is that for a lyric and I only wish I could play my melody for you as you would go nuts over it but will send you a copy as soon as the song is published and you can get some of your friends to play it over for you and I know you will like it though it is a different melody when I play it or when somebody else plays it.

Well girlie you will see how busy I have been and am libel to keep right on being busy as we are not going to let the grass grow under our feet but as soon as we have got this number placed we will get busy on another one as a couple like that will put me on Easy st. even if they don't go as big as we expect but even 25 grand is a big bunch of money and if a man could only turn out one hit a year and make that much out of it I would be on Easy st. and no more hammering on the old music box in some cabaret.

Who ever we take the song to we will make them come across with one grand for advance royaltys and that will keep me going till I can turn out another one. So the future looks bright and rosey to yours truly and I am certainly glad I come to the big town though sorry I did not do it a whole lot quicker.

This is a great old town girlie and when you have lived here a wile you wonder how you ever stood for a burg like Chi which is just a hick town along side of this besides being dirty etc. and a man is a sucker to stay there all their life specially a man in my line of work as N. Y. is the Mecca for a man that has got the musical gift. I figure that all the time I spent in Chi I was just wasteing my time and never really started to live till I come down here and I have to laugh when I think of the boys out there that is trying to make a liveing in the song writeing game and most of them starve to death all their life and the first week I am down here I meet a man like Sears and the next thing you know we have turned out a song that will make us a fortune.

Well girlie you asked me to tell you about the girlie up on the Drive that tried to make me and asked me to come and see her again. Well I can assure you you have no reason to be jealous in that quarter as I have not been back to see her as I figure it is wasteing my time to play round with a dame like she that wants to go out somewheres every night and if you married her she would want a house on 5th ave. with a dozen servants so I have passed her up as that is not my idea of home.

What I want when I get married is a real home where a man can stay home and work and maybe have a few of his friends in once in a wile and entertain them or go to a good musical show once in a wile and have a wife that is in sympathy with you and not nag at you all the wile but be a real help mate. The girlie up on the Drive would run me ragged and have me in the poor house inside of a year even if I was makeing 25 grand out of one song. Besides she wears a make up that you would have to blast to find out what her face looks like. So I have not been back there and don't intend to see her again so what is the use of me telling you about her. And the only other girlie I have met is a sister of Paul Sears who I met up to his house wile we was working on the song but she don't hardly count as she has not got no use for the boys but treats them like dirt and Paul says she is the coldest proposition he ever seen.

Well I don't know no more to write and besides have got a date to go out to Paul's place for dinner and play some of my stuff for him so as he can see if he wants to set words to some more of my melodies. Well don't do nothing I would not do and have as good a time as you can in old Chi and will let you know how we come along with the song.

Chas. F. Lewis.

Chicago, Ill., Aug. 23.

Dear Mr. Man: I am thrilled to death over the song and think the words awfully pretty and am crazy to hear the music which I know must be great. It must be wonderful to have the gift of writing songs and then hear people play and sing them and just think of making $25,000 in such a short time. My, how rich you will be and I certainly congratulate you though am afraid when you are rich and famous you will have no time for insignificant little me or will you be an exception and remember your "old" friends even when you are up in the world? I sincerely hope so.

Will look forward to receiving a copy of the song and will you be sure and put your name on it? I am all ready very conceited just to think that I know a man that writes songs and makes all that money.

Seriously I wish you success with your next song and I laughed when I read your remark about being busier than a one armed paper hanger. I don't see how you can think up all those comparisons and crazy things to say. The next time one of the girls asks me to go out with them I am going to tell them I can't go because I am busier than a one armed paper hanger and then they will think I made it up and say: "The girl is clever."

Seriously I am glad you did not go back to see the girl on the Drive and am also glad you don't like girls who makes themselves up so much as I think it is disgusting and would rather go round looking like a ghost than put artificial color on my face. Fortunately I have a complexion that does not need "fixing" but even if my coloring was not what it is I would never think of lowering myself to "fix" it. But I must tell you a joke that happened just the other day when Edith and I were out at lunch and there was another girl in the restaurant whom Edie knew and she introduced her to me and I noticed how this girl kept staring at me and finally she begged my pardon and asked if she could ask me a personal question and I said yes and she asked me if my complexion was really "mine." I assured her it was and she said: "Well, I thought so because I did not think anybody could put it on so artistically. I certainly envy you." Edie and I both laughed.

Well, if that girl envies me my complexion, why I envy you living in New York. Chicago is rather dirty though I don't let that part of it bother me as I bathe and change my clothing so often that the dirt does not have time to "settle." Edie often says she cannot see how I always keep so clean looking and says I always look like I had just stepped out of a band box. She also calls me a fish (jokingly) because I spend so much time in the water. But seriously I do love to bathe and never feel so happy as when I have just "cleaned up" and put on fresh clothing.

Edie has just gone out to see a picture and was cross at me because I would not go with her. I told her I was going to write a letter and she wanted to know to whom and I told her and she said: "You write to him so often that a person would almost think you was in love with him." I just laughed and turned it off, but she does say the most embarrassing things and I would be angry if it was anybody but she that said them.

Seriously I had much rather sit here and write letters or read or just sit and dream than go out to some crazy old picture show except once in awhile I do like to go to the theater and see a good play and a specially a musical play if the music is catchy. But as a rule I am contented to just stay home and feel cozy and lots of evenings Edie and I sit here without saying hardly a word to each other though she would love to talk but she knows I had rather be quiet and she often says it is just like living with a deaf and dumb mute to live with me because I make so little noise round the apartment. I guess I was born to be a home body as I so seldom care to go "gadding."

Though I do love to have company once in awhile, just a few congenial friends whom I can talk to and feel at home with and play cards or have some music. My friends love to drop in here, too, as they say Edie and I always give them such nice things to eat. Though poor Edie has not much to do with it, I am afraid, as she hates anything connected with cooking which is one of the things I love best of anything and I often say that when I begin keeping house in my own home I will insist on doing most of my own work as I would take so much more interest in it than a servant, though I would want somebody to help me a little if I could afford it as I often think a woman that does all her own work is liable to get so tired that she loses interest in the bigger things of life like books and music. Though after all what bigger thing is there than home making a specially for a woman?

I am sitting in the dearest old chair that I bought yesterday at a little store on the North Side. That is my one extravagance, buying furniture and things for the house, but I always say it is economy in the long run as I will always have them and have use for them and when I can pick them up at a bargain I would be silly not to. Though heaven knows I will never be "poor" in regards to furniture and rugs and things like that as mother's house in Toledo is full of lovely things which she says she is going to give to Sis and myself as soon as we have real homes of our own. She is going to give me the first choice as I am her favorite. She has the loveliest old things that you could not buy now for love or money including lovely old rugs and a piano which Sis wanted to have a player attachment put on it but I said it would be an insult to the piano so we did not get one. I am funny about things like that, a specially old furniture and feel towards them like people whom I love.

Poor mother, I am afraid she won't live much longer to enjoy her lovely old things as she has been suffering for years from stomach trouble and the doctor says it has been worse lately instead of better and her heart is weak besides. I am going home to see her a few days this fall as it may be the last time. She is very cheerful and always says she is ready to go now as she has had enough joy out of life and all she would like would be to see her girls settled down in their own homes before she goes.

There I go, talking about my domestic affairs again and I will bet you are bored to death though personally I am never bored when my friends tell me about themselves. But I won't "rattle on" any longer, but will say good night and don't forget to write and tell me how you come out with the song and thanks for sending me the words to it. Will you write a song about me some time? I would be thrilled to death! But I am afraid I am not the kind of girl that inspires men to write songs about them, but am just a quiet "mouse" that loves home and am not giddy enough to be the heroine of a song.

Well, Mr. Man, good night and don't wait so long before writing again to

Yours (?)

Mabelle.

N. Y., Sept. 8.

Dear Girlie. Well girlie have not got your last letter with me so cannot answer what was in it as I have forgotten if there was anything I was supposed to answer and besides have only a little time to write as I have a date to go out on a party with the Sears. We are going to the Georgie White show and afterwards somewheres for supper. Sears is the boy who wrote the lyric to my song and it is him and his sister I am going on the party with. The sister is a cold fish that has no use for men but she is show crazy and insists on Paul takeing her to 3 or 4 of them a week.

Paul wants me to give up my room here and come and live with them as they have plenty of room and I am running a little low on money but don't know if I will do it or not as am afraid I would freeze to death in the same house with a girl like the sister as she is ice cold but she don't hang round the house much as she is always takeing trips or going to shows or somewheres.

So far we have not had no luck with the song. All the publishers we have showed it to has went crazy over it but they won't make the right kind of a deal with us and if they don't loosen up and give us a decent royalty rate we are libel to put the song out ourselves and show them up. The man up to Goebel's told us the song was O. K. and he liked it but it was more of a production number than anything else and ought to go in a show like the Follies but they won't be in N. Y. much longer and what we ought to do is hold it till next spring.

Mean while I am working on some new numbers and also have taken a position with the orchestra at the Wilton and am going to work there starting next week. They pay good money $60 and it will keep me going.

Well girlie that is about all the news. I believe you said your father was sick and hope he is better and also hope you are getting along O. K. and take care of yourself. When you have nothing else to do write to your friend,

Chas. F. Lewis.

Chicago, Ill., Sept. 11.

Dear Mr. Lewis: Your short note reached me yesterday and must say I was puzzled when I read it. It sounded like you was mad at me though I cannot think of any reason why you should be. If there was something I said in my last letter that offended you I wish you would tell me what it was and I will ask your pardon though I cannot remember anything I could of said that you could take offense at. But if there was something, why I assure you, Mr. Lewis, that I did not mean anything by it. I certainly did not intend to offend you in any way.

Perhaps it is nothing I wrote you, but you are worried on account of the publishers not treating you fair in regards to your song and that is why your letter sounded so distant. If that is the case I hope that by this time matters have rectified themselves and the future looks brigher. But any way, Mr. Lewis, don't allow yourself to worry over business cares as they will all come right in the end and I always think it is silly for people to worry themselves sick over temporary troubles, but the best way is to "keep smiling" and look for the "silver lining" in the cloud. That is the way I always do and no matter what happens, I manage to smile and my girl friend, Edie, calls me Sunny because I always look on the bright side.

Remember also, Mr. Lewis, that $60 is a salary that a great many men would like to be getting and are living on less than that and supporting a wife and family on it. I always say that a person can get along on whatever amount they make if they manage things in the right way.

So if it is business troubles, Mr. Lewis, I say don't worry, but look on the bright side. But if it is something I wrote in my last letter that offended you I wish you would tell me what it was so I can apologize as I assure you I meant nothing and would not say anything to hurt you for the world.

Please let me hear from you soon as I will not feel comfortable until I know I am not to blame for the sudden change.

Sincerely,
Mabelle Gillespie.

N. Y., Sept., 24.

Dear Miss Gillespie: Just a few lines to tell you the big news or at least it is big news to me. I am engaged to be married to Paul Sears' sister and we are going to be married early next month and live in Atlantic City were the orchestra I have been playing with has got an engagement in one of the big cabarets.

I know this will be a surprise to you as it was even a surprise to me as I did not think I would ever have the nerve to ask the girlie the big question as she was always so cold and acted like I was just in the way. But she said she supposed she would have to marry somebody some time and she did not dislike me as much as most of the other men her brother brought round and she would marry me with the understanding that she would not have to be a slave and work round the house and also I would have to take her to a show or somewheres every night and if I could not take her myself she would "run wild" alone. Atlantic City will be O. K. for that as a lot of new shows opens down there and she will be able to see them before they get to the big town. As for her being a slave, I would hate to think of marrying a girl and then have them spend their lives in druggery round the house. We are going to live in a hotel till we find something better but will be in no hurry to start house keeping as we will have to buy all new furniture.

Betsy is some doll when she is all fixed up and believe me she knows how to fix herself up. I don't know what she uses but it is weather proof and I have been out in a rain storm with her and we both got drowned but her face stayed on. I would almost think it was real only she tells me different.

Well girlie I may write to you again once in a wile as Betsy says she don't give a damn if I write to all the girls in the world just so I don't make her read the answers but that is all I can think of to say now except goodbye and good luck and may the right man come along soon and he will be a lucky man getting a girl that is such a good cook and got all that furniture etc.

But just let me give you a word of advice before I close and that is don't never speak to strange men who you don't know nothing about as they may get you wrong and think you are trying to make them. It just happened that I knew better so you was lucky in my case but the luck might not last.

Your friend,
Chas. F. Lewis.

Chicago, Ill., Sept. 27.

My Dear Mr. Lewis: Thanks for your advice and also thank your fiance for her generosity in allowing you to continue your correspondence with her "rivals," but personly I have no desire to take advantage of that generosity as I have something better to do than read letters from a man like you, a specially as I have a man friend who is not so generous as Miss Sears and would strongly object to my continuing a correspondence with another man. It is at his request that I am writing this note to tell you not to expect to hear from me again.

Allow me to congratulate you on your engagement to Miss Sears and I am sure she is to be congratulated too, though if I met the lady I would be tempted to ask her to tell me her secret, namely how she is going to "run wild" on $60.

Sincerely,
Mabelle Gillespie.

Questions for Discussion

1. How is the epistolary form used as a comic device? Consider the language and the method of presenting the subject matter.

2. In what way is the sudden announcement in Mr. Lewis' last letter prepared for at the beginning of the story? Is there any progression in the story's action?

3. What makes Miss Gillespie and Mr. Lewis comic characters? To what extent does the author employ irony in portraying them?

4. Could this story be considered a comedy of manners? Refer to the discussion of this type of comedy in the Introduction. In this connection compare Horner (in *The Country Wife*) and Mr. Lewis. Do you find any similarities?

5. How does the last sentence of the story (which concerns running "wild" on $60) expose in a humorous fashion the pretensions of both Mr. Lewis and Miss Gillespie?

Thomas Gray (1716-1771)

Ode on the Death of a Favorite Cat

Drowned in a Tub of Gold Fishes

'Twas on a lofty vase's side,
Where China's gayest art had dyed
  The azure flowers, that blow;
Demurest of the tabby kind,
The pensive Selima reclined,
  Gazed on the lake below.

Her conscious tail her joy declared;
The fair round face, the snowy beard,
  The velvet of her paws,
Her coat, that with the tortoise vies, 10
Her ears of jet, and emerald eyes,
  She saw; and purred applause.

Still, had she gazed; but 'midst the tide
Two angel forms were seen to glide,
  The genii of the stream;
Their scaly armor's Tyrian hue[1]
Through richest purple to the view
  Betrayed a golden gleam.

The hapless nymph with wonder saw:
A whisker first and then a claw, 20
  With many an ardent wish,
She stretched in vain to reach the prize.

---

1 Purple. It was made by the people of Tyre from the juice of a shell-fish.

What female heart can gold despise?
  What cat's averse to fish?

Presumptuous maid! with looks intent
Again she stretched, again she bent,
  Nor knew the gulf between.
(Malignant Fate sat by, and smiled)
The slippery verge her feet beguiled,
  She tumbled headlong in. 30

Eight times emerging from the flood
She mewed to every watery god,
  Some speedy aid to send.
No dolphin[2] came, no nereid[3] stirred:
Nor cruel Tom, nor Susan heard.
  A favorite has no friend!

From hence, ye beauties, undeceived,
Know, one false step is ne'er retrieved,
  And be with caution bold.
Not all that tempts your wandering eyes 40
And heedless hearts, is lawful prize;
  Nor all, that glisters, gold.

---

[2] An allusion to the legend of the friendly dolphin that carried the poet Arion to shore after pirates had forced him from his ship.

[3] A nymph, daughter of Nereus, the Old Man of the Sea.

Questions for Discussion

1. The style of this poem is important; it is more elevated than the subject demands. Note several instances of the elevated diction.
2. Could the poem be rewritten in a plain style and still be comic?
3. Discuss the basis of the wit in the sixth stanza.
4. To what extent is the poem more than a poem on a cat? Explain.
5. Is the generalization in the last stanza prepared for?

Theodore Roethke (1908-1963)

The Kitty-Cat Bird

The Kitty-Cat Bird, he sat on a Fence.
Said the Wren, your Song isn't worth 10¢.
You're a Fake, you're a Fraud, you're a Hor-rid Pretense!
—Said the Wren to the Kitty-Cat Bird.

You've too many Tunes, and none of them Good:
I wish you would act like a bird really should,
Or stay by yourself down deep in the wood,
—Said the Wren to the Kitty-Cat Bird.

You mew like a Cat, you grate like a Jay;
You squeak like a Mouse that's lost in the Hay,
I wouldn't be You for even a day,
—Said the Wren to the Kitty-Cat Bird.

The Kitty-Cat Bird, he moped and he cried.
Then a real cat came with a Mouth so Wide,
That the Kitty-Cat Bird just hopped inside;
"At last I'm myself!"—and he up and died
—Did the Kitty—the Kitty-Cat Bird.

You'd better not laugh; and don't say, "Pooh!"
Until you have thought this Sad Tale through:
Be sure that whatever you are is you
—Or you'll end like the Kitty-Cat Bird.

Questions for Discussion

1. Why does Roethke choose these particular birds for his poem? Would any others serve the purpose?

2. What does the poet gain by his nursery rhyme idiom—the singsong rhythms and simple diction?

3. Is the Wren a disinterested critic of the Kitty-Cat Bird?

4. Why is the fourth stanza longer than the others?

5. Discuss the human theme mentioned in the last stanza. Is this really a "Sad Tale"?

6. How similar is Roethke's use of the Kitty-Cat Bird to that of Gray's use of the Cat for the purpose of creating humor and making a moral point?

Thomas Hardy (1840-1928)

The Ruined Maid

"O 'Melia, my dear, this does everything crown!
Who could have supposed I should meet you in Town?
And whence such fair garments, such prosperi-ty?"—
"O didn't you know I'd been ruined?" said she.

—"You left us in tatters, without shoes or socks,
Tired of digging potatoes, and spudding up docks[1];
And now you've gay bracelets and bright feathers three!"—
"Yes: that's how we dress when we're ruined," said she.

—"At home in the barton[2] you said 'thee' and 'thou,'
And 'thik oon,' and 'theas oon,' and 't'other'; but now   10
Your talking quite fits 'ee for high compa-ny!"—
"Some polish is gained with one's ruin," said she.

—"Your hands were like paws then, your face blue and bleak
But now I'm bewitched by your delicate cheek,
And your little gloves fit as on any la-dy!"—
"We never do work when we're ruined," said she.

—"You used to call home-life a hag-ridden dream,
And you'd sigh, and you'd sock[3]; but at present you seem
To know not of megrims[4] or melancho-ly!"—
"True. One's pretty lively when ruined," said she.   20

---

[1] Spading up dockweed.
[2] Farmyard.
[3] Groan.
[4] Blues.

—"I wish I had feathers, a fine sweeping gown,
And a delicate face, and could strut about Town!"—
"My dear—a raw country girl, such as you be,
Cannot quite expect that. You ain't ruined," said she.

Questions for Discussion

1. Describe the two speakers in the poem and comment on their fitness for the role of a comic figure.

2. Is 'Melia's friend envious of her fine graments and prosperity? What is 'Melia's attitude toward her friend?

3. How precisely is the word *ruined* used in the poem? Has 'Melia gained some "polish" with her "ruin"?

4. What use does Hardy make of different kinds of speech?

5. Comment on the speech rhythms of the poem. Are they in any way appropriate to the speakers?

6. What is the basic incongruity of the poem which makes it comic?

X. J. Kennedy (1929-   )

In a Prominent Bar in Secaucus One Day

To the tune of "The Old Orange Flute"
or the tune of "Sweet Betsy from Pike"

In a prominent bar in Secaucus one day
Rose a lady in skunk with a topheavy sway,
Raised a knobby red finger—all turned from their beer—
While with eyes bright as snowcrust she sang high and clear:

"Now who of you'd think from an eyeload of me
That I once was a lady as proud as could be?
Oh I'd never sit down by a tumbledown drunk
If it wasn't, my dears, for the high cost of junk.

"All the gents used to swear that the white of my calf
Beat the down of the swan by a length and a half. 10
In the kerchief of linen I caught to my nose
Ah, there never fell snot, but a little gold rose.

"I had seven gold teeth and a toothpick of gold,
My Virginia cheroot was a leaf of it rolled
And I'd light it each time with a thousand in cash—
Why the bums used to fight if I flicked them an ash.

"Once the toast of the Biltmore, the belle of the Taft,
I would drink bottle beer at the Drake, never draft,

And dine at the Astor on Salisbury steak
With a clean tablecloth for each bite I did take. 20

"In a car like the Roxy I'd roll to the track,
A steel guitar trio, a bar in the back,
And the wheels made no noise, they turned over so fast,
Still it took you ten minutes to see me go past.

"When the horses bowed down to me that I might choose,
I bet on them all, for I hated to lose.
Now I'm saddled each night for my butter and eggs
And the broken threads race down the backs of my legs.

"Let you hold in mind, girls, that your beauty must pass
Like a lovely white clover that rusts with its grass. 30
Keep your bottoms off barstools and marry you young
Or be left—an old barrel with many a bung.

"For when time takes you out for a spin in his car
You'll be hard-pressed to stop him from going too far
And be left by the roadside, for all your good deeds,
Two toadstools for tits and a face full of weeds."

All the house raised a cheer, but the man at the bar
Made a phonecall and up pulled a red patrol car
And she blew us a kiss as they copped her away
From that prominent bar in Secaucus, N.J. 40

Questions for Discussion

1. Is the speaker sympathetic towards the lady in the bar?
2. Does she retain any dignity?
3. Are some of the details of her history exaggerated?
4. How do the rhythms of the poem keep it from being sentimental?
5. Compare the lady in Kennedy's poem with 'Melia in Hardy's poem. Does either one have any idea that she is comic?

Philip Larkin (1922-   )

If, My Darling

If, my darling were once to decide
Not to stop at my eyes,
But to jump, like Alice,[1] with floating skirt into my head,

She would find no tables and chairs,
No mahogany claw-footed sideboards,
No undisturbed embers;

The tantalus would not be filled, nor the fender-seat cosy,
Nor the shelves stuffed with small-printed books for the Sabbath,
Nor the butler bibulous, the housemaids lazy:

She would find herself looped with the creep of varying light, 10
Monkey-brown, fish-grey, a string of infected circles
Loitering like bullies, about to coagulate;

Delusions that shrink to the size of a woman's glove
Then sicken inclusively outwards. She would also remark
The unwholesome floor, as it might be the skin of a grave,

From which ascends an adhesive sense of betrayal,
A Grecian statue kicked in the privates, money,
A swill-tub of finer feelings. But most of all

---

[1] Alice from *Alice in Wonderland.*

She'd be stopping her ears against the incessant recital
Intoned by reality, larded with technical terms, 20
Each one double-yolked with meaning and meaning's rebuttal:

For the skirl of that bulletin unpicks the world like a knot,
And to hear how the past is past and the future neuter
Might knock my darling off her unpriceable pivot.

Questions for Discussion

1. What is the speaker's attitude toward his sweetheart?

2. What is the source of the allusion to Alice? Is this appropriate to the situation?

3. The first sentence runs almost fourteen lines. Does this arrangement help to dramatize the speaker's state of mind?

4. What is the speaker's attitude toward himself?

5. The word *skirl* is dialect ("a shrill sound, as from a bagpipe"). Explain the line in which this word occurs.

6. To what extent is this a comic poem?

Biographical Notes

Geoffrey Chaucer (ca. 1343-1400) was born in London, the son of a wealthy middle-class wine merchant. He spent most of his life in aristocratic and court circles and held a number of positions including that of a page in one of the great households of England, a soldier in France, an envoy for the King of Italy and France, Controller of the Customs at the post of London, Justice of the Peace for Kent, and Clerk of the King's Works. Such a variety of experiences brought him in contact with continental literature and enabled him to write on all aspects of English society in both high and low styles. His two most important works are *Troilus and Criseyde* (1385) and *The Canterbury Tales*, which he worked on during the last fourteen years of his life.

William Wycherley (ca. 1640-1716) was born near Shrewsbury, England. He was educated at Queen's College, Oxford. During the Restoration he was close to the court and indeed was favored by Charles II's mistress, the Duchess of Cleveland, but his secret marriage to the Countess of Drogheda displeased the King. He spent several years in prison for debts. His plays are *Love in a Wood* (1671), *The Gentleman Dancing-Master* (1672), *The Country Wife* (1675), and *The Plain Dealer* (1676). The rest of his literary career was spent in writing mediocre verse.

George Gordon, Lord Byron (1788-1824) was born in London, the son of a dissolute father and a stern mother; his childhood was unhappy. He was educated at Harrow and Cambridge. His first volume of poems, *Fugitive Pieces*, was published in 1806 and immediately suppressed. But his career was well under way, and in 1809 he brought out his satirical *English Bards and Scotch Reviewers*, which put him into the midst of the literary controversies of the period. After a period of extensive travel on the Continent he published the first two Cantos of *Childe Harold* (1812), an autobiographical poem which made him famous. Unfortunately his private life (never very private) was marred by a divorce scandal, and in 1816 he left England, never to return. In Italy in 1818 he began *Don Juan*, and this long poem was his chief work during his remaining years. He died from fever in 1824 as a result of his participation in the Greek war for independence from the Turks.

Nikolai Gogol (1809-1852), one of the early masters of Russian fiction, was greatly esteemed by Dostoevsky, Turgenev, and Chekhov. He was born in the province of Poltava of a family of Ukrainian Cossack gentry. His famous comic drama, *The Inspector General*, was produced in 1836; it was quite adversely received by the government officials, and Gogol left Russia immediately and lived for twelve years in Europe, mainly in Rome, where he wrote most of his novel *Dead Souls* (1842). He spent the next ten years writing its sequel, which he burned just before his death in Moscow.

James Joyce (1882-1941) was one of the most important novelists of this century; his influence on other writers has been very extensive. He was born and educated in Dublin, which he left in 1904. This city provided the setting for all of his work, beginning with *Dubliners* (1914) and *A Portrait of the Artist as a Young Man* (1916). He lived first in Trieste, then, after the outbreak of the war in 1914, in neutral Zurich (he was a British citizen), and then in Paris. It was here that he finished and published *Ulysses* in 1922. Most of the remainder of his life was spent on *Finnegans Wake* (1939), which takes his experiments with language to an advanced stage.

Aldous Huxley (1894-1963) was a member of a famous intellectual family which included his grandfather, Thomas Huxley, and his mother's uncle, Matthew Arnold. He was educated at Eton and Balliol College, Oxford. His first two novels, *Chrome Yellow* (1921) and *Antic Hay* (1923) established him as one of the bright young satirists of the 1920's in London. The best-known of his later novels are *Point Counter Point* (1928) and *Brave New World* (1932). He has also published many books of essays and short stories. Before World War II he came to the United States, and he lived in California until his death.

Ring Lardner (1885-1933) was born in Michigan and educated in Chicago. He became a successful sports writer, but gradually moved into a literary career. His work is almost entirely in the form of the short story. Among his collections are *You Know Me, Al* (1915), *Gullible's Travels* (1917), *How to Write Short Stories* (1924), *The Love Nest* (1926), and *Round-Up* (1929).

Thomas Gray (1716-1771) was a scholarly man who spent most of his life in Cambridge University as student and professor. His studies led him to explore such literary fields as old Welsh and Norse, and his translations from these languages are of some importance in the early stages of Romanticism. His most famous poem of course is the "Elegy Written in a Country Churchyard" (1751).

Theodore Roethke (1908-1963) was born in Saginaw, Michigan. He received his B.A. and M.A. from the University of Michigan. Like many other contemporary poets he was a university teacher, and from 1947 until his death he was in the Department of English at the University of Washington. As a poet he was much honored: the Pulitzer Prize in 1954 for *The Waking: Poems, 1933-1953;* the Bollingen Prize in 1958 for *Words for the Wind;* and posthumously the National Book Award in 1965 for *The Far Field.*

Thomas Hardy (1840-1928) was born in Dorset, that county of southwest England which was later incorporated in the "Wessex" of his novels and poems. After attending the local schools, he became an apprentice to an architect. But he turned to the literary art as a profession, and by 1872 he was a successful novelist with the publication of *Under the Greenwood Tree.* This important period of his work ended with *Jude the Obscure* (1896), which was attacked by many of its first reviewers. Hardy then returned to verse with *Wessex Poem* (1898), and he produced a large body of short poems during the remaining thirty years of his life.

X. J. Kennedy (1929—) was born in New Jersey and was educated at Seton Hall and Columbia University. He spent several years in the U.S. Navy and a year in Paris at the Sorbonne, then did further graduate study at the University of Michigan. He now teaches at the University of California at Irvine. His first book of poems, *Nude Descending a Staircase* (1961), received the Lamont Prize of the Academy of American Poets. He has also published *An Introduction to Poetry* (1966) and co-authored *Mark Twain's Frontier* (1963).

Philip Larkin (1922—) was born in England. He is one of the most distinguished poets of his generation and made his reputation with a small volume, *The Less Deceived,* in 1955. A later volume, *The Whitsun Weddings* (1964), has been similarly acclaimed. He is a librarian at Hull.